BLAMESTORMING, BLAMEMONGERS AND SCAPEGOATS

Allocating blame in the criminal justice process

Gavin Dingwall and Tim Hillier

First published in Great Britain in 2015 by

Policy Press
University of Bristol
1-9 Old Park Hill
Bristol
BS2 8BB
UK
t: +44 (0)117 954 5940
pp-info@bristol.ac.uk
www.policypress.co.uk

North America office:
Policy Press
c/o The University of Chicago Press
1427 East 60th Street
Chicago, IL 60637, USA
t: +1 773 702 7700
f: +1 773 702 9756
sales@press.uchicago.edu
www.press.uchicago.edu

British Library Cataloguing in Publication Data
A catalogue record for this book is available from the British Library

Library of Congress Cataloging-in-Publication Data
A catalog record for this book has been requested

ISBN 978 1 44730 500 2 hardcover

Cover design by Qube Design Associates, Bristol
Front cover image: www.istock.com
Printed and bound in Great Britain by CPI Group (UK) Ltd, Croydon, CR0 4YY
Policy Press uses environmentally responsible print partners

Contents

About the authors

Gavin Dingwall was born and brought up in Edinburgh. He studied law at Warwick and Aberystwyth Universities and lectured at Aberystwyth before moving to De Montfort University in 2005. He is the author of *Alcohol and crime* (Willan, 2006) and (with Chris Harding) of *Diversion in the criminal process* (Sweet and Maxwell, 1998). Gavin claims to be an accomplished guitar player. He has also had the misfortune to be witness to some of the worst moments in the history of Hibernian F.C. (and there have been more than a few).

Tim Hillier was born and brought up in Yorkshire. He studied law at the School of Oriental and African Studies and University of Sheffield. During the 1980s he worked for three years as a researcher for a human rights organisation in the West Bank. He moved to Leicester in 1988 and in 2011 became Associate Head of Leicester De Montfort Law School. He has published in the area of international law. Tim has endured the fluctuating fortunes of Leeds United but has been heartened by the recent return to cricketing success of Yorkshire. Five years ago he foolishly took up horseriding.

Preface

Blame as a concept informing domestic and international criminal justice has fascinated us for some time. Through our work researching and teaching criminology and penology and our individual interests in criminal law jurisprudence (GD) and international criminal justice (TH) it became evident that a systematic account of the role blame plays in the criminal justice process would constitute an important contribution to contemporary debates surrounding the use of the criminal law and, by implication, of punishment. It is accepted that recourse to the criminal law has become increasingly prevalent over the past 20 years and that notions of blameworthiness have often been employed to justify such intervention. Sometimes criminalisation was obviously necessary and overdue. Other developments, however, do not stand up to scrutiny and appear to be a blunt response to an illusory or over-stated problem. Like many commentators, we are perturbed by a trend to criminalise in the absence of compelling justification. This work will argue that this development is explained in part by a greater willingness to attribute blame for events, to demand that blame is imputed onto an individual or other legal actor, and that severe consequences should then follow. More will be said about definitions in Chapter One, but we employ the modern term **blamestorming** to describe the deliberate process of attribution. That 'blamestorming' is followed in the book's title by **blamemongers** and **scapegoats** emphasises the fact that blamestorming is not a value-neutral exercise and that significant disparities in power are often involved.

Blame is used in this work as a prism which affords one way to view contemporary criminal justice policy and practice. We readily acknowledge that blame is not the only ground on which recent policy has been justified. When clear tension exists between blame and alternative explanations or claims, this will be explored further but dictates of space mean that our analysis of other possible accounts could not always be developed as fully as we would have liked.

Another function can be fulfilled by blame: it can be used to explain and it can be used to evaluate. Blaming someone for something may be a process worthy of examination but, because of the potentially adverse consequences of this process, it is imperative to assess whether the process is necessary and the finding and consequences warranted. Just as politicians and the media invoke blame too readily to justify potentially repressive measures, some criminologists are guilty of dismissing all instances of criminalisation as further proof of invidious state control. Both accounts dissolve when exposed to the complexity of contemporary criminal justice. A meaningful assessment has to be more nuanced and context-specific. If this hinders the ability to make broad claims, so be it.

Prior to commencing, we were confident that a book about the centrality of blame in the criminal justice process would be valuable. We were equally aware that writing such a work would be a complex undertaking and we would like to record our thanks to those who originally reviewed the proposal for their valuable suggestions to our initial proposal. Like all projects of this size, the contents and layout evolved as the work progressed – new areas cried out for inclusion and this inevitably came at the cost of some topics which we had planned to cover.

Two key decisions were taken at the start. The first was that the book would address both domestic and international criminal justice: any study on blame which failed to consider how society apportions blame for the very worst crimes imaginable would be seriously deficient. Jurisprudence on the topic now exists as does a considerable secondary literature and we have been able to draw on both at various points. Second, the approach would be inter-disciplinary as blame interests those working in a variety of diverse areas of scholarship. One area which required fairly detailed analysis was criminal law theory, despite the book not being a legal study. It can easily be forgotten how dependent the criminal justice process is on the substantive criminal law. Deliberate decisions taken by parliament or the courts set the parameters of the criminal law and therefore determines what conduct can be responded to. Evaluating some crucial legal determinations demonstrated how judges also commonly invoke notions of blame when deciding whether particular forms of conduct should be viewed as criminal. As judicial interpretation influences decisions taken by police and prosecutors, one cannot sensibly divorce criminal law from criminal justice in this context.

The book is organised as follows. Chapter One expands on the terms and concepts adopted in the title, considering 'blamestorming', 'blamemongers' and 'scapegoats' in turn. Through the use of contemporary and historical examples, we document how society seems more ready to hold individuals to account for their, and sometimes others', actions. We start the chapter by detailing the tragic facts surrounding the death of a 22-year-old man. Justice seemingly demanded the punishment of his mother, but a causal analysis shows that her actions were but part of a factually and morally complicated story. Even if one could agree on how factual blame could be apportioned in such a case, determining the extent to which she should be deemed blameworthy is highly problematic. That blame plays a vital role in the criminal justice system, that blame is inherently complex, and that society is prepared to find blame more easily than in the past are themes that emerge at the start of the study and ones to which we return throughout.

Chapter Two provides an overview of the role of blame in English criminal justice. Although the chapter cautions against viewing the criminal trial as the normal response to deviant behaviour (most offenders are diverted pre-trial or admit guilt), the trial remains paradigmatic and the chapter's structure follows the process from mode of trial to sentence. It is argued that blame informs, though does not fully explain, both of these decisions. At this point in the book the value of blame both to illuminate and to evaluate becomes apparent. Sentencing represents a determination which will adversely affect the offender; as harm is being inflicted, it needs moral justification. The extent to which the offender is seen to be deserving of blame often frames a justification for sentence. Moreover, despite considerable residual discretion, sentencers must act within the law: statutes must be followed and guidelines generally heeded. To what extent does the law rely on notions of blame? Even if there is a gap between the statute and implementation, if sentencing law is based on blameworthiness, this is a notable finding. Our conclusion is that, despite a myriad of rival objectives, the law provides thresholds for different penalties (custody, community sentences and so on) based primarily on personal culpability. The relevant law is not so much accommodating to blame as a determinant of sentence, but usually demands that it is the sole or primary consideration.

Situations where individuals are excluded from criminal liability even though they are factually responsible are considered in Chapter Three, which we entitle 'blame and the blameless'. Two categories of person often incur no criminal liability or are treated differently on the basis of a perceived lack of blame: children and those who lack mental capacity. The chapter considers both in turn, investigating the basis for such claims and assessing whether the law is consistent with the findings of other disciplines such as psychology. It is the case that arbitrary decisions are made. The reluctance to raise the minimum age of criminal responsibility in England and Wales from 10 (which is low compared to most jurisdictions), for example, highlights a change in attitude towards those exceptional cases when children kill. We are not the first to explore the effect of the James Bulger case on public sentiment towards juvenile offenders, but by drawing comparisons with earlier cases a hardening of opinion is discernible: there is little sympathy for the fact that the perpetrators were severely disadvantaged children. A study of insanity and other defences which rest on lack of blame throws up legal inconsistencies and situations where the law fails to accord with principle. Finally, attention is paid to the concept of **moral luck**, an under-researched topic of great relevance to our study. Often the outcome of an individual's deliberate action cannot be foreseen: a blow to the head can bruise, injure or kill. Does this arbitrary consequence affect blame? The likely sentence will be highly dependent on the result, but is an individual not as blameworthy if she shoots and misses than if she hits the intended target?

Chapter Four turns to what we term **blameless crime**. Offences typically stipulate a state of mind that must have been present at the time of commission; examples include intention, knowledge and **recklessness**. It can be argued that these states provide some kind of moral hierarchy whereby the intentional harm-causer is seen to be more blameworthy than the risk taker or the incompetent. Some correlation can be found between the seriousness of the offence (and the likely severity of the punishment) and the state of mind prescribed. The most serious crimes, most notably murder, demand an intention to cause the specified harm whereas many comparatively minor offences require no fault on the part of the offender. Blameless crimes therefore exist in considerable number, although it is also the case that the courts have interpreted many key concepts in a way which gives primacy to blame. Two examples are recklessness and **strict liability**. Statute does not specify whether recklessness can be found when the unjustified risk taken is obvious to the **reasonable man** or whether subjective appreciation is necessary. If the former approach is taken, individuals who foresaw no risk and were perhaps incapable of foreseeing any risk would be liable. Examples will be provided of the injustice caused when patently blameless individuals were convicted in this way. In a landmark ruling, the House of Lords held that subjective appreciation was central to a finding of recklessness and based this conclusion largely on the understanding that blame should help determine criminal liability. This perception is also evident in cases dealing with strict liability. Although this category of offence ostensibly requires no fault on the part of the offender, the courts have created a series of conditions that need to be fulfilled if this is to be the case. A **blame requirement** will effectively be read in if the offence is stigmatic and carries significant punishment.

Thus far the book has shown how blame has been used to justify the expansion of the criminal law (often after lobbying by politicians and the media) and how it has been used (primarily by the courts) to constrain the punishment of the **blameless** through distinguishing certain exceptional offenders or situations (Chapter Three) or through the interpretation of key legal concepts (Chapter Four). Blame is thus employed to neutralise or mitigate the scope and the effect of the law. The next two chapters consider how this can work in reverse.

Chapter Five conceptualises blame amplification. It starts with a detailed review of offence-severity and how this can be quantified objectively. Calculating a sentence on the grounds that it should be commensurate to the seriousness of the offence would be consistent with many people's perceptions of justice. The problem is that the assessment of how serious an offence is and the subsequent determination of an appropriate sentence appear subjective. How serious is theft relative to criminal damage? What is a proportionate response to burglary? What is central to this chapter is the relevance of particular factors present in a given case which may make it more serious than usual. These aggravating factors are seen to amplify the offender's blame. We consider the factors that the public identified when determining the seriousness of sexual offences and how these correspond to the factors sentencers should consider when passing sentence. All of this pre-supposes rational decision-making on the part of the offender. Social science research suggests, though, that this distorts the process which calls into question whether issues of aggravation and mitigation can be calibrated with any accuracy.

Context cannot be ignored. The chapter ends by considering 'extraordinary crime' (that is, genocide, war crimes and crimes against humanity). Their exceptionalism does not stem from their rarity. Millions of victims have been directly affected and atrocities continue to occur daily. There are distinctive features underlying this criminality: the brutality is widespread and has few parallels in domestic crime; the targeting is deliberate; and swathes of the population are involved actively or passively as perpetrators. Research suggests that few would resist participating in such events for a variety of reasons. Given this insight, how does blame assist us in finding an appropriate response to extraordinary crime?

In Chapter Six we consider scenarios where the individual puts herself in a position which heightens the risk of her offending. This can take a variety of forms such as joining a criminal gang (where subsequent offending is certain) to becoming intoxicated (there is a correlation between intoxication and offending). We are not aware of any other attempt to synthesise more than one such activity and the conclusions that can be drawn are fascinating. The legal issue is whether the precursory conduct should have an impact on the defendant's criminal liability either in the sense that the offence might not be made out or that a defence may be available. There may be a sense of injustice if someone who was to blame for putting themselves in this position subsequently avoided conviction. A number of tensions are evident: the desire to maintain the integrity of the criminal law and the recognition that a strict application of the law could lead to injustice; the need to protect the public from violence and the acceptance that the violence may not have been intended; and the question of whether blame attaches to the initial act or to the offence that followed. Blame, it will be argued, is often used uncritically in an attempt to remedy some profoundly problematic legal issues. Comparative material will show that other countries do not always arrive at the same conclusions; indeed there are examples where blame has been used to justify departure from English law in other Commonwealth jurisdictions. Blame may or may not point in different directions but it has led the courts to distinct destinations.

One of the central themes of the book is that there has been a growth in the culture of blame and an increased need for scapegoats. We try to account for this phenomenon in Chapter Seven. Examples are taken from cases where children suffered harm or neglect and it is shown that 'justice' now entails blaming not only those who directly caused the harm (all of whom were dealt with fully by the criminal law) but those whose alleged inaction or incompetence provided a space for the abuse to occur. Lessons should be learnt and the incompetent should not be kept in post if their presence risks further abuse taking place but allocating personal responsibility beyond the individual abuser risks creating scapegoats. Why is it no longer sufficient to punish those who actually neglected or abused the child? The chapter also documents two parallel trends namely a shift from civil to criminal liability and from human rights to the international criminal court. All of the developments in this chapter have occurred in a brief timeframe which highlights the relevancy of the approach which we adopted.

Chapter Eight concludes the book by expanding on the process of blamestorming and the role played by the blamemongers. There are many reasons to become dispirited. Too often the allocation of blame is simplistic and arbitrary and reflects little more than the ability of the powerful to coerce the marginalised or vulnerable. Too often the force of the rhetoric drowns out the lack of substance behind the claim. Critically, these scenarios are becoming more common as society loses the ability to appreciate that individual blame cannot always be found when harm occurs. We also document, however, many instances where the law has evolved in order to protect the blameless and the courts still display the confidence to justify their decisions on this basis. It is on this note that the book ends. Although the blame culture is insidious and the criminal law has been allowed to mushroom as a consequence, blame can and should inform progressive criminal justice reform. Blame may be a contested and a complex concept, but it has resonance and power and there would appear to be widespread agreement that it should play some role in setting the parameters of the criminal law. Rather than challenging this, reformers would be best advised to deconstruct the process of attribution and formulate a more compelling alternative.

We wish to thank all those who have assisted us directly or indirectly while we worked on this book and our colleagues at Policy Press for their professionalism and enthusiasm throughout.

Gavin Dingwall and Tim Hillier
July 2014

ONE

Introduction and the centrality of blame

The Case of Mrs Inglis

On 21 November 2008 Frances Inglis killed her 22-year-old son, Thomas, by injecting him with heroin, having been unsuccessful in an earlier attempt. On 20 January 2010 she was convicted of murder and attempted murder and sentenced to life imprisonment with a minimum specified term of nine years. The killing of children by their parents is almost universally regarded as especially wrong and there is usually widespread public condemnation of mothers who kill their own children. On the face of it, Frances Inglis could expect considerable blame to be attached to her actions. Many might consider that her blame would be increased by the fact that she committed the murder while on bail for the attempted murder and that a condition of that bail was that she had no contact with her son. The Sentencing Council guidelines indicate that there is greater culpability when offences are committed on bail (Sentencing Guidelines Council, 2004). Yet the facts surrounding the case outlined in the Court of Appeal judgment in Frances Inglis's appeal (*R v Inglis* [2010] EWCA Crim 2637) show the attribution and assessment of blame to be far more complicated.

On 7 July 2007 Thomas Inglis was involved in a fight in which he was struck on the head. Against his wishes an ambulance was called and he was taken to hospital. According to the facts disclosed in the Court of Appeal judgment, during the journey to the hospital the back doors of the ambulance opened three times. On the third occasion Thomas fell out of the back and sustained severe head injuries which left him in a coma. At the inquest, the Hertfordshire Coroner found that on all three occasions the doors had been opened by Thomas himself and that on the third occasion he had jumped from the ambulance. Thomas required two life-saving operations to relieve pressure on his brain and a portion of the front part of his skull was removed. The Court of Appeal accepted that the appearance of Thomas following the second operation was 'distressing' but the view of the consultants at that time was that there was every possibility that Thomas could recover sufficiently to lead an independent life. Frances, who was separated from her husband, Thomas's father, had been opposed to the operations and took the view that Thomas should have been allowed to die naturally. She was considerably distressed by Thomas's condition and believed him to be suffering and in pain. In August 2007 the medical team concluded that Thomas was not yet ready to be moved to a rehabilitation unit as he was still unable to swallow on his own. The medical team also took the view that Thomas would probably require long-term dependent care.

On 4 September 2007 Frances Inglis visited her son in hospital and following the visit he suffered cardiac arrest and was clinically dead. He was resuscitated and subsequent tests showed the cause of the cardiac arrest to be street heroin. Frances was arrested and interviewed and initially denied all knowledge of the heroin or any idea of ending Thomas's life. The Court of Appeal pointed out that she was 'content to allow suspicion to fall onto Thomas's father or his brother or those responsible for his care at hospital' (para 17). She was subsequently charged with the attempted murder of her son and granted bail subject to the condition that she did not visit her son. In May 2008 her solicitors indicated that Frances Inglis would plead guilty on the basis that her action was motivated by a desire to end what she saw as Thomas's suffering. Her only regret was the fact that she had failed in her attempt. While there was some doubt about Thomas's prognosis before 4 September 2007, after the cardiac arrest his condition and prognosis was extremely poor.

On 21 November 2008 Frances Inglis gained access to the hospital which was providing care for Thomas. The hospital was short staffed and, although staff were aware that Frances was not permitted to see her son, a photograph which would have enabled staff to identify her had been removed some time earlier. Frances asked to see Thomas and was allowed in without suspicions being raised. She then injected Thomas with heroin and, calculating the time needed for it to take effect, waited for the staff to leave the room and then superglued the lock and barricaded the door.

At her trial Frances Inglis argued that she felt she had had no choice. Her actions had been motivated by love for her son who she did not wish to continue suffering a living death. She was particularly concerned about the possibility that hydration and nutrition would be withdrawn from Thomas if his vegetative state persisted beyond a 12-month period. There was also evidence given at the trial to show that Frances had suffered from depressive disorder in the past and was suffering from depression at the time of her actions. At the end of the trial she was convicted of murder and attempted murder and sentenced to life imprisonment with a minimum period of nine years specified for the murder. She appealed both against conviction and against sentence. The appeal against conviction was dismissed and the Court of Appeal focused more on the appeal against sentence. The judgment was delivered by the then Lord Chief Justice, Lord Judge.

Having been convicted of murder the only sentence available to the court was life imprisonment, but the court could still reflect the level of blame to be attached to Mrs Inglis by the minimum period specified. The Court of Appeal confirmed the conventional view that premeditation increases the quantity of blame as does the abuse of a position of trust: both were present in Mrs Inglis's case. They also found, as an aggravating factor, that Mrs Inglis continued to show a lack of remorse for what she had done. On the other hand, the Court of Appeal accepted that Mrs Inglis was suffering from an impaired ability to cope with the situation of her son and that she genuinely believed that she was carrying out an act of mercy. By weighing the aggravating and mitigating factors together the Court of Appeal came to the conclusion that the initial sentence had overvalued the amount of culpability and reduced the recommended minimum term to five years imprisonment.

Had Thomas Inglis not sustained serious head injuries in November 2008 it seems unlikely that his mother, Frances, would be currently serving a sentence of life imprisonment for his murder. Had Thomas not received a blow to the head during a fight in a pub an ambulance would not have been called. Evidence at the inquest suggests that Thomas had been drinking and that, either as a result of alcohol or the blow to his head, his judgement was impaired. In other circumstances he would probably not have attempted to leave a moving ambulance by the back door. Had the light warning the driver of an open door been working properly then the driver might have stopped when the back doors opened. Had the photograph of Mrs Inglis not been removed from the hospital which was treating Thomas then she might have been recognised and escorted from the premises before administering the fatal dose of heroin. Had the hospital not been short staffed it may have been more difficult for Mrs Inglis to see Thomas unaccompanied. Clearly the main person to *blame* for Thomas's death is Frances Inglis. The questions as to whether any others in the tragic story are deserving of blame and the quantity of blame to be attributed to Frances Inglis are more complex.

The Case of Baby P

In 2007 in England and Wales 574 children died between the ages of one and four (ONS, 2007). Of those, 21 were victims of unlawful killing. One of the victims became particularly known to the public. Peter Connelly was born on 1 March 2006 and was found dead in his cot on 3 August 2007. The death of 'Baby P', as he came to be known, received considerable media attention, far more than the other 20 young children whose lives were unlawfully ended in 2007. During his life, concerns had been expressed on a number of occasions about the quality of his care. He was repeatedly seen by members of Haringey's Children and Young Persons Service and by NHS healthcare professionals. On two occasions his mother was arrested in connection with injuries sustained by Peter but both times she was released without charge. The post mortem examination of Peter identified 22 separate injuries including fractures to his ribs, a broken spinal cord, a broken tooth and a removed toenail (*R v B, C and Jason Owen* (2009)).[1] In November 2007 Tracey and her partner, Steven Barker, together with Barker's brother, Jason Owen, were convicted of 'allowing or causing the death of a child or vulnerable adult' under section 5 of the Domestic Violence, Crime and Victims Act 2004. Connelly and Barker were given indeterminate sentences of imprisonment for public protection, Owen received a sentence of three years imprisonment.

Unlike the case of Thomas Inglis, a successful criminal prosecution of those directly responsible for the death did not bring matters to a close. Seven years earlier, Haringey Social Services had been heavily criticised following the death of eight-year-old Victoria Climbié in February 2000. The death of Peter Connelly seemed to be an awful repetition of many of the events surrounding Victoria Climbié's death. Following Peter's death, Haringey Council launched an internal Serious Case Review and the Secretary of State for Children, Schools and Families ordered Ofsted, the Healthcare Commission and the Chief Inspector of Constabulary to carry out an inspection of safeguarding in Haringey. The inspection report was delivered to the Secretary of State on 1 December 2008 and acting on their findings he ordered the immediate removal of the Director of Children's Services, Sharon Shoesmith.[2] On 8 December 2008 Sharon Shoesmith was dismissed by Haringey Council and in April 2009 the Council announced that it had also dismissed the Deputy Director of Children's Services, two managers and a social worker. Two of the healthcare professionals involved in the case were also subject to sanctions. One is left to wonder whether, had it not occurred within the jurisdiction of Haringey

Social Services, the tragedy of Baby P would have received the same media attention. Had it not received the media attention it did, one also wonders whether Haringey Council would have been so minded to dismiss the Director and Deputy Director of Children's Services, the two managers and the social worker.

The case of Baby P raises important issues relating to blame. It also provides an example of public scapegoating. Baby P was not the only young child to die in 2007 yet his case received considerable media attention. Those directly responsible for his death received long terms of imprisonment, yet that did not seem sufficient to assuage a public (or certainly media-led) desire to allocate blame. What is also striking is the fact that the tone of the inquiries into the deaths of Peter Connelly and Victoria Climbié was markedly different to that of the first modern child abuse inquiry and this difference was reflected in the respective reports. In 1973 Maria Colwell was killed by her stepfather following systematic abuse. The case received considerable media coverage and a Committee of Inquiry was established, chaired by Thomas Fisher. In 1974 the *Report of the Committee of Inquiry into the care and supervision provided in relation to Maria Colwell* (the Fisher Report) was published (HMSO, 1974). It was considerably shorter than the two inquiries chaired by Lord Lamming into the deaths of Victoria Climbié and Peter Connelly. The written style of the later reports is much more personalised and there is a greater willingness to identify the guilty and the innocent. In 1974 the authors of the Fisher Report could conclude: 'The overall impression created by Maria's sad history is that while individuals made mistakes it was "the system", using the word in the widest sense, which failed her. Because that system is the product of society, it is on society as a whole that the ultimate blame must rest' (HMSO, 1974, para 242).

The later reports seem to be keen to protect society as a whole from blame by identifying specific individuals and organisations deserving of blame. It will be a central tenet of this book that the increasing willingness to attach blame to specific individuals and organisations is inextricably linked to a desire to exonerate the rest of us.

Blamestorming

Among the new words identified by the Oxford English Dictionary in 2003 was 'blamestorming' which was defined as 'The process of investigating the reasons for a failure and of apportioning blame, esp. by means of discussion or debate'. The first use of the word was traced to a section in *Wired Magazine* by Gareth Branwyn entitled Jargon

Watch. On 20 January 1997 Branwyn identified blamestorming: 'To sit around and discuss why a deadline was missed or a project failed and who's responsible. Like brainstorming, from which it is derived, blamestorming is done with little regard for the quality of contributions to the discussion' (Branwyn, 1997). The *Daily Telegraph* reported on 29 January 2008 that 'blamestorming' was among a number of new buzzwords to enter office jargon identified by a survey carried out by the recruitment firm Office Angels:

> When times get tough, when people get stressed, and when they are faced with a crisis, it is interesting to observe how many people seem to suddenly become skilled in the Art of Blamestorming. Loosely defined Blamestorming is a meeting of like-minded people who enjoy sitting around in meetings, deciding who or what they are going to blame for their current plight. How many good Blamestorming sessions have you had in your own organization recently? You probably know some people who are highly skilled at Blamestorming. Some people are so proficient that they do not even need an organized meeting in order to practice their art. They do it at the water cooler, in the elevator, on the phone and some are even skilled enough to record it on paper or send out by email. In our current economic climate it is not difficult to become a skilled Blamestormer as there are so many easy targets to pick from: Wall Street; The Government; Over Spending Home Owners; Greedy CEOs; Oil Prices and the like. (Meredith, 2009)

Undoubtedly blamestorming has its origins in the workplace and particular management styles yet the concept has a relevance in wider society. Meredith's linking of blamestorming and times of crisis seems apt. Yet the increased readiness to blamestorm and blame seems a particularly modern phenomenon. A review of the British press coverage of the urban unrest of August 2011 by PressEurop was headlined 'Blamestorming Britain'[3] and the overall tone of the press coverage reflected a readiness or even desire to allocate blame to specific individuals and organisations. This is in marked contrast to the attitude of the press following unrest in the St Paul's area of Bristol in April 1980. Then *The Times* editorial published on Monday 7 April 1980 attempted to understand the weekend of disturbances and considered the effects of deprivation and unemployment and the nature of police–public relations:

But whatever the causes of it, and however blame for the causes of it is distributed, the fact of this high unemployment rate, which can only worsen in the months ahead, is a contributory factor in petty crime, dropping out, and resentment of authority – and authority means first and foremost the police. (p 9)

This shift in public attitudes is perhaps encapsulated by words, often misquoted, spoken by the then Prime Minister, John Major, in an interview given to the *Mail on Sunday*: 'Society needs to condemn a little more and understand a little less' (*Mail on Sunday*, 21 February 1993). The condemnation is expressed in blame. Increasingly, in all aspects of life there seems to be a desire, almost a need, to allocate blame when things appear to go wrong. We live in a society that is increasingly preoccupied with allocating blame. Scientific and technological developments appear to give humans increasing control over their own destiny. An important consequence of this appears to be that when things go wrong someone must be to blame. Stan Cohen refers to 'a denaturalization of nature' (Cohen, 2002, 38). Cohen argues that disasters and environmental problems are increasingly treated as social events:

> These 'technical' disasters are 'the new species of trouble', in contrast to traditional 'natural' disasters. They have become 'normal accidents', catastrophes embedded within the familiar: the collapse of a football stand, a rail crash, a bridge falling, the sinking of a channel ferry, a botched cancer screening programme. The resultant reactions are not as homogenous, automatic or simple as they are supposed to be in contrast with the complexities of moral discourse. Indeed the reactions are similar to the highly contested terrain of all moral panics. (Cohen, 2002, 38)

In 1976 Kai T Erikson published his study of the effects of the Buffalo Creek flood (Erikson, 1976). The flood occurred on 26 February 1972 when the Pittston Coal Company's coal slurry impoundment dam collapsed in West Virginia. The resultant flood engulfed the small village of Buffalo Creek, killing 125 people and injuring 1,121. Of the population of 5,000, 4,000 were left homeless. The Pittston Coal Company called the disaster an act of God. The two enquiries into the disaster were fairly inconclusive although the Pittston Coal Company did agree to pay compensation to the survivors. Erikson was concerned with the effect of the disaster on social integration. Before the disaster the community of Buffalo Creek had been a very close-knit one and social integration was extremely high. That high level of social integration was reflected in high levels of social regulation. The disaster had a devastating effect on both. Following the disaster, the people of Buffalo Creek had far less confidence and Erikson found that people suffered from a high level of *anomie*.

Some six years before the Buffalo Creek flood soon after 9.00 am on 21 October 1966 a colliery spoil tip above the village of Aberfan in South Wales collapsed. The rock and shale slurry quickly covered the village including the classrooms of Pantglas Junior School; 116 children and 28 adults were killed as a direct result of the disaster. On 26 October 1966 the Secretary of State for Wales appointed a tribunal of inquiry under the chairmanship of Lord Justice Edmund Davies. The Tribunal reported on 3 August 1967 (HMSO, 1967). The Report was clear where blame was to be allocated:

> Blame for the disaster rests on the National Coal Board. This is shared, though in varying degrees, among the NCB headquarters, the South Western Divisional Board, and certain individuals...The legal liability of the NCB to pay compensation of the personal injuries, fatal or otherwise, and damage to property, is incontestable and uncontested. (para 74)

The Report also commented:

> [T]he Aberfan Disaster is a terrifying tale of bungling ineptitude by many men charged with tasks for which they were totally unfitted, of failure to heed clear warnings, and of total lack of direction from above. Not villains, but decent men, led astray by foolishness or by ignorance or by both in combination, are responsible for what happened at Aberfan. (Para 73)

Nine individual NCB employees and officials were identified and singled for particular criticism. The report made clear, however, that it was a tale 'not of wickedness but of ignorance, ineptitude and a failure of communications'. There were no criminal proceedings following the disaster. On the day of the disaster itself the chairman of the National Coal Board, Lord Robbens of Woldingham chose to attend his investiture as Chancellor of the University of Surrey rather than going to the scene of the disaster. He did not arrive at Aberfan until the evening of 22 October. It is hard to believe that a comparable disaster today would not result in a massive 'blamestorm' leading to resignations, dismissals or criminal prosecutions.

Both Aberfan and Buffalo Creek had high levels of social integration at the time of the disasters and perhaps this provides a clue to the puzzle of blame and blamestorming. Although potential targets for blame were clearly visible in both disasters the 'blamestorm' never developed. Socially cohesive societies are unused to looking to the outside for either praise or blame and so when disaster strikes there is greater introspection and a fracturing of belief systems. Increasing blame and blamestorming may itself be a reflection of lower levels of social cohesion. Another possibility is raised by Cohen's suggestion that in sudden unexpected forms of deviance or disaster, blame and responsibility can be shifted upward. Cohen's focus was the series of disturbances that occurred in a number of south coast resorts and which involved clashes between the rival groups of Mods and Rockers. Cohen noted that there was generally widespread support for the police and the courts and blame was directed towards the government: 'Students of natural disasters have noted a similar scapegoating process: those involved in the disaster are usually exonerated – 'they only did their job' – and government figures become targets for attack and protest in a situation for which they had no conceivable direct responsibility' (Cohen, 2002, 186).

Cohen wrote those words in 1972 and the studies of the natural disasters to which he referred were published in 1943 and 1957 (Veltfort and Lee, 1943; Bucher, 1957). It is possible that, in the 40 years since the publication of *Folk devils and moral panics*, those in power have become more sophisticated in deflecting blame back downwards. In Chapter Five we discuss how a refusal to accept superior orders as a defence to war crimes and crimes against humanity may have the effect of downshifting blame and responsibility.

Blamemongers

We coin the term 'blamemonger' to focus attention on those who blamestorm and allocate blame in society. In the immediate aftermath of the Aberfan disaster there was considerable bitterness. The risks posed by the spoil tip above the village had been known about for a long time and many in the village had asked for action to be taken to prevent the very kind of disaster that ultimately occurred. The *Merthyr Express* reported on public sentiment at the inquest into the deaths:

The brave front of the people of Aberfan cracked on Monday at an inquest on 30 of the children. There were shouts of 'murderers' as the Coroner of Merthyr, Mr Ben Hamilton, began reading out the names of the dead children. As one name was read out and the cause of death given as asphyxia and multiple injuries, the father of the child said 'No, sir, buried alive by the National Coal Board'. One of the only two women among the 60 people at the inquest at Sion Primitive English Methodist Chapel at Aberfan, shouted out through her tears, 'They have killed our children.' Then a number of people called out and got to their feet. The coroner tried to restore order and said: 'I know your grief is such that you may not be realising what you are saying.' The father repeated: 'I want it recorded – "Buried alive by the National Coal Board." That is what I want to see on the record. That is the feeling of those present. Those are the words we want to go on the certificate.' (*Merthyr Express*, 1966)

Those immediately affected were in no doubt as to who was to blame. Yet criminal prosecutions did not occur and media reports were much more measured. Contemporary society is more pre-occupied with blame, but it is important to have an understanding of who in society is in a position effectively to allocate blame.

There are very great parallels here with the concept of moral entrepreneurs first identified by Howard Becker. For Becker, 'Rules are the products of someone's initiative and we can think of the people who exhibit such enterprise as *moral entrepreneurs*' (1963, 168). Becker considers there to be two types of moral entrepreneur: rule creators and rule enforcers. The rule creators he regards as moral crusaders who 'typically believe that their mission is a holy one' (p 168). Successful crusaders create new rules and new groups of outsiders. With the creation of a new rule there are new problems of enforcement and the need for rule enforcers who become part of the crusade.

Deviance – in the sense I have been using it, of publicly labelled wrongdoing – is always the result of enterprise. Before any act can be viewed as deviant, and before any class of people can be labelled and treated as outsiders for committing the act, someone must have made the rule which defines the act as deviant. Rules are not made automatically. Even though a practice may be harmful in an objective sense to the group in which it occurs, the harm needs to be discovered and pointed out. People must be made to feel that something ought to be done about it. Someone must call the public's attention to these matters, supply the push necessary to get things done, and direct such energies as are aroused in the proper direction to get a rule created…Once a rule has come into existence, it must be applied to particular people before the abstract class of outsiders created by the rule can be peopled. Offenders must be discovered, identified, apprehended and convicted (or noted as "different" and stigmatized for their nonconformity…). This job ordinarily falls to the lot of professional enforcers who, by enforcing already existing rules, create the particular deviants society views as outsiders. (pp 183–4)

Becker argues that only by focusing attention on both those who break the rules and those who enforce and make them will we achieve a full understanding of deviant behaviour. In a similar way only by exploring how blame is allocated – and by whom – will we achieve a full understanding of the behaviour that attracts blame.

To some extent the legitimacy of the allocation of blame is dependent on the legitimacy of the blamemongers: 'Blame is morally appropriate only when the blamer has standing' (Bell, 2013, 262). Bell identifies a number of writers, including Antony Duff and TM Scanlon, who defend this 'standard account' requiring would-be blamers to have standing to blame and there are some analogies with the concept of *locus standii* in legal proceedings. For Bell standard accounts of blame articulate a number of conditions that must be met for a blamemonger to have standing.

The first condition identified by Bell is the **business condition**: we can only legitimately blame when it is 'our business' to do so. In its narrowest meaning, to satisfy the business condition the blamemonger needs to demonstrate that he or she has been directly injured by the act or omission being blamed. This condition has the closest parallels with legal standing or *locus standii* and for similar reasons has also been the target of criticism. There may be practical reasons for limiting the amount of litigation but those practicalities do not seem as relevant to the allocation of blame. The 'business condition' has also been used in the context of discussions of blame and privacy: some behaviour is private and therefore should not attract blame. Angela Smith argues that this respect for privacy and a reluctance to allocate blame to acts or omissions which are 'private' and therefore 'none of our business' helps the smooth running of society (Smith, 2007). Clearly in recent years there has been an increasing blurring of the boundaries between public and private, not least as a result of the emergence of widespread use of social media and almost instant communication. In the past it might have been true to argue, as Smith does, that: 'The rights of privacy are such that it is generally not our business to reproach others for their minor moral faults unless we stand in a special relationship to them and/or have a relevant stake in the matter. (Smith, 2007, 478, n18)

In the days of Facebook and Twitter it may be that many more people feel that they have a 'special relationship' or 'relevant stake' and thus a business standing to blame.

The second condition Bell identifies is the **contemporary condition**:

> [T]he blamer must inhabit the same moral community as the person blamed. Very roughly, two persons can be said to inhabit the same moral community if they see the same considerations as reason-giving and employ the same moral concepts. If the target is dead or inhabits a moral community far removed from the critic's community, it would be impossible for the target to give criticism uptake. (Bell, 2013, 271)

Yet a functional view of blame might see considerable value in the blaming, even where the target is dead. One only has to consider the allegations made in respect of Jimmy Savile to see how blame can be allocated to dead targets. Those who defend the contemporary condition argue that if the blame cannot be received by the target it is pointless and morally inappropriate. A less functional view of blame would not raise such an objection.

Bell's third condition is the **nonhypocrisy condition** according to which 'one forfeits one's standing to blame if one manifests the same flaw that one attempts to criticise in another' (Bell, 2013, 272). There are echoes here of the techniques of neutralisation identified by Sykes and Matza (1957) and the condemnation of the condemner. Clearly the blamed may be able to respond to blame by pointing out the hypocrisy of the blamer but that in itself is surely not enough to negative the blamer's standing. Those blaming may themselves be blameworthy but that does not logically imply that they are incapable of blaming. The final condition identified by Bell is the **noncomplicity condition**: one cannot blame in situations where one is complicit in the wrongdoing. This would seem to rule out the possibility of self-blame which undoubtedly exists and can be criticised on the same grounds as the nonhypocrisy condition.

It is clear, though, that possessing the standing to blame is important: whether a person is in a position to blame does intuitively appear to depend on the relationship between blamemonger and blamed. The arguments for the standard account are underpinned by the same ideas which underpin legal standing: if there are not strict rules on standing we shall be overrun with blame. Bell argues for a more functional view of blame while accepting that relative position is important: 'Blame helps to shield and protect us from the moral damage wrought by wrongdoing. Rather than attempting to limit blame by appealing to the objectionable notion of standing, we should take seriously our special responsibility as critics, targets, and bystanders' (Bell, 2013, 281).

Subsequent chapters attempt to shed some light on this discussion to which we will return in the final chapter.

Scapegoats

The origins of the word 'scapegoat' are to be found in the translation of the Bible undertaken by William Tyndale in the sixteenth century. Tyndale's translation reached a wider public in the King James Bible authorised by King James I and completed in 1611. Chapter 16 of the Book of Leviticus includes the following verses:

8. And Aaron shall cast lots on the two goats; one lot for the LORD, and the other lot for the scapegoat.
9. And Aaron shall bring the goat on which the LORD'S lot fell, and offer him for a sin offering.
10. But the goat, on which the lot fell to be the scapegoat, shall be presented alive before the LORD, to make an atonement with him, and to let him go for a scapegoat into the wilderness.

'Scapegoat' was invented by Tyndale to express the literal meaning, as he saw it, of the Hebrew word 'azazel'. The verses in Leviticus are describing the ritual for the Day of Atonement as laid down by Mosaic Law. Two goats are to be brought to the altar of the Tabernacle: one goat is sacrificed for the Lord and the other goat is used for the atonement of sins. The priest transfers the sins of the people to this other goat, the scapegoat, and it is driven or allowed to escape into the wilderness. By transferring the sins to the scapegoat, the community was cleansed of it sins. Tom Douglas (1995, 29) sees particular significance in the fact that in ancient Hebrew society the scapegoat was not killed. It was only by leaving the community alive that the goat could carry with it the sins of the community: 'The idea of the scapegoat being allowed to live is of particular importance when we consider current practice, where victims are pushed to the periphery of a group or a community but not driven away completely because their function as a focus of blame may need to be repeated' (Douglas, 1995, 29).

The practice of scapegoating was not confined to ancient Hebrew society: 'All through human history there have been ceremonies, if that is the right word, which have been and are described as scapegoating, and there have been victims' (Douglas, 1995, 29). Even though modern society bears little resemblance to the communities of biblical times, scapegoating continues to occur.

For Douglas:

> [I]n order to state that a person, a group or an organisation is being scapegoated it is absolutely essential that there should be clear evidence that the allegations of responsibility and of causation are untrue, or at least partially so. This, in effect, means that any rational and real involvement in causing difficulties and problems is sufficient to dismiss any accusation of scapegoating. A scapegoat has to be innocent of causing the events, behaviour or situations for which he or she is being blamed. (Douglas, 1995, 55)

The authors argue that proving innocence is not always an easy task and that very often the allocation of blame is done quickly and without all necessary care in order to achieve the fundamental purpose of scapegoating: relieving the burden on the rest of the community. Douglas himself makes reference to the case of Beverley Allitt. In 1993 Beverley Allitt was convicted of murdering four children, attempting to murder three children and causing grievous bodily harm to six other children while working as a nurse on the children's ward of Grantham and Kesteven Hospital. She received 13 life sentences. As in the Baby P case the conviction of the person directly responsible for the deaths of children appeared to be insufficient to assuage the anger of the community. Following the trial and conviction of Beverly Allitt, the Secretary of State for Health appointed an inquiry chaired by Sir Cecil Clothier QC. The Clothier Report made it clear that the tragic events at the hospital were the product of a malevolent, deranged criminal mind and that a determined and secret criminal may defeat the best regulated organisations. Nevertheless, the Report criticised failures of management and communication within the hospital and described a 'general lack in the qualities of leadership, energy and drive in all those most closely associated with the management of ward four (the children's ward)'. Before the Report was published in February 1994, two consultant paediatricians and one nursing manager at the hospital had been made redundant and another nursing manager had taken early retirement. Parents of some of the children expressed anger at the 'scapegoating' of the consultants and managers while the senior management criticised in the Report remained in their jobs:

> The Allitt case was clear: cause-and-effect responsibility and blame are all too horribly obvious. What is most important is how blame was apportioned between those who were generally regarded as having failed to prevent such a monstrous series of events occurring. Whether or not the Health Authority action in making the two consultants and two other staff redundant was designed to imply that these people were responsible is not relevant. What is relevant is that the public, and to some extent the media thought they were being offered as sacrifices to enable the matter to be closed at the cost of four people's careers and, in some cases, their present and future quality of life. (Douglas, 1995, 59)

Significantly Douglas then continues: 'There may have been some culpability on the part of the four who had been dispensed with' thus casting doubt on whether the four can be considered scapegoats according to Douglas's own narrow definition. It is for this reason that the authors suggest that a scapegoat does not need to be entirely innocent but merely to be carrying blame for others who might also be blamed.

> The death of children is always a highly charged and emotional affair...No amount of cold fact will obliterate the overwhelming need to blame. Allitt was found guilty, so she cannot be much of a focus for blame because she is so obviously grossly disturbed. Thus the blame must go to those who should have prevented her from being able to take such lethal actions. (Douglas, 1995, 59)

We shall return to the situations where those clearly directly responsible cannot be a focus for blame in Chapter Three. The need to blame might also go some way to explaining the investigations into allegations of sexual abuse made against the former BBC disc jockey, Jimmy Savile.[4] Savile's death means no criminal proceedings can be brought against him, but investigation might identify police officers, managers and fellow disc jockeys at the BBC who are still alive and who are capable of being the focus for blame. It is our hope that this book will go some way to explaining the nature of this need to blame. We return to the investigation of allegations made against Jimmy Savile in Chapter Seven.

Blame

> [Uncontroversial] is the fact that blame is, for better or worse, a central part of human relationships. (Coates and Tognazzini, 2013, 3)

> Blame is as common as water and as transparent to the gaze. We all know what it is but we cannot explain what we know by describing the experience. Often there is no experience to describe. We also cannot explain what we know by specifying blame's purpose, since genuine blame is always impotent because always after the effect. Given its ubiquity, its elusiveness, and its evident moral importance, we might expect philosophers to have scrutinised blame carefully. But strikingly, they have not. (Sher, 2006, vii)

This book is fundamentally concerned with blame. Blame *is* a central part of human relationships, as significant as jealousy and love. Yet, as George Sher points out, discussion of blame has been minimal: 'the absence of a significant literature on [blame] is really quite remarkable.' (Sher, 2006, vii). We perhaps should point out that we are not saying blame is inevitable. A human society which does not blame is theoretically possible yet one cannot find an example: a *society* without blame may well be an oxymoron.

The anthropologist, Mary Douglas, suggested such a society is not possible. She offers three types of blame or 'blame situation'. Imagine, she says, that a woman dies. The mourners will inevitably ask: 'Why did she die?' Douglas suggests the framing of the question and the response will depend on the type of society in which one lives. One possible explanation is, 'moralistic: she died because she has offended the ancestors, she had broken a taboo, she had sinned' (Douglas, 1992, 4). In such a society blame attaches to the victim. The 'harm' is evidence of the 'blame'. A second explanation is that the woman died because she had individual adversaries:

> [The] reason she died can be traced back to her not having been quick enough or clever enough in looking after her own interests; rival magic was more powerful than hers. The rivals who killed her are hardly being blamed when the finger of causation points to them, for there is not much moral concern: everyone is expected to do the same to promote their interests. (Douglas, 1992, 6)

The third possibility is that blame is attached to 'an outside community': 'In this case the answer is she died because an enemy of the community got her, not necessarily one who actually comes from outside but a hidden disloyal traitor' (Douglas, 1992, 6).

Contemporary society relies on the third type of blame. Blame is about identifying the outsider, the 'enemy within' or the 'other' just as the concept of the scapegoat relies on the idea of insiders and outsiders. The Biblical account of scapegoating was that the goat that was not to be sacrificed was cast to the 'outside'. The work of Tajfel and Turner on social identity theory shows how important the need 'to belong' can be and how destructive a focus on the out-group or 'other' may become (1986).

In 1960 PF Strawson delivered a lecture to the British Academy entitled 'Freedom and Resentment'. Strawson himself noted that the lecture was 'one of my very few ventures into moral philosophy' (Strawson, 2008, xxvi). The 'venture' received considerable attention and is seen by many as 'the founding document of contemporary work on blame' (Coates and Tognazzini, 2013, 5). In his lecture Strawson was attempting to reconcile two opposing views on the implications for blame on the truth or otherwise of determinism. Strawson characterised the two views as pessimism and optimism, more often referred to as incompatibilists and compatibilists. The pessimists argue that if determinism is true and human beings do not have free will, then blame and punishment and expressions of moral condemnation and approval are unjustified. The optimists counter this position by arguing that blame remains valid even if determinism is true. Some optimists argue that the justification for blame is to be found in its efficacy in 'regulating behaviour in socially acceptable ways' (Strawson, 2008, 92). The pessimists reply 'that just punishment and moral condemnation imply moral guilt and guilt implies moral responsibility and moral responsibility implies freedom and freedom implies the falsity of determinism'(Strawson, 2008, 93). For Strawson, the optimists accept the requirement of freedom but understand freedom to mean merely the absence of conditions which would make moral condemnation or punishment inappropriate:

> [Conditions] like compulsion by another, or innate incapacity, or insanity, or other less extreme forms of psychological disorder, or the existence of circumstances in which the making of any other choice would be morally inadmissible or would be too much to expect of any man. To this list they are constrained to add other factors which, without exactly being limitations of freedom, may also make moral condemnation or punishment inappropriate or mitigate their force: as some forms of ignorance, mistake or accident. (Strawson, 2008, 93)

Strawson's reconciliation of the two positions relies on the fact that 'The existence of the general framework of attitudes itself is something we are given with the fact of human society. As a whole, it neither calls for, nor permits, an external 'rational' justification' (Strawson, 2008, 145). Both optimist and pessimist 'over-intellectualise' the notion of blame. For Strawson, human society without blame is an impossibility: '[In] the absence of any form of these attitudes it is doubtful whether we should have anything that we could find intelligible as a system of human relationships, as human society' (Strawson, 2008, 148).

The reconciliation of the two positions comes from a radical modification of the optimists' position. Strawson accepts the important role of moral condemnation in regulating behaviour but argues that the optimists 'forget that these practices, and their reception, the reactions to them, really *are* expressions of our moral attitudes and not merely devices we calculatingly employ for regulative purposes. Our practices do not merely exploit our natures, they express them' (Strawson, 2008, 150). For Strawson, therefore, blame and moral responsibility are not matters of belief which are capable of being assessed for objective truth but, rather, they are attitudes and, as such, neither true nor false.

Strawson's lecture was an attempt to resolve arguments about the relationship between blame and determinism and the extent to which blame could exist in the absence of free will. David Hume had attempted to answer the question 220 years earlier. According to Hume the reason we are justified in blaming wrongdoers is that the badness of their acts is traceable to corresponding defects in their characters. In *The Treatise of Human Nature*, Hume wrote:

Actions are by their very nature temporary and perishing; and where they proceed not from some cause in the characters and disposition of the person, who performed them, they infix not themselves on him, and can neither redound to his honour, if good, nor infamy, if evil. The action itself may be blameable; it may be contrary to all the rules of morality and religion: But the person is not responsible for it; and as it proceeded from nothing in him, that is durable or constant, and leaves nothing of that nature behind it, 'tis impossible he can, on its account, become the object of punishment or vengeance. (Selby-Brigge, 1960, Book II part III sec II, 411)

Strawson places blame at the centre of our moral lives but there still remains the question of what it actually means to blame somebody. A number of writers express a view of blame as a sort of moral ledger (for example, Feinberg, 1970; Glover, 1970; Ishtiyaque Haji, 1998; Zimmerman, 1988):

Moral responsibility, so conceived, is liability to charges and credits on some ideal record, liability to credit or blame (in the sense of 'blame' that implies no action). Just as it is, as we say, 'forever to the credit' of a hero or saint that he performed some noble act, so a man can forever be 'to blame' for his fault. This, then, is what it is to be morally responsible for something on this conception: it is to be liable not to overt responses, but to a charging against one's record as a man. This record in turn can be used for any one of a variety of purposes – as a basis for self-punishment, remorse, or pride, for example; but a person can avoid putting it to those further uses, leaving responsibility simply a matter for the record. (Feinberg, 1970, 30)

Blame can be seen thus as the negative counterpart of praise. According to JJC Smart:

Praising a person is...an important act in itself – it has significant effects. A utilitarian must therefore learn to control his acts of praise and dispraise, thus perhaps concealing his approval of an action when he thinks that the expression of such approval might have bad effects, and perhaps even praising actions of which he does not really approve. (Smart, 1973, 49–50)

Such a view is implicit in the practice of considering mitigating factors when deciding on sentence following conviction. Someone of previous good character might receive a lesser punishment for the same act committed by a habitual wrongdoer.

In addition, this view might seem to undermine Strawson's characterisation of blame as 'attitude'. Yet when we blame another we do more than simply record the fact that he or she has fallen below some standard. The blamer as moral bookkeeper is to suggest an objective attitude and:

> To adopt the objective attitude to another human being is to see him, perhaps, as an object of social policy: as a subject for what, in a wide range of sense, might be called treatment; as something certainly to be taken account, perhaps precautionary account of; to be managed or handled or cured or trained; perhaps simply to be avoided, though this gerundive is not peculiar to cases of objectivity of attitude. The objective attitude may be emotionally toned in many ways, but not in all ways; it may include repulsion or fear, it may include pity or even love, though not all kinds of love. But it cannot include the range of reactive feelings and attitudes which belong to involvement or participation with others in inter-personal human relationships; it cannot include resentment, gratitude, forgiveness, anger, or the sort of love which two adults can sometimes be said to feel reciprocally, for each other. (Strawson, 2008, 109)

The view of blame as some sort of moral account or sanction has been criticised by a number of writers. PF Strawson himself argued against a view of blame as either an assessment or a form of sanctioning activity but saw it instead as a 'distinctive emotional response we have to perceived manifestations of ill will or disregard on the part of others' (Smith, 2013, 28). For Strawson, blame is closely related to attitudes such as resentment, indignation, guilt and forgiveness. Blame is not just an objective evaluation, it is connected to desire, emotion, expectation and disposition: 'we not only evaluate when we blame, but we also respond' (Coates and Tognazzini, 2013, 10). More recently, alternative accounts of blame have been put forward by George Sher (2006) and TM Scanlon (2008).

For George Sher '[Blame] is a stance or attitude that a person takes toward himself or another on the basis of a judgment that that person has in some way failed to conform to some moral standard' (Scher, 2006, 7) and further, 'To blame someone…is to have certain affective and behavioural dispositions, each of which can be traced to the combination of a belief that that person has acted badly or has a bad character and a desire that this not be the case' (Sher, 2006, 115). Sher sees blame to be about the person rather than the act and the issue of whether blame attaches to act or actor is discussed elsewhere in this book. Sher also sees a relationship between blame and forgiveness: 'The absence of blame would indeed mean we could not forgive anyone… because forgiving presupposes blame' (Sher, 2006, 4).

Scanlon, like Strawson, views blame as attitudinal in character but is less concerned with resentment and indignation. For Scanlon:

> To claim that a person is blameworthy for an action is to claim that the action shows something about the agent's attitudes toward others that impairs the relations that others can have with him or her. To blame a person is to judge him or her blameworthy and to take your relationship with him or her to be modified in a way that this judgment of impaired relations holds to be appropriate. (Scanlon, 2008, 128–9)

As Sher, Scanlon believes blame can take many forms and it is the relationship between the blamemonger and blamed that determines the precise form the blame takes. Reactive attitudes might be a possible response to impaired relations but other responses are possible: rather than resentment and indignation, one might feel sadness or a desire to end contact with the target of blame.

Seeing much merit in Scanlon's and Sher's account of blame, Angela Smith argues that both fail to identify the important aspect of protest inherent in blame and offers an amendment to their accounts:

> To blame another is to judge that she is blameworthy (that is, to judge that she has attitudes that impair her relations with others) and to modify one's own attitudes, intentions, and expectations towards that person as a way of protesting (that is, registering and challenging) the moral claim implicit in the conduct, where such protest implicitly seeks some kind of moral acknowledgement on the part of the blameworthy

agent and or on the part of others in the moral community. (Smith, 2013, 43)

Smith therefore draws a distinction between being blameworthy and being blamed: 'When I say of someone, "I know he's blameworthy, but I just can't bring myself to blame him", I am confessing that I find it hard to protest the meaning of his actions' (Smith, 2013, 43).

Smith's clear distinction is blurred by the definition of **culpable** offered by the Oxford English Dictionary. Initially 'culpable' is defined as 'guilty, criminal: deserving as punishment or condemnation' or to be deserving blame or censure: to be culpable is to be blamed or blameworthy.

Culpability is an important concept for contemporary penology. S143(1) Criminal Justice Act 2003 provides: 'In considering the seriousness of any offence, the court must consider the offender's culpability in committing the offence and any harm which the offence caused, was intended to cause or might foreseeably have caused.'

Von Hirsh is clear that punishment is inextricably linked to blame: 'The penal sanction clearly does convey blame. Punishing someone consists of visiting a deprivation (hard treatment) on him, because he supposedly has committed a wrong, in a manner that expresses disapprobation of the person for his conduct' (Von Hirsch, 2000, 9).

We are left with a certain circularity here since punishment will reflect the seriousness of any offence which in turn reflects the level of the offender's culpability. In this book we will explore the extent to which it is possible to assess the amount of blame attributed to a wrongdoer independently of any sanction (formal or informal) imposed.

Preliminary reflections

The idea for this book first emerged as the authors were engaged in researching the punishment of those responsible for crimes against humanity. It seemed to us that traditional justifications for punishment proved unsatisfactory when guidance on how to punish those responsible for extraordinary crimes was needed. The fact that many of those responsible for some of the worst atrocities had, until the critical moment in their lives, led fundamentally blameless lives raised further problems in relation to punishment. Could one really find mitigation for someone who had murdered hundreds in the fact that they had previously been a caring and compassionate prison officer? The idea that it is ordinary people who commit extraordinary crimes is nothing new. The psychological experiments of Stanley Milgram and Philip Zimbardo suggest we are all (or at least nearly all of us) capable of committing blameworthy acts given the right circumstances (Milgram, 1974; Zimbardo, 2007). Christopher Browning's study of the behaviour of a German police reserve unit in occupied Poland supports those experimental findings (Browning, 2001). Central to discussion about these extraordinary crimes seemed to be the allocation of blame: to what extent are those who are responsible also culpable? This led us to consider blame in a more general, less extraordinary context and, like George Sher, we were surprised at the comparative lack of relevant literature.

In 1999 Mark Langford launched the Accident Group, a personal injury claims management business. It is perhaps best known for its advertising slogan 'Where There's Blame, There's a Claim'. The slogan lasted longer than the company, which went into liquidation in 2003. The slogan seemed to epitomise contemporary, claim driven society. It also reflects a modern preoccupation with blame: if blame leads to claims it can also be said that claims lead to blame. A **claim culture** is also a **blame culture**. Our view is that over the last 35 years we have moved to a more judgemental, less sympathetic, and more punitive society. This change is reflected in a growth in criminalisation. Central to the change is blame. We suggest that the flow of blame in society increases as levels of uncertainty increase and social cohesiveness decreases.

A recent manifestation of this blame culture can be found in the reaction to the Berwick Review into Patient Safety. The Review was prompted by a number of allegations relating to the safety of those who found themselves under the care of Mid Staffordshire NHS Foundation Trust. The immediate response to publication of the Review was the announcement by David Cameron of the creation of a new criminal offence of wilful neglect for those working within the health service. The media coverage of the announcement was exemplified by the headline in the *Independent*: '"Neglect is unacceptable": NHS staff face jail if patients are abused' (*Independent*, 16 November 2013). In fact the Review had been keen to promote a culture of openness and transparency within the NHS and the reference to legal sanctions came towards the end of the Review:

> *We believe that legal sanctions in the very rare cases where individuals or* organisations are unequivocally guilty of wilful or reckless neglect or mistreatment of patients would provide deterrence while not impeding a vital

open, transparent learning culture. Our proposals aim to place wilful or reckless neglect or mistreatment of all NHS patients on a par with the offence that currently applies to vulnerable people under the Mental Capacity Act. (DH, 2013, 33)

The Berwick Review had suggested that important lessons could be learned from the no-blame culture that had improved aviation safety. When addressing the House of Commons, the Secretary of State for Health reflected the overall tone of the Berwick Report: 'That is not about penalising staff for making mistakes; it is about enabling them to learn from them' (Hansard, 19 November 2013, column 1096). By then, however, it was the new criminal offence that had entered public consciousness. David Cameron's initial response set the tone and was consistent with current practice: when faced with an apparent crisis the temptation to draft a new law seems almost overwhelming. The public could be forgiven for believing the Review to be another attempt to increase the number of criminal offences and to blame individuals. A letter to the *Guardian* made the following point:

So, five years for wilful neglect of patients. How long one wonders for wilful neglect (or is that destruction) of an entire health service? On the assumption that our elitely educated government cannot possibly be simply incompetent, there must be a reason for the continuing assault on the NHS. All I can come up with is that by the next election they will, in all honesty, be able to say that the NHS is no longer worth saving. (John Main, Clinical Director, Renal Medicine, James Cook University Hospital, Middlesbrough: *Guardian*, 19 November 2013)

John Main raises the further issue of the extent to which blame is attached to individuals or wider society. One feature of contemporary society has been to focus more on **person blame** and less on **system blame**, although on occasion the focus is wider and we shall explore this theme in subsequent chapters. An adequate account of blame needs to provide some understanding of the circumstances when system blame is preferred to person blame and also, when both system and person are blamed, in what proportion that blame is to be allocated.

Philip Zimbardo, who conducted the Stanford Prison Experiment in 1971, wrote: 'The most important lesson to be derived from the Stanford Prison Experiment is that Situations are created by Systems.

Systems provide the institutional support, authority, and resources that allow Situations to operate as they do' (Zimbardo, 2007, 226).

Zimbardo continues by arguing that it is those 'who had the power to design the behavioural setting and to maintain its operation in particular ways' that should be held responsible for consequences and outcomes. In the context of the Stanford Prison Experiment, it was not the individual guards that should shoulder most of the blame, but rather the one who created the system: Zimbardo himself. Similarly, Zimbardo argues, abuses that occurred in Abu Ghraib prison in Iraq were the responsibility of those who created the system. As we have already suggested, blaming others exonerates the rest of us; blaming the person rather than the system leaves the system unchanged and the possibility of further wrongdoing remains.

In recent years a new approach to criminology has emerged with a focus on social harm. Hillyard et al (2004) criticised criminology for the failure to pay adequate attention to social harm and sought to argue that the criminal justice system failed to protect us from harm while at the same time inflicting harm on those who are processed through the system. We argue that blame has similarly been neglected by criminology and has a similar central importance to an understanding of crime and criminalisation. We seek to show how blame acts as a lever for criminalising and marginalising behaviour and as such is legally transformative. We argue that an increasing pre-occupation with blame leads to an increasing resort to litigation. An understanding of blame will assist in a greater understanding of the criminalisation process.

This book was being completed as the death of Nelson Mandela was announced. Among the countless tributes made to him, the prevailing theme concerned his dignity and forgiveness and the fact that he sought to bring about reconciliation. Mandela's view was that the future of South Africa would not be advanced by recrimination and blamestorming. The interests of South Africa would not be served by identifying scapegoats for the evils of apartheid. Instead there was the establishment of a Truth and Reconciliation Commission. Victims of wrongdoing are often far more concerned that their story be told and that the truth is established than with the identification of individuals who can be blamed.

Notes

[1] http://news.bbc.co.uk/1/shared/bsp/hi/pdfs/22_05_09_sentencing_remarks_baby_p.pdf

[2] www.theguardian.com/society/2008/dec/01/baby-p-ed-balls-statement

[3] www.presseurop.eu/en/content/article/848681-blamestorming-britain

[4] www.bbc.co.uk/news/uk-20026910

TWO

Blame in the criminal justice process

This chapter provides an overview of the role of blame in the criminal justice process in England and Wales. Although many view the orthodox trial as the usual state response to criminal behaviour, it is important to recognise that in many ways it represents the exception (Kirchengast, 2010). The criminal justice system, it has been argued, is designed to facilitate trial avoidance (Cammiss, 2013) by, for example, rewarding those who confess and then plead guilty to the offence. In order to recognise this reality, it is necessary to consider both the orthodox criminal trial and some of the most common ways in which offenders are otherwise processed. Dingwall and Harding (1998) have argued that the criminal justice process should be viewed as a path which allows and facilitates departure at various points from charge to sentence. While it may be possible to justify some of these departures – for example a criminal trial may be a disproportionate response to a particularly trivial offence – no systematic or holistic approach can be discerned. Instead, the process has developed in a reactive and haphazard fashion and has been driven by a number of potentially competing demands, including the desire to use limited resources sensibly. In our current analysis, we seek to evaluate the extent to which blame has an impact on and influences this process. This analysis would appear to be apposite if the system seeks to operate in a morally justifiable manner. Some of the themes introduced in this chapter will be revisited later in the book when attention is paid to particular types of offender whose blameworthiness could be viewed as atypical.

As many offenders avoid prosecution, the chapter will start by considering pre-trial diversion. A distinction will be drawn between diverting individuals who might be said to have limited blame and certain activities which are criminal but which are routinely diverted. After a consideration of pre-trial diversion, attention will be given to the trial. Decisions relating to mode of trial, or the court in which the case is heard, will be studied as this depends on a number of factors, some of which are allied to blameworthiness. Finally, the sentencing process will be analysed from both a philosophical and a legal perspective. A number of rationales influence sentence such as retribution, rehabilitation, deterrence and public protection. Throughout the book it will be seen that these competing objectives help to explain the variable importance of blame in the criminal justice process. In this chapter the key facets of each potential justification will be outlined and it will be shown that, while blame is central to some of these aims, it is of marginal importance to others.

Pre-trial diversion: removing those of limited culpability

Later chapters will have more to say about how the criminal justice system responds to certain categories of offender such as juveniles and the mentally disordered post-conviction. It is, however, usually the case that such offenders do not face trial in a criminal court. There is a long tradition of young offenders being dealt with informally by the police through a system of cautioning which involved no more than a warning by a senior police officer which was recorded and which could then influence future decisions to prosecute (see further Dingwall and Harding, 1998; Muncie, 1999). Guidelines stipulated that cautions could only be imposed in appropriate cases and when the offender admitted guilt. Research, however, demonstrated that police forces differed greatly in the extent to which they cautioned young offenders, raising suspicions that force culture was the most likely determinant of whether a caution would be imposed (Ball, 2004; Wilkinson and Evans, 1990). It also emerged that repeat cautioning was commonplace which suggested that it had limited deterrent effect. Repeat cautioning also undermined the underlying justification. Each caution did require an admittance of guilt on the offender's part. Similarly, a defining characteristic which explained why the offender was less blameworthy (for example, relative immaturity) could often be found. Nonetheless, a caution carried with it an implicit message that the offender was being dealt with in an exceptional manner and this message became increasingly implausible with repetition.

A more formal system of pre-trial diversion for juveniles was introduced in the Crime and Disorder Act 1998. Cautioning was abolished and replaced with reprimands and warnings. Reprimands were reserved for less serious cases and were similar in effect to a caution; however, a reprimand could only be issued if an offender had not received a reprimand before (s65(2)). If the case was adjudged by the police to be more serious (s65(4)) or if the offender had previously been reprimanded, a warning would be considered. The Act limited the use of warnings to situations where the offender had not previously been warned or, where the offender had been warned, the offence was committed more than two years after the date of the previous warning and the police officer considered the offence insufficiently serious to require a charge to be brought (s65(3)). A warning required the offender to be referred to a youth offending team who would arrange for him or her to participate in a rehabilitative programme (s66(2)).

This new model has the virtue of providing a framework where the individual's blame, determined in part by his past record, is central to the decision whether to reprimand or warn. Ostensibly, this guarantees greater protection than the arbitrary system of cautioning. Peuch and Evans (2011, 804), however, reported that young offenders and youth offending team workers found the system to be 'arbitrary, unfair and disproportionate, especially as it may involve compulsory participation in a rehabilitation (change) programme'. Research by Fox et al (2006) also found that the system could operate oppressively and discriminate against marginalised groups. Koffman and Dingwall (2007) recognised that reprimands and warnings were more punitive than cautioning (although there is case law which establishes that reprimands and warnings are not forms of punishment) but sought to argue that the framework could potentially be justified if it was used proportionately. Minor offenders would be subject to a minimal response while those who admit to a more serious offence would face a more invasive intervention. Which response is appropriate would depend, at least theoretically, on the offender's culpability. Repetition is also a critical factor which suggests that the government viewed recidivism as sufficiently blameworthy to exclude some outcomes. Blame may dictate whether a warning can be issued but the terms of the rehabilitative intervention are assessed according to need. Therefore, a less blameworthy individual could receive a more onerous regime than an offender who committed an identical offence but with more personal responsibility. The effect of introducing this more involved diversionary scheme has, paradoxically, been to accelerate young offenders' involvement with the criminal justice system. Where a caution would have sufficed, a warning may have to be issued which entails the involvement of a youth offending team. It is not unreasonable to ask whether the outcomes adequately reflect the culpability of young offenders or whether they are often disproportionate and counter-productive.

Cautioning remains an option for adult offenders. The decision to issue a caution is taken by the police except for the most serious category of offences which are classified as indictable only and which otherwise would be tried at the Crown Court. A Crown Prosecutor determines whether a caution is appropriate for these offences. According to Crown Prosecution guidance:

> When considering the Public Interest in any case, consideration will be given as to whether the matter can be appropriately dealt with out of court. What is appropriate in the circumstances of each individual case will depend on the seriousness of the offence, the results of the offending behaviour, the antecedents of the offender and the likely outcome at court. Where an out of court disposal offers an outcome appropriate to the circumstances of the case, it should be considered and any relevant guidance taken into account. Whenever possible, the views of the victim should also be obtained and taken into account. In cases that are referred to a prosecutor for a charging decision, the CPS may recommend the case is dealt with by a simple caution or a conditional caution if that is considered appropriate. (CPS, 2013a, para 9)

In 2012, 168,260 adult offenders were cautioned (Ministry of Justice, 2013). As one would expect, most offenders were cautioned for comparatively minor offences such as common assault (25%), possession of a controlled drug (17%) and theft and handling stolen goods (16%). Small numbers, though, were cautioned for serious offences including threat or conspiracy to murder (93 offenders), wounding or other acts endangering life (53 offenders) and sexual activity with a child under 13 (30 offenders). One offender was cautioned for rape. It is apparent that offence gravity dictates most cautioning decisions which is consistent with the advice above. The data mask other factors which may have influenced the police or the Crown Prosecution Service particularly in the cases involving serious offences. By definition, these must be exceptional cases and it is likely that some factor personal to the offender meant that prosecution was not deemed to be in the public interest. The guidelines above, however, do not specifically mention the offender's blameworthiness as a relevant consideration. The seriousness of the offence would clearly favour prosecution in such a case and it is difficult to see how the conduct would not cause significant harm. Presumably prosecutors base their decisions either on the fact that the exceptional circumstances associated with the case would mean that any sentence imposed would be minimal or on a more holistic interpretation of what is in the public interest.

Conditional cautions are also available for adult offenders. After changes in the Legal Aid, Sentencing and Punishment of Offenders Act 2012, the police can issue a conditional caution for any offence apart from indictable offences and offences involving hate crime or domestic violence. In the rare cases where it might be appropriate for an indictable offence, the Crown Prosecution Service must make the determination and the rules stipulate that this power can only be used exceptionally. Unlike standard cautions, conditional cautions contain rehabilitative, reparative or restrictive conditions. Conditional cautions are issued very infrequently. Nationally only 192 conditional cautions were issued pre-charge and 180 were issued post-charge in the first quarter of 2013/2014 (CPS, 2013b, 2). Of the conditional cautions, 52% contained compensation conditions which is not surprising when 34% of the offences related to damaging or destroying property.

These statistics show that many minor offenders avoid any contact with the criminal court and suggest that care must be taken when discussing the 'typical' criminal justice process: prosecution and punishment are never seriously entertained for many minor offenders. To describe such a process as 'diversionary', as is usual, is therefore misleading as the term suggests a departure from the norm (Dingwall and Harding, 1998, 102–8); prosecution may more accurately be described as 'diversion' in such a context. What these statistics also suggest is that a simple caution is seen as an appropriate response to a significant amount of criminal behaviour. This recognises that the trial process itself would be a disproportionate response for many adult offenders. In deciding who should avoid trial, blame is an implicit consideration.

Pre-trial diversion: fixed penalties for particular categories of offence

The previous section considered situations where a general diversionary measure, such as a caution, could be justified because of the offender's limited culpability. Often blame was limited as the harm caused was minor or the offender was a juvenile. Cautioning has a lengthy history (Dingwall and Harding, 1998, 102–8) and, while the processes have become more defined and invasive, reprimands and warnings continue a diversionary approach of long standing. Fixed penalty notices are not novel, either, as they have been used extensively for minor road traffic offences such as speeding and parking violations for some time. In recent years, however, fixed penalties have been used in an increasing range of circumstances. Their status in the criminal justice system is interesting. As the payment of a fixed penalty is not taken as an admittance of guilt a criminal conviction is avoided, although the financial impact (which to many individuals would be considerable) would be identical to a fine of the same amount. Fixed penalty notices are interesting in another regard. Sometimes such a measure is genuinely diversionary in that it avoids prosecution. The question in such cases may be whether this form of diversion is more appropriate than a traditional approach such as cautioning. Fixed penalties are, however, more onerous and their availability may partly explain why conditional cautions are used so sparingly. More controversially, the growth of fixed penalties demonstrates an increased willingness to use the law to control 'undesirable' behaviours such as excessive noise in residential areas. The expansion of fixed penalty notices evidences a trend towards social regulation through an increasing use of coercive measures, even if care is taken to disguise this through the use of semantic legal distinctions between civil and criminal responses.

The most significant development has been the introduction of penalty notices for disorder in the Criminal Justice and Police Act 2001. Fixed penalty notices can be issued to offenders aged 18 and over for a considerable number of listed offences, such as being drunk and disorderly in a public place. 'Lower-tier' offences attract a fixed penalty of £60 while 'higher-tier' offences attract a £90 penalty. As the fixed penalty notice does not technically constitute a fine, prompt payment avoids a criminal conviction. Non-payment results in the fixed penalty being lodged as an unpaid fine at the magistrates' court. As this system avoids prosecution and guarantees that the individual will not get a criminal record, there is an obvious incentive to pay the fixed penalty. This inducement carries the possibility that people will pay even if they are not guilty of the offence, however.

Another category of offence which can be dealt with by a fixed penalty are minor environmental crimes such as littering and graffiti. The number of environmental offences which can be resolved by paying fixed penalties has grown substantially over the past decade, most notably through the Anti-Social Behaviour Act 2003 and the Clean Neighbourhoods and Environment Act 2005. Also important in this context is the Noise Act 1996 which gives local authorities the power to investigate and issue fixed penalty notices for excessive night noise following complaints by neighbours.

The most controversial development relates to truancy. Section 23 of the Anti-Social Behaviour Act 2003 allows head teachers, the local authority and the police to issue a £50 or a £100 fixed penalty notice to a parent who fails to ensure that their child attends school regularly. It has been argued that this power emphasises the punishment of 'flawed' parents, pays insufficient regard to the reality of low-income, and often single-parent, families and offers a simplistic response to a complex socio-economic problem (Donoghue, 2011). Arguably, resorting to the criminal law in this way fails to take account of the parent's blameworthiness and demonstrates a naive belief in the ability of a sanction to ensure compliance when support may prove more effective. Granting a head teacher the right to impose a fixed penalty also allows head teachers to discipline parents and pupils, a strategy that is hardly conducive to fostering a positive relationship between a struggling parent and school staff.

Pre-trial diversion: the routine diversion of some types of criminal conduct to specialist state agencies

Some types of deviant conduct are not investigated by the police or prosecuted in the usual manner. Examples would include offences linked to tax evasion, benefit fraud and health and safety breaches. There may be compelling reasons why such activities are policed differently, but it is important to ensure that there is some parity of approach: it would be unjust if offenders were being convicted and sentenced for 'routine' offences if more blameworthy offenders were dealt with in a less public way and were not subject to the same degree of public condemnation and punishment. Conversely, as there are significant attractions for the individual in avoiding a trial, one has to ensure that adequate safeguards are in place to protect the innocent. The threat of prosecution may be a powerful weapon for law enforcement agencies but, for this reason, care has to be taken in establishing that the individual has indeed broken the law. There is, therefore, a common rationale for diverting such activities based on a mutual desire on the part of all stakeholders to arrive at a speedy and fair settlement. Against this, there is the danger that excessive discretion allied to the implicit threat of prosecution could undermine the protection to which an accused person is entitled. A more general question is why these factors favour diversion and not prosecution in these particular instances. If the case for diversion is so compelling, why is this approach not used more widely (Braithwaite, 2002)?

Tax evasion is often presented as the archetypal crime which is seldom prosecuted by the authorities. Revenue raising bodies do not perceive their function to be prosecutorial. Rather, their aim is to recover taxes owed and a pragmatic approach reserves prosecution for a limited number of exceptional cases, often involving serial evaders or particularly elaborate evasionary schemes. According to HM Revenue & Customs:

> [The] law allows us the discretion to deal under a civil penalty regime with an offence which would otherwise require prosecution as a criminal offence. This not only provides an incentive for the taxpayer to co-operate with us once the fraud has been discovered, but prevents needless expense in taking cases involving small amounts of tax to the criminal court. (HM Revenue & Customs, 2013)

Ordinarily:

> [HM Revenue & Customs] will try and reach an agreed figure…covering the amount of tax, interest and penalties due. We will only suggest adjustments that we consider to be reasonable in light of the information we hold…We will invite [the individual] to sign a letter offering to pay an agreed sum and if we agree the sum we will issue a letter of acceptance. This exchange of letters is a legal contract. (HM Revenue & Customs, 2013)

Research has shown that this strategy is effective if judged on purely economic grounds (Feld and Frey, 2007; Franzoni, 2004; Leviner, 2008). This may be explained on the basis that there is little academic agreement about whether the threat of prosecution serves as a deterrent in tax cases (Klepper and Nagin, 1989), although one must not lose sight of the fact that a criminal offence has been committed. A broader concern is whether someone who deliberately breaks the criminal law, and in the process often goes to considerable lengths to deceive the authorities, should escape prosecution and punishment when other offenders, who are perhaps less blameworthy, do not.

A legal distinction is drawn between tax avoidance, a legal enterprise designed to minimise tax liability, and tax evasion which is a criminal offence. Few people enjoy paying tax and traditionally it would probably have been accurate to say that most people would not have regarded tax evasion as 'criminal' behaviour. More recently, however, there has been a widespread shift in attitudes towards the aggressive tax avoidance strategies which have been employed by some multi-national companies and wealthy individuals. The significant reputational damage caused has led to the 'voluntary' payment of taxes and public apologies. An obvious explanation is that these practices are taking place at a time of public austerity. The public mood seems to go beyond this, though, as the revulsion relates to avoidance and not evasion; deliberately taking steps to use the law to one's personal advantage has widely been seen as morally blameworthy and deserving of condemnation even if the actions are lawful.

It does not necessarily follow from this that the public will view illegal tax evasion more harshly than legal tax avoidance (Orviska and Hudson, 2003). The legal and financial advice on which wealthy tax avoiders depend is beyond the means of most of the public, leading, perhaps, to a sense of injustice. Paying cash for work in the knowledge that it will not be declared to the revenue may resonate more with the average person and, because of its ubiquity, be perceived as less blameworthy. Shifts in what is believed to be acceptable behaviour can lead to legislative reforms designed to close particular tax 'loopholes' that avoiders have exploited. These changes, though, reflect a desire to criminalise such behaviour in order to block one avenue for avoiding tax liability rather than a change of strategy which would mean that such offenders are routinely prosecuted and punished.

A comparison has sometimes been drawn between tax evasion and benefit fraud, an activity committed disproportionately by the poor and which often involves small sums of money. Benefit fraudsters are proportionately more likely to be prosecuted than tax evaders, but prosecution remains far from certain. A common tactic is for an agreement to be reached whereby prosecution will be avoided on condition that the benefit is no longer claimed. This may appear sensible but two concerns emerge. The first is that many claimants are vulnerable and are not in a position to challenge the assertion that they are not entitled to the benefit. When the Liverpool Welfare Rights Centre did challenge a number of cases, every benefit was subsequently reinstated (Moore, 1981, 139). A secondary issue is that considerable discretion remains as to whether an offender is prosecuted. Prosecution is less exceptional for welfare fraud, heightening the risk of arbitrary decision-making. The public mood is also hardening with regards to welfare fraud. Dingwall and Harding (1998) have suggested that benefit fraud may be perceived as more serious than tax evasion because it involves taking as opposed to withholding public money. This has meant that it is easier to conceptualise benefit fraud as 'criminal'. Whereas many would have regarded benefit fraud as a crime, there may have been some sympathy for perpetrators as they are often marginalised and carry little blame due to their financial plight. Jones (2011) has argued powerfully that this view has hardened and benefit claimants have become demonised, primarily by the media, in recent years and that this has led to a common belief that a lot of lawful welfare is undeserved.

Environmental offences are also investigated and selectively prosecuted by agencies other than the police, such as the Environment Agency and local government departments. This arrangement allows for expert involvement but again raises concerns about how this type of offending, which can have considerable impact on community well-being, is dealt with in comparison to other types of crime. One possible rationale for differentiation is the difficulties of proving causality and intent on the part of the polluter. Negligence may have led to the pollution, but how much blame should attach to a failure to take adequate precautions? There are instances where such concerns do not arise, 'fly tipping' providing an obvious example, but the picture is often far from straightforward. Limited resources necessitate an extremely selective approach to prosecution which raises questions about how decisions to proceed are taken. The seriousness of the offence would appear to be central but should this be measured only with reference to the damage caused? Individual blame, or lack thereof, would demand that the assessment went beyond the harm to consider matters such as whether the individual's actions were deliberate or negligent or whether an employer turned a blind eye to the practices of his or her employees.

A final category of offences which are seldom prosecuted are those relating to health and safety. If the inspectorate finds breaches of health and safety law, the preferred response is to issue a notice requiring rectification. Prosecution is reserved for the worst cases, usually following an accident. The working culture of the inspectorate is to work with employers to avoid harmful and illegal practices. Constructive dialogue may be the most appropriate way to secure compliance and limited resources may mean that inspectors have no practical alternative. Similar issues concerning blame, previously discussed with reference to environmental offences, arise. Negligence or ignorance of the law may be more common than deliberate attempts to avoid health and safety legislation and, in any event, proving the latter at trial would often be difficult. Another interesting dimension to health and safety law is that the inspectorate is often dealing with incidents which could have caused significant injury as opposed to situations where injury occurred. The individual's blame in failing to comply with the law, whether innocently or intentionally, may have been identical but, when harm occurs, one instinctively appears to be dealing with a more serious offence.

Most of the inspectorate's work attracts no public attention. If anything, health and safety has become a concept worthy of scorn even though there might be a tacit recognition that measures are necessary to protect public safety. It is only when a major incident, such as a railway accident, occurs that the adequacy of the official response is questioned. Yet, by definition, major incidents are complicated and unusual events making it difficult to apportion responsibility and blame. One of the broader themes of this book is that there has become a greater readiness to apportion blame for incidents and that this urge leads to scapegoating. The way in which those who breach health and safety law are routinely dealt with appears not to cause public concern, even if this acceptance may be explained by ignorance, however the law is perceived to be wanting when a high-profile accident occurs leading to death or significant injury. Finding out where blame lies in the context of health and safety is admittedly complex. Yet this fails to capture the prevailing mood as it usually will be easier to apportion blame for an accident in a workshop or a factory. Perhaps the decline in manufacturing has meant that the public find it easier to identify with the victims of a transport disaster than an industrial accident.

Mode of trial: deciding which court will hear a case

Assuming that the case has not been diverted by this point, the next procedural decision relates to mode of trial. Criminal offences in England and Wales fall into one of three categories depending on their perceived seriousness. The least serious offences are classified as summary only and must be tried in the magistrates' court. The gravest offences are classified as indictable offences and can only be tried before a jury in the Crown Court. Occupying the middle ground are triable either way offences which, as the name suggests, can be heard either in the magistrates' court or in the Crown Court. Determining which court hears such cases is important for practical reasons – a Crown Court trial is far more expensive and the sentencing options available to the judge are more extensive (and potentially more expensive as well). Broader policy questions are as important: who should determine where a triable either way case is heard? What are the criteria for selection if the determination is to be made by an individual other than the accused?

This section will address these points by considering the relevant law before reviewing empirical research which has challenged the extent to which decision-making in practice satisfies the need for full consideration of each case. There is a broader political context to the law relating to mode of trial (see Cammiss, 2013). Governments have been keen to encourage the use of magistrates' courts for financial reasons and this has led to the reclassification of certain common offences and to more overt inducements to plead guilty at the earliest opportunity. Both of these developments compromise the defendant's right to a fair trial as the first development restricts the right to a jury trial and the second effectively penalises those who elect to plead not guilty as their penalty on conviction will be greater than those imposed on offenders who elect not to exercise this right.

The legal process starts with the defendant entering a plea of guilty or not guilty to the offence in the magistrates' court (s17A Magistrates' Courts Act 1980). If the defendant enters a plea of not guilty, the magistrates have to decide whether the case should be heard by the magistrates' court or in the Crown Court. The Magistrates' Courts Act 1980 states that regard should be had to the nature and seriousness of the offence, whether the magistrates' court would be able to impose an appropriate sentence if the defendant was convicted, and any other factors that appear relevant. Considerable discretion rests with the magistrates at this stage as all of these factors are inherently subjective. The nature and seriousness of the offence would allow for an appraisal of the defendant's blame (even though the defendant maintains complete innocence) and a determination about the adequacy of sentencing options is again related to the individual's culpability if guilt were to be established. Other factors could also cover specific issues related to blame, such as the fact that the defendant was elderly. The relationship between offence-severity and the residual category is interesting: should individual culpability, as distinct from the harm caused by the offence, inform an assessment of offence-severity or is it a distinct concern? The case is automatically sent to the Crown Court if the magistrates decline jurisdiction. Where the magistrates elect to hear the case, the defendant is granted the opportunity to consent to summary trial or can instead elect jury trial in the Crown Court. Most defendants accept the magistrates' decision given the danger that a more exacting punishment could be imposed following a conviction in the Crown Court: around 80% of triable either way offences remain in the magistrates' court (Cammiss, 2013).

Research by Cammiss (2009) found that there was rarely disagreement about where a case would be tried and that magistrates followed the prosecution's recommendations in 96% of cases. This meant that decision-making was quick. However, Cammiss also found evidence that courts tended to follow their own working culture even where this went against official guidance. Citing domestic burglary as an example, the magistrates routinely declined jurisdiction even though national guidelines state that a Crown Court trial is only appropriate if specified aggravating factors are present (Sentencing Guidelines Council, 2008, 219). Guidelines are not prescriptive, but Cammiss' finding that decisions relating to seriousness and the appropriateness of available sentencing powers are determined according to local practice rather than national standards raises the issue of whether geographical disparity leads to injustice. The generic guidelines could hardly be described as illuminating or detailed: the 'definitive' guideline on allocation is only two pages long and the section dealing with mode of trial amounts to little over a hundred words (Sentencing Council, 2012a). More comprehensive guidance is provided in the *Magistrates' Court Sentencing Guidelines* (Sentencing Guidelines Council, 2008) which considers each offence separately. Arson, for example, should be tried in the magistrates' court where the damage is minor or moderate but jurisdiction should be declined where the damaged is judged to be serious (Sentencing Guidelines Council, 2008, 23). Slavish devotion to the guidelines would undermine the statutory test that magistrates should follow in so far as the test deliberately grants magistrates discretion to arrive at the correct decision. The danger is that, rather than make determinations on a case by case basis, magistrates may feel constrained not by the national guidelines but by local custom.

How do these findings relate to the defendant's blameworthiness? The fact that there is broad agreement between prosecution, defence and the magistracy suggests that either determining offence-severity is relatively easy or that the exercise is not being undertaken with due diligence. Official statistics suggest that many decisions are easy in that the bulk of triable either way cases remain in the magistrates' court. There is also often a consensus of opinion among the prosecution, defence and the magistracy (Cammiss, 2009). There are, however, benefits for all parties if a Crown Court trial is avoided which has led to accusations that defence lawyers may exert considerable pressure on their clients to enter a guilty plea (McConville et al, 1994). Magistrates' courts do have the ability to impose a short custodial sentence and magistrates may well believe that this usually gives sufficient scope to deal appropriately with most triable either way offences. What this means is that determinations about individual culpability are ordinarily taken after conviction at the sentencing stage.

Justifying sentence: the normative background

Punishment can be justified on a number of grounds which are usefully summarised in the Criminal Justice Act 2003:

(a) The punishment of offenders,
(b) The reduction of crime (including its reduction by deterrence),

(c) The reform and rehabilitation of offenders,

(d) The protection of the public, and

(e) The making of reparation by offenders to persons affected by their offences. (Criminal Justice Act 2003, s142(1))

Sentencers in England and Wales are supposed to take all of these aims into account when deciding what sentence to impose. The list does not provide a hierarchy; instead sentencers are meant to perform a balancing act between these diverse objectives. Problems arise, though, because each aim seeks a distinct end with the result that balancing renders the exercise futile. Prioritisation is essential if any of the justifications are to be realised. The fact that the 2003 Act fails to specify either an overriding objective or a hierarchy of aims engenders inconsistency as sentencers are forced to make such choices themselves.

Considering each objective in turn demonstrates why there are issues of incompatibility. A primary distinction can be drawn between retributive and utilitarian justifications. Retributive justifications rest on the notion that punishment is a deserved response to offending behaviour. Crucially, no future benefit has to accrue from the punishment. Utilitarian justifications, by contrast, demand future benefit on the basis that the harm of punishment can only be acceptable if a future harm of greater magnitude is avoided. Deterrence, rehabilitation and public protection are all utilitarian justifications.

Retribution attempts to justify punishment with reference to the offence committed. Punishment has to be proportionate to the seriousness of the offence in order to ensure that the offender receives his 'just deserts'. Offence-severity then is crucial to retribution as a disproportionate sentence (regardless of whether it is too lenient or, more commonly, too severe) cannot be justified. The harm caused by the offence is obviously central to quantifying the severity of the offence, but most retributivists would recognise that the offender's blameworthiness is also relevant. Blame does not just relate to the gravity of the harm caused but could include variables such as age or, more controversially, whether the offender has a prior record. Issues surrounding blame could legitimate the imposition of a lesser sentence or an increased sentence even if the harm caused by the offence was identical. A retributive approach would also allow for the pre-trial diversion of certain individuals for whom any form of punishment would be a disproportionate response.

Blame is of less direct importance to the utilitarian justifications, although those advocating such an approach would no doubt baulk at the punishment of the blameless. With each of the utilitarian justifications, the focus shifts to the means of achieving the future benefit. Deterrence, for example, would legitimate a sentence calculated to make the offender desist from committing like offences in the future (specific deterrence) or to make others minded to engage in such conduct refrain (general deterrence). It has been argued that deterrence is deeply problematic in that sentences which do not reflect the gravity of the offence, and hence the offender's blameworthiness, could be justified. It is consistent with this aim that a more blameworthy offender who is less likely to offend in future receives a lesser sentence than a less blameworthy offender who, perhaps through no fault of his own, is more likely to reoffend. Taken to extremes, utilitarianism might sanction the 'punishment' of an innocent individual if that harm was outweighed by a significant reduction in offending by others.

Public protection is similarly problematic. Here the (usually lengthy) confinement of 'dangerous' offenders is justified and determined by the perceived risk the individual would pose if at liberty. The offence for which the offender is being sentenced is usually of some relevance in that incapacitative sentences are not generally available for minor offences. If blame, though, has any relevance it is marginal. Legislation is often framed broadly so as to allow the possibility of incapacitating those who commit moderately serious violent or sexual offences. Sometimes little discretion is given to the court if certain specified criteria are met, as was the case with the notorious Imprisonment for Public Protection in England and Wales. The point here is that, logically, blame should play no part if public protection is the goal as it has no direct bearing on perceived risk as someone with limited culpability may nonetheless pose a vivid danger.

It is possible to argue that blame is of more relevance to the final utilitarian justification – rehabilitation – as it may help determine the most appropriate provision for the offender. Rehabilitative schemes for juvenile offenders may well differ from those for adult offenders, for example. As a utilitarian justification, however, the focus is on the future benefit of the punishment imposed. The aim, as with deterrence and public protection, is desistance and the method employed is to address underlying factors that may account for the offending behaviour. There may sometimes be a perception that offenders who are given probation rather than a custodial sentence have particular characteristics which make them less culpable and that providing assistance outside prison is likely to be more effective. Sentencers certainly have the scope to pass a non-custodial sentence in most cases, although there is little empirical evidence about the factors which determine whether an offender is imprisoned.

Justifying sentence: the legal background

Having considered the possible philosophical justifications for sentencing offenders, this section provides an overview of sentencing law in England and Wales. It will be shown that, although the main Act of Parliament requires sentencers to consider all of the objectives listed in the previous section, the framework for determining which disposition is appropriate favours a retributive approach. As a consequence, the individual's blame should be highly relevant in the sentencing process.

The Criminal Justice Act 1991 provides a useful starting point as this Act, which was the first to state explicitly the aims of sentencing, provided that the primary determinant of sentence was the seriousness of the offence. The Act was welcomed by commentators both for providing clarity to the process and for attempting to curb the potential injustice of sentencing on utilitarian grounds (Koffman, 2006a). Increasingly there had been concern that sentences justified on the basis of rehabilitation were disproportionate to the gravity of the offence committed. Sentencers were now required to assess the seriousness of the offence and, having done so, determine whether it met the threshold for different types of punishment. Imprisonment, for example, could only be imposed if 'the offence, or the combination of the offence and one other offence associated with it, was so serious that only such a sentence can be justified for the offence' (s1(2)(a)). The term had to be that which was 'commensurate with the seriousness of the offence' (s2(2)(a)). An offence could not be regarded as more serious on the basis of 'any previous convictions of the offender or any failure of his to respond to previous sentences' (s29(1)). Mitigation could still be taken into account by sentencers (s28(1)). A potential weakness with the Act was that no guidance was provided about how the seriousness of an offence should be measured and early guidance from the Court of Appeal added little of value (see *Cox* (1993) 14 Cr App Rep (S) 749).

It was not long before the government amended the law which diluted the singularity of approach contained in the 1991 Act (see further Hudson, 1995; Koffman, 2006a). After sustained judicial lobbying, and a lack of political nerve, two fundamental provisions were abolished in the Criminal Justice Act 1993. The first was the requirement that sentencers could not take account of previous convictions when deciding on the seriousness of an offence. Now they could (s66). This re-opened the danger that offenders could be sentenced on the basis of their record as opposed to the seriousness of the current offence. More broadly, it sent a signal that a repeat offender was more blameworthy than a first offender and deserved a harsher sentence to reflect this.

The 1991 Act also contained an innovative and progressive system of **unit fines** which took into account both the seriousness of the offence and the offender's means. In order to determine the amount of a fine a two-stage process had to be followed. First, the sentencer had to calculate the seriousness of the offence and attribute this a unit value. The unit value would then be multiplied by the offender's disposable income to arrive at the amount of the fine. Equality of impact is an important notion in sentencing and taking full account of the offender's income meant that financial penalties would affect offenders who had committed offences of similar gravity in the same way. The results were, however, ridiculed in the media as offenders who were of limited means but had committed relatively serious offences were fined smaller amounts than more affluent offenders who were guilty of lesser crimes. In the popular imagination, the system was unjust because it did not reflect the blame of the offender. The irony was that that it did, but in a more sophisticated manner. Rather than modify the unit system, or seek to defend the underlying philosophy, the government abolished the system while maintaining the general principle that the offender's means should be taken into account when setting the level of a fine (s65).

Abolishing unit fines did not represent a rejection of the principle that a proportionate fine has to incorporate the wealth of the offender. Instead the 1993 Act retained the principle, but jettisoned a formulaic system. Returning discretion to sentencers did not mean that sentencers could ignore an offender's income, instead it gave them the discretion to determine how to modify the amount of a fine to accommodate means. In practice, considerable ground was conceded. Legislating for a unit system represented a clear acknowledgement that fairness demanded that offenders of equal blame were treated consistently and that uniform fines were unjust on this basis. There was value in a system which saw this as a two-stage process: first a determination of the gravity of the offence (where the offender's blame was key) followed by a consideration of a proportionate sentence (where the offender's financial means was fundamental). Although the revised provision suggested that these two stages had to be followed, the absence of a defined process made it difficult for sentencers, even if so minded, to undertake a meaningful financial assessment prior to setting the amount of a fine. Perhaps it is best to view the change of procedure as a way of minimising the effect of the realisation that equal impact required setting different fines for offenders with similar culpability.

The accepted account is that the Criminal Justice Act 1993 was the first incremental step in a process which reduced the importance of retribution in the sentencing process (Koffman, 2006a). Subsequent Acts did expand the opportunity for other sentencing aims to be pursued, particularly the incarceration of 'dangerous' offenders. Such individuals did not have to be especially blameworthy if they were perceived to pose a risk to the public. The efficacy of this approach depends on whether it is legitimate or desirable to punish on the basis of a potential future offence, even if this offence is likely to be serious. Research shows that risk is inherently difficult to predict which means that many of those classed as 'dangerous', and incapacitated on this basis, would not offend if at liberty (Braithwaite and Pettit, 1990; Golash, 2005; Mathiesen, 2006). Incapacitative sentencing represents a direct challenge to notions of proportionality in that the offence for which the offender is being sentenced – and for which he may be said to be blameworthy – is of marginal concern. There is a rich body of work on what has been termed the 'risk penology' which has sought to account for what is an international trend in criminal justice (Ericson, 2007; Garland, 2001; Simon, 2007). Given the lack of a sound empirical basis, the moral justification becomes weak and it is regrettable that governments have become increasingly willing to embrace such an approach.

Despite this undeniable shift towards public protection, it has been argued by one of the present authors that retribution still dominates the current sentencing framework (Dingwall, 2008). The law is mainly found in the Criminal Justice Act 2003. In order to pass any particular sentence, the sentencer has to assess the seriousness of the offence. Section 143(1) states that: 'In considering the seriousness of any offence, the court must consider the offender's culpability in committing the offence and any harm which the offence caused, was intended to cause or might foreseeably have caused.'

The offender's culpability is then distinct from the harm (whether realised, intended or foreseen). Section 143(2) stipulates that courts are to view previous offences as aggravating factors which should increase the sentence. Whether a particular sentence can be imposed depends on whether or not a threshold has been met and this in turn depends on the seriousness of the offence. Taking the example of imprisonment:

> The court must not pass a custodial sentence unless it is
> of the opinion that the offence, or the combination of the

offence and one or more offences associated with it, was so serious that neither a fine nor a community sentence can be justified for the offence. (s152(2))

A criticism that was made earlier related to the lack of guidance that sentencers had when deciding how serious a case was. The 2003 Act provides a statutory test that was lacking in the 1991 Act. A more important development, however, is that sentencers now have more detailed guidelines from which to work. At the time of the 1991 Act, the Court of Appeal had issued some **guideline judgments** which offered starting points for sentencing that offence. The problem with this approach was that the guideline judgments concentrated on particularly serious offences, such as armed robbery, where the primary issue was not what type of punishment should be imposed but on the length of sentence. What was lacking was guidance on whether a particular disposition threshold had been met. This was particularly unsatisfactory with regards to certain property offences, notably robbery and domestic burglary, which the court had to sentence on a regular basis. A paucity of guidance meant that, even if the 1991 Act was clear about the purpose of sentencing, its application was likely to be inconsistent. Devising and implementing an alternative framework was always going to be contentious. The judiciary are vocal about the need for discretion so that they can accommodate the variables that each case presents. Similarly, there is a legitimate constitutional debate about the respective roles of the government and the judiciary in determining sentencing policy. It is no surprise that the government's reforms were incremental.

The Sentencing Advisory Panel was established in the Crime and Disorder Act 1998. Their role was to assist the Court of Appeal before a guideline judgment was issued by, for example, providing information to the court on current sentencing practice or on the effectiveness of different punishments (s81(4)(c)). The Court of Appeal was obliged to consider the Panel's views but could depart from them if they saw fit. A Sentencing Guidelines Council was created by the Criminal Justice Act 2003. Comprising mainly, although not exclusively, of judicial members, the Council was charged with drafting guidance which sentencers would have a duty to 'have regard to' (s172(1)). The first guideline passed by the Council (Sentencing Guidelines Council, 2004) related to calculating offence seriousness in recognition of the fact that this judgment remained fundamental to the framework of the 2003 Act. This guideline remains important as it directly addresses individual blame.

It will be recalled that s143(1) of the 2003 Act drew a distinction between the culpability of the offender and the actual, intended or foreseeable harm caused. The guideline dealt with both considerations in turn. Four levels of **criminal culpability** were identified: intention; recklessness; knowledge; or negligence (Sentencing Guidelines Council, 2004, para 1.7). These 'levels' are presumably listed in descending order of culpability. Harm was similarly divided into harm to individual victims, harm to the community and a residual category of other types of harm. Unlike culpability, the guideline did not specify the relative gravity of these harms recognising, correctly, that this was impossible.

The Council recognised that '[a]ssessing seriousness is a difficult task, particularly where there is an imbalance between culpability and harm' (para 1.16). The task was especially problematic either where the harm that materialised was greater than that intended or where the offender's culpability exceeded the harm that arose. Harm, they argued, 'must always be judged in the light of culpability' (para 1.17). Therefore, the initial factor in determining seriousness was the culpability of the offender. Dingwall comments (2006/2007, 308–9) that:

> The use of the word 'initial' is intriguing. Does this imply that culpability should be the *primary* determinant of seriousness? Or does it describe a process whereby culpability should be considered prior to harm in an overall assessment of severity? The latter would certainly appear to reflect the process in section 143(1) of the 2003 Act more accurately, in that culpability and harm are seen as two distinct elements which are to be amalgamated in order to determine seriousness. On the other hand, if the use of the word 'initial' is taken to denote a hierarchy, an apparent way of addressing the two problematic scenarios that were identified in the report is provided. (Italics in the original)

Although the guideline provides a thoughtful appraisal of how seriousness can be quantified, its practical benefit is limited as it fails to provide concrete guidance to sentencers faced with deciding whether a particular offence is so serious that a particular punishment is warranted. Instead, it stated that this guidance would be best provided in discrete guidelines on individual offences (Sentencing Guidelines Council, 2004, para 1.37). Subsequent guidelines do address when particular punishments are appropriate but there is a danger that, by concentrating on particular offences in isolation, broader questions about relative severity are lost (Ashworth, 2005, 132). The Sentencing Guidelines Council and the Sentencing Advisory Panel were abolished in the Coroners and Justice Act 2009 and replaced by a Sentencing Council who maintain a responsibility for producing guidelines. A crucial difference is that courts are now obliged to follow such guidance unless departure can be justified in the interests of justice (s125(1)). The Council has not revisited the issue of determining seriousness at a generic level but has continued to provide guidance on an offence-specific basis.

It is evident that blame remains central to the sentencing process. The Criminal Justice Act 2003 and subsequent guidance from the Sentencing Guidelines Council (2004) both state categorically that offence-severity cannot be measured adequately if one concentrates exclusively on the harm caused, intended or foreseen. This realisation can complicate matters. As the Sentencing Guidelines Council recognised, scenarios can arise where an individual's culpability is low but the ensuing harm is considerable. Conversely, those who intend serious harm can sometimes be thwarted. Individual guidelines do provide a clear framework which, if followed (and that is not certain), would lead to a degree of consistency. Whether the sentences deemed appropriate in the guidelines adequately reflect the blame of individual offenders remains contentious as determining what constitutes a just, proportionate sentence remains subjective.

Conclusions: blame and procedural decision-making

In one of the most influential contributions to criminal justice scholarship, Packer (1968) drew a distinction between **crime control** and **due process** values in the criminal justice process. Although Packer's model is not without flaws, this dichotomy has explanatory value in understanding the inherent tension between the need for a practical and effective system for dealing with alleged law-breakers and the desire for a system which contains robust procedural safeguards at all stages to ensure that justice is achieved. The crime control model is outcome-focused, in so far as any system should be judged on the efficiency with which desired objectives are realised. By contrast, a due process model would prioritise fairness over expediency at each and every stage. Gilchrist (2006, 169) comments:

> This balancing between due process and crime control can be translated into a conflict between 'expediency' and 'legality', which is interesting to consider in terms

of the smaller decision points involved in the prosecution process. This area can also be researched in terms of factors influencing these, and what this might mean in terms of 'justice'. Consideration can also be given to what requires challenge and change, and how this might be achieved.

It has been argued that Packer's models have limited potential for reforming the criminal justice process:

> One of the strands of thought underlying the due process model is a scepticism about how the criminal sanction is used. Packer stated that this scepticism leads in turn to concern about the criminal justice process. Since the range of possible concerns about the use of the criminal sanction is so diverse, however, this strand of thought does not in itself give us any guidance on what form the criminal justice process should take. It simply acts as a catalyst for further evaluation. It is therefore not possible to construct an ideal type with concern about the use of the criminal sanction as a starting-point. That is not to say that concern about the use of the criminal sanction is irrelevant. Not only might it provoke consideration of the criminal justice process, it might also be relevant in making the value judgments that the ideal-types open up. (Macdonald, 2008, 270)

To what extent do these models explain the criminal process outlined in this chapter? Can they help us to evaluate whether blameworthiness, as a factor influencing fairness and justice, is given sufficient weight? Packer himself invoked images of conveyor belts and obstacle courses to describe the criminal justice process and so it makes sense to evaluate the system in a sequential manner.

Determining whether prosecution is in the public interest or whether an alternative diversionary strategy is more appropriate represents the starting point. The processing of offenders in an expedient fashion with minimal financial outlay clearly satisfies crime control objectives, not least as it relieves pressure on the courts to try those who cannot be diverted. It is not necessarily the case that diversionary approaches are inimical to a due process model. What is necessary, though, is that the offender is given adequate protection as there is an obvious temptation to confess to an offence in the knowledge that a denial would lead to prosecution. There are requirements that guilt is established in most cases and many measures demand an admittance of guilt. For example, cautions can only be administered when there is a sufficiency of evidence as well as a confession. The growing use of fixed penalty notices is less easy to accommodate in a due process model as there is no formal admittance of guilt. Expediency is the obvious driver and their use prioritises crime control values. Some may object to this analysis on the basis that the models are inapplicable as fixed penalty notices are not technically punishments, but this ignores the reality: notices are being issued for conduct that is criminal and the financial penalties have an impact in exactly the same way as does a fine. It is suggested that diversionary approaches can be accommodated within a due process model if: (1) meaningful safeguards are in place to ensure that the factually innocent do not 'admit' guilt in order to avoid prosecution; (2) clear national guidelines are provided as to when diversion is appropriate; (3) there is an adequate review process to monitor how any diversionary scheme operates.

These conditions all relate to blame in that they are designed to protect the blameless from any intervention while providing a framework which aims to achieve consistent outcomes for those who can be deemed blameworthy. For justice to be realised though, diversion must be a proportionate response to the gravity of the offence which means that a determination has to be made by some actor as to whether a given offence meets the threshold for prosecution. Inevitably, and despite objective criteria, this involves a subjective value judgement by the police or a crown prosecutor. The cautioning statistics suggest that the correct cases are being dealt with pre-trial, although one does not know how many of those cautioned are factually innocent. Reprimands and warnings are more difficult to evaluate using Packer's models. Keeping juvenile offenders out of court may suggest a pre-occupation with crime control, but the system replaces a less invasive, quicker and cheaper system for dealing with youth offending. From a due process perspective, statutory criteria are listed which offer procedural protection of a degree although key decisions, such as whether a first offence is sufficiently serious to justify a warning rather than a reprimand, remain arbitrary. Blame does appear relevant to this new framework provided decisions on offence-severity do not just measure the harm caused. One cannot, however, ignore empirical evidence from stakeholders which suggests that the process operates inconsistently and unfairly (Peuch and Evans, 2001).

Diverting particular activities from the orthodox criminal process also exposes tensions between crime control and due process values. Some of these offences, for example breaches of health and safety law, require specialist investigation and hence it may well be legitimate to transfer this function from the police to bespoke agencies with the necessary expertise. The benefits of a speedy resolution to some offences are obvious. In that respect, aspects of a crime control model are clearly visible. Due process concerns are not wholly absent, but their role is often limited. Three factors help explain this balance. First, these types of activity are often seen as **quasi-criminal** and attract less stigma than 'normal' criminality. Second, such offences are often classed as strict liability offences (see further, Chapter Four). Conviction is not dependent on proving a particular state of mind on the part of the offender; there is, therefore, no legal requirement for the offender to be blameworthy provided he is factually responsible for the specified harm. Finally, and partly because strict liability commonly suffices, the likely punishment is often comparatively minor. Later chapters will challenge the assertion that these crimes are relatively minor and that those who commit them are less blameworthy than those offenders who are routinely prosecuted. There is the added problem that a vigorous campaign to prosecute deviant organisations could indirectly punish those whom the law is seeking to protect:

> [Corporations] act according to capitalist laws of economic behaviour rather than laws of due process or social justice. If forced to comply with laws which make processes uneconomic (or, more realistically, less profitable) firms will simply scale down or move their business. Regulatory agencies which genuinely care about their true clients (the workers within the industry they regulate) are thus forced into choosing between two unpalatable alternatives: corporate law breaking or reduced economic activity. (Sanders et al, 2010, 420)

Mode of trial decisions have an impact both on the likelihood of conviction (the acquittal rate is higher in the Crown Court) and on the potential punishment (as magistrates' courts' sentencing powers are more limited). The criminal justice system already determines where the least serious and the most serious offences are heard largely on the basis of offence-severity. Although the classification of offences has to be decided at a general level, an assessment of the **typical offence** demands consideration not only of the **typical harm** caused but of the **typical offender**'s blameworthiness. A useful example is fraud where the average financial loss may suggest that this is a comparatively minor offence, yet the fraudster's actions might demonstrate considerable culpability. At a general level, dividing offences into three generic categories has not been questioned presumably on the basis of necessity: unless the magistrates' courts deal with the bulk of cases the criminal justice system would collapse. Nor is this objectionable at a theoretical level as the magistrates' courts have sufficient sentencing powers to deal with most offenders in a just and proportionate manner. It goes without saying that there will be a degree of arbitrariness in the classification of offences as determinations of seriousness are inherently subjective and political. The political dimension means that some offences will be classified as a triable either way, or an indictable offence for symbolic reasons rather than on an objective assessment of seriousness, while others will be classified as summary offences solely because it will help reduce pressure on the Crown Court. Broadly, however, the categorisation appears defensible on grounds of offence-severity.

Many triable either way offences have a wide legal definition and it therefore comes as a surprise that most decisions are uncontested and unproblematic in practice (Cammiss, 2009). If this was because national guidelines were sufficiently clear and were followed sensibly, one might conclude that there was adequate due process protection at this vital juncture. Instead, the fact that court custom was crucial and that the majority of cases remain in the magistrates' court highlights the importance of crime control at this stage. This is not necessarily problematic in that defendants have to consent to summary trial, but the risks associated with a Crown Court trial serve as a powerful disincentive.

Finally, we turn to sentencing. The argument advanced earlier in the chapter was that other writers have over-stated the retreat from retribution in the criminal justice system. This is not to deny the resurgence of public protection over the past 15 years, rather it is to situate it in the everyday reality of sentencing decision-making. In most cases, sentencers are legally bound to determine the seriousness of the offence – which explicitly includes the offender's culpability – before determining whether a statutory threshold for a particular type of punishment is met. In many cases they are assisted in this task by sentencing guidelines which they are required to follow unless the interests of justice demand otherwise. Sentencers are routinely making assessments about seriousness, in part on the basis of individual culpability. Our thesis then is that blame remains central to sentencing and the imposition of punishment.

From decisions to prosecute to determining sentence, blame plays a crucial role in the criminal justice system. It is far from the only factor that dictates policy and, at times, policy appears to prioritise concerns other than blame, perhaps most notably the need to manage the criminal justice system in an expedient manner. Many competing influences are important and it can be justifiable to marginalise or exclude blame from the calculus at times. Blame is used in this book primarily as a means of evaluation rather than an exemplar. That said, a criminal justice system which fails to consider individual blame risks losing any claim to legitimacy. Assessments of blame are sufficiently entrenched in our current system to ensure that this is not the case but it is evident that, when tested on this basis, parts of the system are found wanting.

THREE

Blame and the blameless

Some categories of individual are excluded from criminal liability even though they have caused a criminal harm. In English Law children under the age of 10 cannot be held criminally liable; the International Criminal Court has no jurisdiction over anyone under the age of 18. Most legal systems also recognise that mental capacity affects criminal liability: less or no blame may be attached to those who lack the mental capacity to control their actions. Chapter Three considers the influences and effects of both age and mental capacity on blame. The chapter will also survey a number of additional excuses or justifications to crime to ascertain the extent to which they depend on an absence or reduction of blame. The chapter concludes by exploring the notion of moral luck. Those following the Kantian tradition would argue that intention is the key to moral assessment: HLA Hart posed the question: 'Why should the accidental fact that an intended harmful outcome has not occurred be a ground for punishing less a criminal who may be equally dangerous and equally wicked?' (Hart, 1968, 129). Yet often the person making the unsuccessful attempt is assessed differently from the one who succeeds.

The minimum age of criminal responsibility

On 8 November 2013 the Age of Criminal Responsibility Bill received its second reading in the House of Lords. The bill's sponsor, the Liberal Democrat peer Lord Dhokalia, pointed out during the debate that at 10, the age of criminal responsibility in England and Wales was the lowest in Europe. The introduction of the bill followed the publication of a report by the Centre for Social Justice which had been commissioned by the Secretary of State for Work and Pensions. *Rules of Engagement: Changing the Heart of Youth Justice* (Centre for Social Justice, 2012) considered a number of aspects of the current system of youth justice in England and Wales including the minimum age of criminal responsibility. The Centre for Social Justice pointed out that discussion of the topic has for long been almost taboo in England and Wales and those who have suggested increasing the age have faced vilification from the tabloid press. It is clear that part of the reason for setting a minimum age relates to concerns about the degree to which children are competent to participate in the criminal process. There has also been much discussion about the impact of criminalisation on children. Adopting a minimum age is also fundamentally about allocation of blame: all societies seem to accept that there is some age below which an individual cannot be considered fully responsible for their actions.

> Early to mid-adolescence is a period during which the domains that control and coordinate thoughts, behaviours and emotional responses undergo significant development. In particular, the likelihood of impulsive, sensation-seeking and risk-taking actions is greatly increased. Capacity to accurately gauge the consequences of actions is developing, as is the ability to empathise. Young people are also much more susceptible to the influences of others, especially their peers: they find it harder to resist or say no to behaviours that in the adult world would be called crimes. This does not mean that children bear no responsibility for their behaviour, but that they may be less responsible. (Centre for Social Justice, 2012, 202)

The issue of culpability was considered extensively by the United States Supreme Court in *Roper v Simmons* (543 US 551 (2005)). At the age of 17, Christopher Simmons persuaded a younger friend to help him break into a woman's apartment, tie her up and then throw her over a bridge. He was convicted of murder and sentenced to death by a Missouri court in 1994. Following a number of appeals the case reached the Supreme Court in October 2004 and the opinion of the Court was delivered in March 2005. According to the Court: 'Capital punishment must be limited to those offenders who commit "a narrow category of the most serious crimes" and whose extreme culpability makes them "the most deserving of execution"' (p 14).

Since a major purpose of the death penalty, according to the Supreme Court, is retribution and:

> Whether viewed as an attempt to express the community's moral outrage or as an attempt to right the balance for the wrong to the victim, the case for retribution is not as strong with a minor as with an adult. Retribution is not proportional if the law's most severe penalty is imposed on one whose culpability or blameworthiness is diminished, to a substantial degree, by reason of youth and immaturity. (p 17)

The extent to which the culpability of juveniles is in some way diminished was therefore a central issue in the case. To assist it the Court was able to refer to the brief prepared by the American Psychological Association and the Missouri Psychological Association on behalf of Simmons. The *amicus* brief argued forcefully against imposing adult levels of culpability on juveniles:

> At ages 16 and 17, adolescents, as a group, are not yet mature in ways that affect their decision-making. Behavioral studies show that late adolescents are less likely to consider alternative courses of action, understand the perspective of others, and restrain impulses. Delinquent, even criminal, behavior is characteristic of many adolescents, often peaking around age 18. Heightened risk-taking is also common. During the same period, the brain has not reached adult maturity, particularly in the frontal lobes, which control executive functions of the brain related to decision-making...Developmentally immature decision-making, paralleled by immature neurological development, diminishes an adolescent's blameworthiness. (American Psychological Association, 2004, 2)

The brief cited with approval the work of Jeffrey Jensen Arnett on adolescence. Beginning at the end of childhood at the age of about 10 or 11, adolescence provides the key development bridge to adulthood which is not always achieved until the early 20s (Arnett, 2000). Arnett (1992) found that adolescents as a group were statistically overrepresented in almost every kind of reckless behaviour and that adolescents appear to be particularly attracted to high risk behaviour. As Hirschi and Gottfredson (1983) point out 'One of the few facts agreed on in criminology is the age distribution of crime' (p 552). One of the 'brute facts' (p 552) of criminology which varies little across time or different cultures is that the highest levels of crime occur during late adolescence, typically between the ages of 15 and 18.

The *amicus* brief cited a number of studies which demonstrated that adolescents were 'less future oriented and less likely to consider properly the consequences of their actions' (American Psychological Association, 2004, 7). Furthermore, 'Neuropsychological research demonstrates that the adolescent brain has not reached adult maturity' (p 9):

> Of particular interest with regard to decision-making and criminal culpability is the development of the frontal lobes

of the brain. The frontal lobes, especially the prefrontal cortex, play a critical role in the executive or 'CEO' functions of the brain which are considered the higher functions of the brain…Neurodevelopmental MRI studies indicate this executive area of the brain is one of the last parts of the brain to reach maturity. (p 10)

Ruben Gur of the University of Pennsylvania in Philadelphia has stated: 'The brain's frontal lobe, which exercises restraint over impulsive behaviour doesn't begin to mature until 17 years of age…The very part of the brain that is judged by the legal system process comes on board late' (Beckman, 2004).

The majority in the Supreme Court held that it was unconstitutional to impose the death penalty on offenders who were under the age of 18 at the time of the offence. The decision was partly based on acceptance of the diminished culpability of juveniles. Even O'Connor J, dissenting from the majority opinion, accepted that: 'It is beyond cavil that juveniles as a class are generally less mature, less responsible, and less fully formed than adults, and that these differences bear on juveniles' comparative moral culpability' (*Roper v Simmons*, p 13).

According to Cipriani (2009) the minimum age ranges globally from six to 18. The median age is 12 and this is the minimum age recommended by the Committee on the Rights of the Child (CRC) established by the UN Convention on the Rights of the Child 1989 (CRC, 2007, para 32). The CRC states that even children above the age of criminal responsibility have a lesser culpability than adults because they 'differ from adults in their physical and psychological development, and their emotional and educational needs' (para 10). In England and Wales the minimum age of criminal responsibility is currently set at 10 years by s16 Children and Young Persons Act 1963. Many have pointed to the discrepancy between this age and the minimum age required in respect of other functions and activities. Perhaps the best example is provided by Goldson and Peters (2000, 4) who note:

> Section 3 of the Pet Animals Act 1951 provides that it is not until a child has reached the age of 12 that they may be regarded as being sufficiently responsible, and thus legally entitled, to buy a pet. This seems perfectly sensible. It is curiously anomalous and legally inconsistent therefore, to regard the same child, albeit two years younger, to be sufficiently responsible to face the full rigour of criminal law.

Brooks points to the almost absurd inconsistency that provides that:

> [A] defendant not old enough to legally buy a hamster can be
> tried in an adult court, as though the level of psychological
> sophistication required to look after a domesticated rodent
> is worthy of a longer period of development than the
> capacity to understand the moral responsibility inherent in
> the commission of a serious criminal act. (Brooks, 2011)

Yet criminalising juveniles might appear less absurd viewed through the prism of blame. Juveniles can provide convenient scapegoats. Hendrick (1994) identifies how the social construction of childhood produces two types: the innocent, vulnerable child-as-victim and the impulsive, incorrigible child-as-threat. Arguably the growth of a blame culture has coincided with an increasing awareness and concern with the child-as-threat. Many point to the murder of two-year-old James Bulger in February 1993 as a defining moment in this process. In sentencing 11-year-old Robert Thompson and Jon Venables, Mr Justice Morland stated that their 'cunning and very wicked behaviour' had resulted in an act 'of unparalleled evil and barbarity' (*Guardian*, 25 November 1993).

Sadly, one can probably find many parallel acts of evil and barbarity. Elsewhere in this book there are references to young children who have died under circumstances little less horrific than those endured by James Bulger in his final hours. Yet the fact that his attackers were only 10 at the time seems to have somehow made them more, not less, blameworthy. *The Times* editorial stated on the day after Venables and Thompson were sentenced:

> Childhood has a darker side...children should not be
> presumed to be innately good. In the lexicon of crime
> there is metaphysical evil, the imperfection of all mankind;
> there is physical evil, the suffering that humans cause each
> other; and there is moral evil, the choice of vice over virtue.
> Children are separated by necessity of age from none of
> these. (*The Times*, 25 November 1993)

Shortly after the murder of James Bulger, the then Home Secretary, Michael Howard, described child 'offenders' as 'adult in everything except years' who would not be allowed to 'use age as an excuse for immunity from effective punishment' (cited in Goldson, 1997, 130). Such a view was not uncommon in the UK in the 1990s and represented a growing process of 'responsibilization and adultification' (Goldson, 2013, 113) of juvenile offenders.

Until 1998 offenders between the ages of 10 and 13 had the additional protection of the *doli incapax* presumption. It was for the prosecution to rebut the presumption that the child was aware of the difference between right and wrong by proving, beyond a reasonable doubt, that the child knew that what she or he had done was seriously wrong and not merely naughty or mischievous. The presumption was abolished by the Crime and Disorder Act 1998. The following year saw a 29% increase in the number of 10- to 14-year-old children cautioned and/ or convicted (Goldson, 2013, 114). The change to the law occurred at a time of growing concern about juvenile crime and the existence of a growing number of persistent young offenders.

> Many of the arguments that led to the abolition of the presumption of *doli incapax*...did not address the issue of whether children are developed enough by the age of 10 to be criminally responsible. Instead the focus was on making children take responsibility for their actions. Arguments which related to children's actual capacity to understand the wrongfulness of their actions tended to not go beyond basic appeals to **common sense**, claiming that children develop quicker in modern society and are better able to distinguish right from wrong due to compulsory education. Such claims were made without a thorough examination of whether children today really are mentally or socially mature from an earlier age...A common claim was that it flies in the face of common sense to presume that children cannot distinguish right from wrong. This view of when a child is criminally responsible is, however, a gross simplification of the issue. (Crofts, 2009, 285)

The child-as-threat provides a convenient scapegoat. The 'common sense' view that children develop quicker in modern society and that criminal responsibility is only about distinguishing between right and wrong is, as we have already seen, refuted by the scientific evidence. The Centre for Social Justice Report found that 'young people who offend, particularly those who commit the most serious crimes, are likely to be the most vulnerable (often being victims themselves) and least competent to engage with the criminal justice system' (Centre for Social Justice, 2012, 202). The CSJ argues that questions of culpability are:

[distinct] from the question of the age at which children understand the difference between right and wrong, a question on which the MACR debate often misguidedly centres. Most children can broadly differentiate between right and wrong from a very young age. Children, however, have a limited capacity to judge the magnitude of right and wrong: that is, what is criminal and what is not. This is likely to be particularly true of children who have grown up in highly dysfunctional family circumstances and hence not learned law abiding behaviour in the home. There is also some indication that children who have experienced abuse may 'learn through modelling and reinforcement (social learning theory) that aggressive behaviour is linked to attention and status', leading them to emulate such behaviour themselves. (p 203)

The conclusion drawn by the CSJ is that 'The evidence indicates strongly that the current low MACR in England and Wales is unsafe, unjust and harmful to wider society' (p 210). Yet the report accepts that reform of the law is 'unlikely in the immediate term' (p 211). The second reading of Lord Dhokalia's bill was the last occasion it was discussed in Parliament: with the prorogation of the 2013–14 Parliamentary session, the bill lapsed.

The position of English law in relation to juveniles contrasts with the approach taken by international criminal law. While the CSJ recommends raising the minimum age of criminal responsibility to 12 'for all but the most grave offences (murder, attempted murder, rape, manslaughter and aggravated sexual assault)' (p 211), those under 18 who commit war crimes or crimes against humanity will not find themselves indicted before the International Criminal Court (ICC). The Rome Statute of the ICC provides that the Court shall have no jurisdiction over those who were under the age of 18 at the time of the alleged commission of the offence (Rome Statute, 2002, article 26). This is consistent with the Principles and Guidelines on Children Associated with Armed Forces or Armed Groups 2007 (Paris Principles, 2007). The Paris Principles were drawn up under the auspices of UNICEF and formally endorsed by 58 states in February 2007. Principle 3.6 provides that 'children who are accused of crimes under international law allegedly committed while they were associated with armed forces or armed groups should be considered primarily as victims of offences against international law, not only as perpetrators'.

The Paris Principles themselves are consistent with the United Nations Standard Minimum Rules for the Administration of Juvenile Justice (the Beijing Rules) which were adopted by the United Nations General Assembly on 29 November 1985 (United Nations, 1985). Principle 4 provides:

> 4.1 In those legal systems recognizing the concept of the age of criminal responsibility for juveniles, the beginning of that age shall not be fixed at too low an age level, bearing in mind the facts of emotional, mental and intellectual maturity.

The Commentary to the Beijing Rules indicates that there is a close relationship between notions of responsibility for criminal or delinquent behaviour and other social rights and responsibilities. A minimum age of criminal responsibility set at 10 provides an interesting comparison with a minimum age for giving consent to sexual activity set at 16 and a minimum voting age of 18.

Surprisingly, particularly given the foregoing discussion on the minimum age of criminal responsibility, 'little has been written about the substantive reasons that support a separate policy towards crimes committed by young offenders' (Zimring, 1998, 447). Zimring suggests that the reason for this stems partly from the fact that the different treatment of children seems intuitively right. He goes on to suggest two policy areas which determine official attitudes to youth crime: one aspect is the fact that adolescents may be more susceptible than adults to efforts at rehabilitation; the other aspect relates more directly to the issue of blame. Zimring proposes that age be considered as a species of diminished responsibility: 'Just as psychiatric disorder or cognitive impairment that does not render a subject exempt from the criminal law might still mitigate the punishment justly to be imposed, so a minimally competent adolescent should not be responsible for the whole of an adult's desert for the same act' (p 448).

Zimring argues there are three types of personal attribute affecting decisions to commit crimes where juveniles may lack full adult competency. First, juveniles may not have the fully developed cognitive ability to be able to understand moral and legal rules and apply them to social situations. An infant may lack such ability entirely and for this reason we would not hold a four-year-old child criminally responsible. Cognitive ability develops with age and older children and adolescents have an increased ability but may not possess the full ability of adults. For this reason the degree of criminal responsibility and blame should be diminished. Second, juveniles may not possess full adult ability to exercise self-control: 'Long after a child knows that taking candy is wrong, the capacity to resist temptation when a taking is the only available route to the candy may not be fully operational' (p 448).

Zimring accepts that understanding and knowledge of self-control is limited but argues that it is a behaviour that develops with practice and experience and that bad decisions by juveniles should not be regarded in the same way as similar decisions by adults who have had the time and experience to develop self-control. Third, Zimring identifies the ability to resist peer pressure:

> A teen may know right from wrong and even may have developed the capacity to control his or her impulses if left alone to do so, but resisting temptation while alone is a different task than resisting the pressure to commit an offense when adolescent peers are pushing for the adolescent to misbehave and witnessing whether or not the outcome they desire will occur. (p 449)

We may not yet have sufficient knowledge of developmental psychology to be able to quantify precisely the extent to which blame and responsibility should be diminished in juveniles. It seems incontestable, however, that attribution of blame to juveniles cannot be set at the same level as it is for fully competent adults.

Mental capacity

In March 2013 the Catholic Archbishop of Durban, Cardinal Wilfred Fox Napier was widely criticised for describing paedophilia as a psychological 'illness, not a criminal condition' (BBC, 2013). The main basis for the criticism was the assumption that the Cardinal was attempting in some way to excuse child sex abuse. Barbara Dorries, who as a child was abused by a priest and who works for the Chicago-based Survivors Network of those Abused by Priests told the BBC: 'If it is a disease that's fine, but it's also a crime and crimes are punished, criminals are held accountable for what they did and what they do.' The relationship between illness, mental capacity and blame has a long history.

On Friday, 20 January 1843 Daniel M'Naughten shot Edward Drummond in the back. As he attempted to fire a second shot, M'Naughten was apprehended by a police constable. Edward Drummond, private secretary to the Prime Minister Sir Robert Peel, died five days later. Significantly, in relation to the issue of moral luck discussed later in this chapter, there is some discussion as to the precise cause of death. At the trial of M'Naughten, the doctors who attended Drummond were in no doubt that the shooting was the direct cause of death. Yet there is some suggestion that it would have been possible for Drummond to make a full recovery from his injury and that what killed him was the medical intervention. Had Drummond been treated differently it is possible he might not have died from the bullet wound and the M'Naughten Rules may never have seen the light of day. In any event, M'Naughten was subsequently indicted for the wilful murder of Edward Drummond and his trial took place at the Old Bailey on 27 February 1843 (Old Bailey, 1843). At the trial a number of medical experts gave evidence on the state of M'Naughten's mind. Among the medical experts was William Hutchinson, physician to the Royal Lunatic Asylum in Glasgow who had examined M'Naughten and found him to be suffering from 'morbid delusions' which would fully explain and account for the action of shooting Edward Drummond. Under cross examination Hutchinson was clear: "[M'Naughten] was perfectly incapable of exercising control in any matter connected with the delusion – I am decidedly of opinion that the act flowed immediately out of that delusion."

On the basis of this and similar evidence M'Naughten was found not guilty on the basis of insanity.

The verdict was widely criticised. In a debate on insanity and crime in the House of Lords on 13 March 1843 the Lord Chancellor explained the situation:

> A gentleman in the prime of life, of a most amiable character, incapable of giving offence or of injuring any individual, was murdered in the streets of this metropolis in open day. The assassin was secured; he was committed for trial; that trial has taken place, and he has escaped with impunity. Your Lordships will not be surprised that these circumstances should have created a deep feeling in the public mind, and that many persons should, on the first impression, be disposed to think that there is some great defect in the laws of the country with reference to this subject which calls for a revision of those laws, in order that a repetition of such outrages may be prevented. (HL Deb, 13 March 1843, vol 67, cc714–44)

Part of the concern related to the manner in which the trial was ended and the fact that the issue of insanity was not put to the jury. A number of the medical experts had not examined M'Naughten and based their evidence on what they had heard in court. Yet there was also disquiet at the fact that M'Naughten had seemingly 'escaped with impunity'. Edward Drummond had been *murdered* and yet there appeared to be nobody to blame. The continuing concern led the House of Lords to assert a right to ask abstract questions of law of the trial judges. It is the report of these questions and the answers to them that constitutes the M'Naghten Rules ((1843) 10 CI & Fin 200). The rules provide that there is a presumption of sanity. The burden of proof is on the defence to show that the defendant was labouring under such a defect of reason, due to disease of the mind, as either not to know the nature and quality of his or her act or, if he did know this, not to know that he or she was doing wrong. Where a defence of insanity is successful the verdict of the court will be not guilty by reason of insanity and the Criminal Procedure (Insanity) Act 1964 s.5 provides that where a defendant is found not guilty by reason of insanity the judge may make a hospital order, a supervision order, or an order for the defendant's absolute discharge.

In *Sullivan* [1984] AC 156 Lord Diplock stated that, although 'defect of reason' and 'disease of the mind' might not be terms currently used by the medical profession, the meaning was clear:

> 'Mind'…is used in the ordinary sense of the mental faculties of reason, memory and understanding. If the effect of a disease is to impair these faculties so severely as to have either of the consequences referred to in the latter part of the rules, it matters not whether the aetiology, of the impairment is organic, as in epilepsy, or functional, or whether the impairment itself is permanent or is transient and intermittent, provided that it subsisted at the time of commission of the act. (p 172)

The courts have distinguished between mental impairment caused by disease and other causes by requiring that where impairment is due to disease the immediate cause must be internal to the defendant, although in *Burgess* [1991] 2 QB 92 the Court of Appeal pointed out that this is not always a clear distinction.

The key aspect of the insanity defence as far as blame is concerned is that the defendant was unable to appreciate what he or she was doing or that what was being done was wrong. The jury needs to be satisfied that either the defendant was unaware of the act, or its effects, or the material circumstances in which the act occurred. Even if the defendant is able to appreciate what he or she is doing, the insanity defence will succeed if it can be shown that the defendant was unaware that the action was wrong. This alternative aspect of the defence perhaps causes more problems. In *Windle* [1952] 2 QB 826 it was held that an insanity defence will not succeed if the defendant knew what they were doing was prohibited by law. It may be argued that this would allow relatively few successful pleas of insanity since, as the Butler Committee suggested, even grossly disturbed persons generally know that murder, for example, is prohibited by law and thus legally wrong (Butler Committee, 1975, para 18.8). *Windle* has been criticised and both the High Court of Australia and the Supreme Court of Canada (*Chaulk* (1990) 2 CR (4th) 1) have declined to follow the decision. In *Stapleton v R* (1952) 86 CLR 358 the High Court of Australia took the view that 'wrong' should be taken to mean morally wrong, in the sense of being contrary to the moral views of the majority of the population.

The defence of insanity covered by the M'Naghten Rules is a complete defence to most offences and results in an acquittal. In cases of murder evidence of mental impairment may result in a diminution in the extent to which the defendant is held responsible. S2 of the Homicide Act 1957 as amended by the Coroners and Justice Act 2009 provides:

(1)   A person ('D') who kills or is a party to the killing of another is not to be convicted of murder if D was suffering from an abnormality of mental functioning which –

    (a)   arose from a recognised medical condition,

    (b)   substantially impaired D's ability to do one or more of the things mentioned in subsection (1A), and

    (c)   provides an explanation for D's acts and omissions in doing or being a party to the killing.

(1A) Those things are –

    (a) to understand the nature of D's conduct;

    (b) to form a rational judgment;

    (c) to exercise self-control.

(1B) For the purposes of subsection (1)(c), an abnormality of mental functioning provides an explanation for D's

> conduct if it causes, or is a significant contributory
> factor in causing, D to carry out that conduct.

A successful plea of diminished responsibility under s2 will result in the defendant, otherwise guilty of murder, being convicted of manslaughter. The practical implication of this is that the court has a discretion in regard to sentencing. Under English law a conviction for murder carries a mandatory sentence of life imprisonment. It was the view of the UK government and the Law Commission that establishing diminished responsibility requires a causal connection between the abnormality of mental functioning and the killing (Hansard, 3 March 2009L, Column 414). This had not been clear in the legislation as originally drafted in 1957. In relation to s2(1)(a) it is expected that reference will be made to existing accepted classificatory lists such as the World Health Organisation's international classification of diseases and the American Psychiatric Association's diagnostic and statistical manual of mental disorders.

A particular type of diminished responsibility is provided by the Infanticide Act 1938 (as amended by the Coroners and Justice Act 2009). This provides that a woman who kills her own child under the age of 12 months will be guilty of infanticide rather than murder or manslaughter if, at the time of the act or omission leading to the death of the child:

> [The] balance of her mind was disturbed by reason of her
> not having fully recovered from the effect of giving birth to
> the child or by reason of the effect of lactation consequent
> on the birth of the child. (s1(1))

The law has been criticised on a number of grounds including the fact that it fails to cover situations where the balance of the mother's mind is disturbed by factors connected to but not consequent on the birth of the child (see *Kai-Whitewind* [2005] EWCA Crim 1092). The reference to lactation is regarded as outdated since at the time the legislation was originally introduced it was widely, although it turns out to be incorrectly, believed that post-natal depression was linked to lactation.

The Coroners and Justice Act 2009 also introduced a new partial defence to murder. English common law had long recognised that provocation had a bearing on criminal responsibility and s3 of the Homicide Act 1957 provided:

> Where on a charge of murder there is evidence on which
> the jury can find that the person charged was provoked
> (whether by things done or by things said or by both
> together) to lose his self-control, the question whether the
> provocation was enough to make a reasonable man do as
> he did shall be determined by the jury.

A number of cases resulted in the law on provocation being criticised. In some cases it was felt too broad a view of what constituted provocation was taken: for example, in *Doughty* [1986] EWCA Crim 1 the Court of Appeal accepted that the persistent crying of a 17-day-old baby could constitute provocation. On the other hand, the need to show sudden and temporary loss of control left a number of women who killed persistently violent partners without a defence. S54–56 of the 2009 Act abolishes the partial defence of provocation and replaces it with a new defence of loss of control. The loss of control must result from a 'qualifying trigger' and: 'a person of the defendant (D)'s sex and age, with a normal degree of tolerance and self-restraint and in the circumstances of D, might have reacted in the same or in a similar way to D'.

The 'qualifying triggers' are: where the defendant fears serious violence; when certain things have been said or done which amount to circumstances of an extremely grave character and caused the defendant to have a justifiable sense of being seriously wronged; or, when a combination of the first two situations applies. Unlike with the defence of provocation, the loss of control need not have been sudden but the judge and jury may take any delay into account when deciding on whether there has been a loss of control. The changes to the law here appear to reflect common views about blame. It recognises the fact that in certain circumstances (the qualifying triggers) individuals with otherwise 'normal' levels of tolerance and self-restraint may lose self-control. It is perhaps worth noting that the reforms made to the law here do not appear to have been based on significant amounts of scientific research on self-control. Parallels might be drawn here with the attitude taken toward adolescent self-control discussed earlier in this chapter.

It can be seen that mental impairment and loss of self-control can have an effect on levels of criminal responsibility and, we would argue, blame. In many cases, a finding of diminished responsibility (in its wider sense) reflects a diminution in attribution of blame: a mother suffering from post-natal depression who kills her very young child is regarded as deserving of less blame than the mentally well child-killer.

Yet put like this one raises more fundamental questions about blame and responsibility: to what extent is it possible to refer to the 'normal', 'reasonable', 'self-controlled', 'self-restrained', 'tolerant' child-killer? The reaction to Cardinal Napier's comments regarding paedophiles demonstrates the problem here. There is more than a hint of suspicion that in some cases the demand for blame will outweigh considerations of mental capacity and impairment. The public reaction to Daniel M'Naughten's acquittal was partly based on a sense of outrage that an innocent man had been killed and the *murderer* had 'escaped with impunity'. In May 1981 Peter Sutcliffe was convicted of 13 counts of murder. The murders were carried out in West Yorkshire over a five-year period and involved mutilation. Sutcliffe unsuccessfully put forward a defence of diminished responsibility on the grounds that he was suffering from paranoid schizophrenia and that his killings were carried out as a mission to clear the streets of prostitutes (see *R v Peter William Coonan (formerly Sutcliffe)* [2011] EWCA Crim 5).

The prosecution had intended to accept Sutcliffe's plea after four psychiatrists diagnosed him with paranoid schizophrenia. The trial judge unusually demanded an explanation of the prosecution decision, however, and, having heard legal submissions, rejected the plea and the trial proceeded before the jury. Following conviction and imprisonment Sutcliffe was found to be suffering from paranoid schizophrenia and subsequently transferred to Broadmoor Hospital, a high security psychiatric hospital. Given the fear which Sutcliffe's offences generated and the level of publicity which surrounded the police investigation and trial it is perhaps unsurprising that the defence of diminished responsibility was rejected. This was a case that required someone to be blamed; a successful plea of diminished responsibility would have diminished the blame.

Justifications, excuses and circumstances precluding wrongfulness

> Ann swings her arm and injures Ben. She faces moral condemnation and legal liability unless she can offer an explanation that absolves her of full blame. She might make a claim of justification that, despite initial appearances, her action was desirable or proper, or she might make a claim of excuse that she does not bear full responsibility for injuring Ben. If Ann is fully justified, she will not be subject to blame or to classification as a weak or defective person. If Ann is excused, she may be regarded as wholly

or partly free of blame, but she will have demonstrated weakness or some defect. Because the moral evaluation of a justified actor differs from the moral evaluation of an excused actor, deciding whether Ann is justified or excused is an important moral question. (Greenawalt, 1986, p 89)

In this section we are concerned with the circumstances where what might at first appear to be blameworthy conduct is excused or justified to the extent that no blame is attached. Although a distinction is properly drawn between excuses and justifications both have an effect on blame: as Greenawalt indicates, the extent to which we blame Ann is connected to the extent to which we accept her justifications or excuses.

Consent may provide an excuse to what would otherwise be regarded as wrongful activity. The International Law Commission's Draft Articles on State Responsibility (ILC, 2001) set down the circumstances that will preclude wrongfulness in chapter V and the opening article provides: 'Valid consent by a State to the commission of a given act by another State precludes the wrongfulness of that act in relation to the former State to the extent that the act remains within the limits of that consent' (Article 20).

Within municipal legal systems there is often a recognition that many offences against the person may be excused if the victim gives a valid consent. The least controversial area is probably consent given to reasonable surgical interference. Surgical interference will usually involve permanent or short-term harm to the body but where it is carried out for therapeutic purposes and consent is validly given there is little question of blame arising. Yet where surgery occurs for non-therapeutic reasons the position may be less clear. The Female Genital Mutilation Act 2003 prohibits female circumcision which would therefore be regarded as unreasonable surgical interference to which consent could not be validly given. Those who participate in contact sports are deemed to consent to the risk of such accidental harm as can reasonably be expected. Consent clearly extends to harm sustained within the rules of the sport but may also go beyond that: it is to be reasonably expected that, in the heat of the moment, conduct outside the rules may occur. It seems clear that conduct which in other contexts would be regarded as deserving of blame will be condoned in the context of recognised sporting activity.

In recent years much of the debate about consent has focused on sexual behaviour. The leading English case is *Brown* [1994] 1 AC 212. The defendants had consented to acts of violence against each other for the sexual pleasure of giving and receiving pain. The defendants appealed against their convictions for assault occasioning actual bodily harm and unlawful wounding on the grounds that the acts in question had been carried out in private with the victim's consent. The House of Lords in dismissing the appeals upheld an earlier Court of Appeal decision (*A-G's Reference (no 6 of 1980)* [1981] QB 715) that a person cannot validly consent to non-trivial injuries that were intended and/or caused. The House of Lords took the view that consent would have been relevant if it was in the public interest to permit the intentional causing of harm but it could find no such reasons. Despite their criminal liability the extent to which Brown and the others involved would be 'blamed' for their actions might be more debatable. Clearly there would be a difference in levels of blame between consensual and non-consensual acts of genital torture. The extent to which consent may reduce blame may also be limited by the limits on consent: 'Consent provides an objective reason for allowing a person to make choices that may involve consenting to harm, but consent is not absolute. Consent protects personal autonomy, but it does not allow a person to degrade or destroy the human dignity of the consenting party' (Barker, 2009, p 98).

The two main justifications recognised by criminal law are necessity and public or private defence. Under the ILC Draft Articles on State Responsibility Article 25 (ILC, 2001), necessity arises when a state acts to safeguard an essential interest against a grave and imminent peril. Most legal systems will recognise that in certain situations behaviour which would otherwise be regarded as criminal will not be so regarded if it is done to prevent a more serious harm. A common example would be an ambulance or fire engine exceeding the speed limit in order to attend an emergency. Legal provision for the defence is often quite minimal although public policy considerations and prosecution authority discretion will often mean that in cases where necessity might be an issue charges will be dropped or never brought. Where action is genuinely based on necessity it seems unlikely that blame will arise.

Where someone acts to prevent the commission of a crime, or to effect a lawful arrest then use of a reasonable amount of force may be justified and the action will not be regarded criminal. Similarly, if someone acts in defence against an actual or imminent attack or to defend property against attack then the action may be justified. Action taken to prevent unlawful imprisonment or an imminent or actual trespass may also be justified. While the concept of self-defence and the right to defend and protect others is well recognised, the extent to which any particular defensive action is proportionate and reasonable may be more difficult to ascertain. The reasonableness of the action should be judged on objective grounds taking into account all the immediate circumstances in which the defendant believed he was situated. The case of *Martin (Anthony Edward)* [2003] QB 1 particularly captured the public imagination. Tony Martin was a farmer who shot and killed 16-year-old Fred Barras who was burgling his house. Although the issue of self-defence was raised at his trial it was rejected by the jury who found him guilty of murder. The trial attracted considerable publicity and there was a degree of media sympathy for the farmer who, according to popular view, was merely defending his property. There seemed to be little public sympathy for Barras who was revealed to have a number of previous convictions for burglary. Although Martin was held criminally responsible it seemed the public (or certainly sections of the media) were unwilling to blame Martin for his actions. He appealed against the conviction. The Court of Appeal rejected arguments based on self-defence, but did find Martin to be suffering from depression and a paranoid personality disorder and substituted a conviction for manslaughter on the grounds of diminished responsibility.

In International Law self-defence is recognised as providing justification for military action which would otherwise be unlawful by virtue of Article 2(4) of the United Nations Charter. Article 51 of the Charter refers to the preservation of an inherent right of self-defence 'should armed attack occur'. Here, too, debate often centres on the extent to which action taken in self-defence is proportionate. In recent years the concept of self-defence has undergone some changes as a result of a perceived increased terrorist threat. Following the attack on the World Trade Center on 11 September 2001 military action was taken by the United States and other states against Afghanistan. The justification given was self-defence on the basis that Al Qaeda, largely based in Afghanistan, posed an ongoing military threat to the United States and its allies. The 2003 invasion of Iraq by United States and others was also partly justified on the basis of self-defence. The extent to which the justification was accepted remains a matter for debate.

Blame and luck

The death of Thomas Inglis, discussed in Chapter One, raises some important questions about the relationship between blame and luck. Thomas Inglis died as a result of his mother injecting him with a fatal dose of heroin. At the time that she administered the drug to her son it was clear that she intended to kill him: she wished to put an end to the pain and suffering she believed he was experiencing. Yet, prior to her son sustaining a serious head injury there was never any suggestion that Mrs Inglis harboured any ill feelings towards her son and it seems clear that prior to 7 July 2007 she had had no intention of killing him. The situation changed as a result of a tragic chain of events, most of which were out of Mrs Inglis's control. No single link in the chain was inevitable: what occurred was a catastrophic, but largely unpredictable combination of chance happenings. Had any of the chance happenings not occurred it is likely that Thomas would still be alive today and his mother, Frances Inglis, would not be serving a sentence of life imprisonment for murder. It is clear that the direct cause of Thomas Inglis's death was the administration of the fatal heroin dose by his mother. She is to be 'blamed' for his death because it was her intention and actions that directly caused his death. Yet the ill luck that led to her contemplating killing her son seems to be directly related to the extent of her blame.

In his 2009 study of the concept of causation Michael Moore states 'Causation matters to legal liability' (Moore, 2009, 3) and '[Causation] is a prerequisite of legal liability throughout both the law of torts and the law of crimes' (p 20). Moore then poses a question of central relevance to this book: does causation matter to moral responsibility? To what extent is blame dependent on causation? As Moore points out the issue is one faced by all systems of criminal and civil liability. In criminal law the issue is raised by the attitude taken to inchoate offences: do attempted crimes carry the same degree of culpability as completed offences? Moore suggests that:

> To cause a death that one intends to cause is morally worse than merely intending or trying to cause such a death: to cause a death that one has knowingly and/or unreasonably risked, is worse than merely knowingly and/or unreasonably risking such a death. How much worse? The common legal metric (for attempts) was by a factor of 2: it was believed to be twice as bad to kill, to rape, to hit, and so on as it was to try (unsuccessfully) to do any of these things, which resulted in punishments for these inchoate crimes being put as one-half the punishments of the completed crime analogues. (Moore, 2009, 21)

Although many legal systems (including the California Penal Code section 664) do apply the factor of two to attempts, not all do. The Sentencing Council's Definitive Guidelines on Attempted Murder suggest that offenders in such cases may have high levels of culpability which will be reflected in sentences broadly similar to the terms actually served by those convicted of murder (Sentencing Council, 2009).

Kant argued that moral judgement, and, by implication, blame, should only attach to intention and not to actions: 'The good will is not good because of what it effects or accomplishes or because of its adequacy to achieve some proposed end; it is good only because of its willing, ie, it is good of itself' (Kant, 1959, sec I, para 3).

From this it must logically follow that bad will is bad only because of its willing. The basis of Kant's argument is that we have control over our intentions while our actions are often determined by external factors. Kant's view is linked to the Control Principle: individuals can only be morally assessed or blamed to the extent that the actions for which we are blamed depend on factors under our control. The corollary of this principle is that amounts of blame allocated to two people should not vary if the only differences between them are due to factors beyond their control. If A and B both intend to kill C and A succeeds in killing C but B fails because of factors outside B's control the moral assessment of A is the same as B; B is equally deserving of blame as A.

According to this view one should judge attempts no differently than completed offences. An intention to commit a bad act, a bad will, cannot become good simply because the intended outcome is not achieved. In her analysis of the role of luck in criminal justice, Kim Kessler imagines Alice shooting at Bob with the intention of killing him (Kessler, 1994). She suggests four possibilities:

1. The bullet hits Bob and kills him. Alice is guilty of murder.
2. The bullet hits Bob at exactly the same time Carla's bullet hits Bob, thus frustrating but-for causation. The court will most likely still hold Alice guilty of murder.
3. A large bird flies in the bullet's path. Thus, the bullet misses Bob completely. Alice is only guilty of attempted murder.
4. The same large bird flies in the bullet's path and deflects the bullet. The bullet misses Bob but hits Carla. Alice is guilty of Carla's murder.

This seems, initially at least, to be unsatisfactory: the 'chance' influence of another actor or some act of fate affects Alice's liability. Consistent with Kant, Kessler argues that luck should not play a part in the criminal justice system and that criminal liability should be determined by intention. She offers another hypothetical example:

For example, imagine that Leigh is recklessly driving in a school zone. She does not hit anyone. Patty, on the other hand, recklessly drives through the school zone and hits three children. When Leigh passes by a group of bystanders, they may think that she is a bad driver and should be arrested before she kills someone. When Patty hits the children, they can point to the results of her actions as an indicator of how culpable she is, whereas they can only imagine what Leigh would have done. Such an indicator of culpability (having caused a harm) causes people to recognize that Patty is a bad person. Should people rationally think about the harm that Leigh might have caused, however, they will conclude that there is no distinction to be made between the two women's culpability. (pp 2188–9)

Yet blame is not allocated on a rational basis and often reckless driving is only recognised as such when it results in harm. Kessler accepts that Patty may feel more guilt than Leigh and, arguably, feelings of guilt are closely linked to self-blame. Many people continue to drive with blood-alcohol levels above the legal maximum yet considerably more blame (including self-blame) is attached to the drunk driver who kills someone than to the drunk drivers who manage to navigate themselves safely home.

According to Thomas Nagel:

When we blame someone for his actions we are not merely saying it is bad that they happened, or bad that he exists: we are judging him, saying he is bad, which is different from his being a bad thing. This kind of judgement takes only a certain kind of object. Without being able to explain exactly why, we feel that the appropriateness of moral assessment is easily undermined by the discovery that the act or attribute, no matter how good or bad, is not under the person's control. While other evaluations remain, this one seems to lose its footing. So a clear absence of control, produced by involuntary movement, physical force, or ignorance of the circumstances excuses what is done from moral judgement. (1979, 25)

Nagel offers the hypothetical case of the truck driver who accidentally runs over and kills a child who runs out in front of the truck. If the driver is entirely without fault then no blame will attach. Yet should the driver be guilty of some degree of negligence then blame would arise:

> And what makes this an example of moral luck is that he would have to blame himself only slightly for the negligence itself if no situation arose which required him to brake suddenly and violently to avoid hitting a child. Yet the negligence is the same in both cases, and the driver has no control over whether a child will run into his path. (p 29)

Blame therefore is not about intention or result: it is a moral judgement based on both: 'Actual results influence capability' (p 32). Yet the problem of moral luck remains. Nagel identifies four types of luck: resultant, constitutive, circumstantial, and causal.

Resultant luck: Resultant luck is luck in the way things turn out and is at play in the case of Alice, and Leigh and Patty and the hypothetical truck driver. Leigh and Patty have exactly the same intent, drive in an identical way but the results are very different. Bernard Williams discussed the case of 'a creative artist who turns away from definite and pressing human claims on him in order to live a life in which, as he supposes, he can pursue his art' (Williams, B, 1981, 22). Williams recalls the artist Gauguin. When Gauguin leaves his family to take up a life of painting in Tahiti he has no way of knowing whether or not the decision will result in him becoming a great artist. Yet, Williams argues, we judge Gauguin very differently depending on whether he succeeds in his wish or fails: 'Actual results influence culpability or esteem in a large class of unquestionably ethical cases ranging from negligence through political choice' (Nagel, p 32).

Constitutive luck: Here Nagel is referring to those qualities of temperament and personality we possess over which we have no control. Our personality is partly determined by factors outside our control: our genes, our carers, our peers and other environmental influences. To that extent who we are is largely a matter of luck. Since who we are determines, to some extent at least, how we are and how we behave; our actions are affected by constitutive luck:

> One may want to have a generous spirit, or regret not having one, but it makes no sense to condemn oneself or anyone else for a quality which is not within the control of the will. Condemnation implies that you should not be like that, not that it is unfortunate that you are. (p 34)

Yet although this argument is entirely rational, Nagel accepts that it is intuitively unacceptable. We blame the coward for failing to intervene to prevent a fight even though cowardice maybe a character trait over which the non-intervener has no control.

Circumstantial luck: We have already seen how a combination of circumstances led Mrs Inglis to murder. Nagel raises the example of Nazi Germany:

> Ordinary citizens of Nazi Germany had the opportunity to behave heroically by opposing the regime. They also had the opportunity to behave badly, and most of them are culpable for having failed this test. But it is a test to which citizens of other countries were not subjected, with the result that even if they, or some of them, would have behaved as badly as the Germans in like circumstances they simply did not and therefore are not similarly culpable. Here again one is morally at the mercy of fate, and it may seem irrational on reflection, but our ordinary moral attitudes would be unrecognizable without it. We judge people for what they actually do or fail to do, not just for what they would have done if circumstances had been different. (p 34)

Causal luck: In many respects causal luck is a combination of constitutive and circumstantial luck:

> If one cannot be responsible for consequences of one's acts due to factors beyond one's control, or for antecedents of one's acts that are properties of temperament not subject to one's will, or for the circumstances that pose one's moral choices, then how can one be responsible even for the stripped down acts of the will itself, if they are the product of antecedent circumstances outside of the will's control? (p 36)

This returns us to the problem of free will outlined in Chapter One and Nagel does not provide any real answers seeking only to make the links with the other types of moral luck.

For Nagel the existence of moral luck undermines blame and the distinction drawn between causing harm and merely intending or risking harm. Michael Moore sees a solution in denying the existence of *moral* luck and instead relying on the doctrine of proximate causation. Proximate causation limits responsibility and liability, and thus blame, to those events which are normal or routine. 'Luck' and the exclusion of liability only arises when events are too 'freakish':

> When a defendant negligently operates a train too fast, so that he cannot stop it before it hits another's railroad car, there is no luck involved in his injuring the second car because that is how such things normally happen. When, however, the same negligently speeding defendant causes the same damage to the same car, but does so because the first collision (which does no damage) throws the defendant against the reverse throttle of his engine, thereby knocking him unconscious, whereon his engine goes in reverse around a circular track, colliding with the other's car and then causing it damage, there is luck involved because of the abnormal conjunction of events taking place between the defendant's act and the harm. (Moore, 1997, 216)

In many cases this may provide a solution but there remains the difficulty of the precise assessment of proximity.

We have seen how blame and criminal responsibility often run alongside one another but at times their paths can diverge. While Durkheim may be correct in asserting that crime offends sentiments which are found among all normal individuals within a society, there may sometimes be a time delay before moral sentiments are accurately reflected in criminal law. In some ways blame may be seen as a safety valve for moral sentiment. In this chapter we have seen that on occasion clearly criminal behaviour may attract little or no blame; on other occasions conduct which is perfectly lawful may still attract blame. One final thing to note here is the fact that although levels of blame arising from similar activities may vary considerably, the task of accurately quantifying blame may be impossible.

FOUR

Blameless crime

In order to understand the operation of the criminal justice process it is necessary first to consider the substantive criminal law because the criminal justice system can only respond to those who transgress it. The definition of crime is not only a concern for criminal lawyers but sets the boundaries of criminology. What constitutes criminal behaviour is particularly important when the criminological analysis is theoretical as forms of culpable and harmful behaviour that are not defined as criminal tend to escape criminological study on the basis of legalistic, and often arbitrary, definitions. A further complication is that the criminal law does not remain static: behaviours which were once tolerated are criminalised while acts that were deemed worthy of punishment become legalised. Parliament and the courts also have to respond to new threats, for example, those posed by the internet. Finding commonality between the thousands of offences in existence is impossible; the only certain link is that all of these behaviours have been defined as crimes by Parliament or the courts. In many cases, the case for criminalisation is beyond dispute; variants of the most serious offences are found in most, if not all, jurisdictions. The necessity of many other offences is far less obvious. Sometimes this is because the conduct appears innocuous and sometimes because criminalisation seems a disproportionate response even though the behaviour is culpable.

The parameters of the criminal law are clearly important to this work. If one wishes to investigate the role that blame plays in the criminal justice system one first has to evaluate the extent to which it informs the criminal law. If, for example, the criminal law protects the blameless from conviction, an exploration of the role of blame in the criminal justice process would be unnecessary. Conversely, if the blameless are routinely convicted, one would be bound not only to review why this was occurring and how it was justified but would also force an assessment of how such individuals were then processed and punished.

Offences usually specify a particular mental state, or **mens rea**, that the prosecution must prove beyond reasonable doubt (see generally Ashworth, 2009; Card, 2012; Ormerod, 2011; Simester et al, 2010). Common examples include **intention**, recklessness and **dishonesty**. A failure to prove that the defendant acted in the way required should result in an acquittal. The existence of a mens rea requirement, however, does not always mean that a blameless individual will be acquitted. 'Intention' is a common form of mens rea. A relative distraught at the sight of a family member facing a prolonged and painful death and an assassin may both intend to kill, thereby satisfying the mens rea for murder, despite having very different motives. Some may regard the relative as morally blameless but the courts would still find that the mens rea had been satisfied. There are powerful reasons for excluding motive from assessments of intent (Kaufman, 2003), although judicial practice, as will be shown, has not been wholly consistent. Recklessness has also sometimes been interpreted in a way which failed to protect the blameless (Norrie, 1992; Williams, 1988). Conviction was possible where an individual failed to see a risk that was obvious to others. A final category of offence, those of strict liability, poses perhaps the greatest challenge to the idea that the blameless should not be convicted. Strict liability offences are those which specify no mens rea in their definition with the result that the incompetent, the naive, the incapable and the young have no escape. Parliament, however, sometimes fails to make its intention clear and the failure to specify mens rea does not mean that the courts will always deem the offence to be one of strict liability. Particularly where the offence is seen to be a 'real crime' which carries stigma on conviction and the likelihood of serious punishment, the courts have been willing to hold that there is a presumption of mens rea. As will be shown later, the justification for imposing mens rea has been the need to protect the blameless from conviction in such cases.

This chapter will start with an analysis of motive in the Criminal Law and, in particular, with its relationship to intention. Although conceptually distinct and seemingly of limited legal relevance, it will be shown that motive has been considered, albeit in limited situations, to spare the blameless from conviction. Recklessness will then be analysed. The key debate with recklessness has been whether the test should be subjective (in which case account is taken of the defendant's perception at the time) or objective (in which case conviction does not necessarily depend on the defendant's perception). Objectivism would allow for the conviction of the blameless and, after a series of cases where vulnerable and blameless individuals were held criminally liable, the test reverted to a subjective one in recognition of the potential for individual injustice. After considering recklessness, attention will be given to negligence and gross negligence. Negligence relates to conduct and not to the individual's state of mind and so it is important to consider why it is appropriate to disregard the individual's perceptions in determining liability. Finally, strict liability will be considered. Blame would appear to be totally irrelevant in such cases but judicial interpretation has limited the scope for injustice for the more serious offences which fail to specify mens rea. As with recklessness, a desire to spare the blameless from conviction is evident in the jurisprudence from the courts. The conclusion will argue that the courts are mindful that convicting the blameless is unjust and that this has informed the judicial interpretation of key concepts, most notably recklessness, and in the way in which parliamentary ambiguity with regards to whether an offence is one of strict liability has granted the courts authority to require mens rea if they believe it is necessary.

Perceptions of blame on the part of the judiciary have, therefore, shaped the substantive criminal law. The legal definitions discussed in this chapter affects pre-trial decision-making as it will inform charging and prosecuting decisions. There will also be defendants who will be acquitted at trial. The issues which concern this chapter have considerable implications on the role of blame in the criminal justice process and, therefore, on the analysis throughout this book.

Motive: criminalising the well-intentioned

The previous chapter discussed situations where particular categories of individual could be classed as blameless, or at least lacked sufficient blame to be dealt with by the criminal justice process in the usual manner (although Chapter Two cautions that it can be difficult to determine what the 'usual' process for dealing with offenders is). Motive could potentially have informed some of the discussion in the last chapter as motive may have partly explained the extraordinary blame in some cases. Here it is discussed in the context of criminal liability. According to criminal law theory, motive is generally irrelevant to whether or not an individual is criminally liable (see further, Gardner, 1993; Husak, 1989; 2010, Chapter 2). Glanville Williams, the pre-eminent criminal lawyer of the twentieth century explains it thus:

> If we say that a man shot and killed his aunt with the motive of benefitting under her will, the immediate intent, which makes the act murder, is the intention or desire to kill, while the further intent or motive, which forms no part of the definition of the crime of murder, is the intention or desire to benefit under the will. Other motives are the desire to obtain the satisfaction of revenge, or to get rid of a rival, or to promote a political object. Such motives may also be

expressed in abstract terms: 'he killed her from a motive of greed/revenge/jealousy'. Motive in this sense is irrelevant to responsibility (guilt or innocence), though it may be relevant to proof, or to the quantum of punishment. The prosecution may prove a motive for the crime if it helps them to establish their case, as a matter of circumstantial evidence; but they are not legally bound to prove motive, because a 'motiveless' crime is still a crime. Conversely, the defendant may adduce evidence of his good motive in order to reduce his punishment, perhaps to vanishing-point. (Williams, 1983, 75)

Kaufman (2003) provides a robust defence of this orthodox position arguing that it accords with moral theory. Motive is relevant to criminal liability in some situations. A theft does not occur, for example, if an individual genuinely believes that a property owner would consent to him taking the property (Theft Act 1968, s2; see Ormerod and Williams, 2007, 105). There are also a number of situations where the individual's motive is seen, rightly or wrongly, to make the crime especially serious and this is reflected in the creation of an aggravated offence (see further, Chapter Five) or in an enhanced sentence.

Whenever motive in English law is raised two controversial, and unusual, cases are mentioned which appear to introduce motive as a central concern. The first of these cases is *Steane* [1947] KB 997. Summoned by the Nazis in war-time Germany, Steane was asked to make a series of propaganda broadcasts which he did as he had been told that his wife and children would have been sent to a concentration camp had he refused. He was charged after the war with assisting the enemy and, despite the fact that he had clearly assisted the enemy when making the broadcasts, the Court of Criminal Appeal dismissed his conviction. It is easy to see why the Court was desperate to allow his appeal given Steane's predicament. On the facts, however, the Court had a perfectly justifiable option at their disposal; the defence of duress would appear to have been made out. Regrettably, the Court elected to quash the conviction on the dubious basis that he did not intend to assist the enemy. Surely he was desperate to do so in order to spare his family? According to Lord Goddard CJ:

In our opinion it is impossible to say that where an act was done by a person in subjection to the power of others, especially if that other be a brutal enemy, an inference that he intended the natural consequences of his act must be drawn merely from the fact that he did it. The guilty intent cannot be presumed and must be proved. The proper direction to the jury in this case would have been that it was for the prosecution to prove the criminal intent, and that while the jury would be entitled to presume that intent if they thought that the act was done as the result of the free uncontrolled action of the accused, they would not be entitled to presume it, if the circumstances showed that the act was done in subjection to the power of the enemy, or was as consistent with an innocent intent as with a criminal intent, for example, the innocent intent of a desire to save his wife and children from a concentration camp. (p 1006)

The first part of this statement is undoubtedly correct: intention to commit an act cannot be inferred from the commission of an act. The requirement that the prosecution must prove intent where this is an element of the offence also accords with the rules of criminal procedure. Thereafter the reasoning becomes less convincing. Intent, if one accepts Lord Goddard's logic, should not be found 'if the act was done in subjection to the power of the enemy' or was consistent with an 'innocent' intent such as seeking to save his family's lives. Talking of the 'enemy' does not help (although in a case dating from 1947 is understandable) because the argument is more general as it would, presumably, apply to other situations where an individual commits an act under threat of death or serious injury. The objection to *Steane* is basic: he did intend to make the broadcasts, which would have assisted the enemy, even if his desire was driven by external pressure rather than commitment to the Nazi cause. There is no denying that his motive was relevant, as was his lack of blame, but this should have determined whether he had a possible defence rather than whether he intended to commit the offence. Following *Steane* to its logical conclusion, there would be no need for a defence of duress as defendants in such cases would presumably have an 'innocent' intent.

Gillick v *West Norfolk and Wisbech Area Health Authority and Department of Health and Social Security* [1986] 1 AC 112, the other leading case, concerned a challenge to the right of medical professionals to prescribe contraceptives to girls under the age of consent without parental approval if a clinical judgement was made that this was in the patient's best interests. Among other arguments, it was submitted that a doctor who prescribed contraception in the knowledge that the girl would engage in sexual intercourse would be guilty of aiding and abetting unlawful sexual intercourse. The House of Lords focused on the doctor's motive:

> The *bona fide* exercise by a doctor of his clinical judgement must be a complete negation of the guilty mind which is an essential ingredient of the criminal offence of aiding and abetting the commission of unlawful sexual intercourse… If the prescription is the *bona fide* exercise of his clinical judgement as to what is best for his patient's health, he has nothing to fear from the criminal law or from any public policy based on the criminality of a man having sexual intercourse with her. (p 190)

Public policy can be a useful explanation for judgments which ostensibly conflict with legal precedent. Sometimes it is invoked to justify radical departure but, more commonly, it is used to qualify or limit a law that if applied to a particular case would create obvious injustice. No injustice was caused in *Steane* or in *Gillick* due to the exceptional nature of the first scenario and the policy ramifications had the second been decided otherwise. It is, however, legitimate to ask whether the means employed to reach these outcomes were proper. It has already been argued that duress could have been invoked in *Steane*. A lack of a potential defence meant that the House of Lords in *Gillick* had to introduce motive into an assessment of intent so that clinical decisions would not be open to challenge in a criminal court.

There are also situations where public policy has required the courts to conclude that someone acting for the best of motives may nonetheless commit an offence intentionally. The case of *Yip Chin-Cheung* v *R* [1994] 3 WLR 514 serves as a useful example. An American drug enforcement agent acting undercover and, according to the Privy Council with courage and good motive, arranged to meet with Yip Chin-Cheung in order to take a consignment of heroin from Hong Kong to Australia. Conspiracy, the offence with which Yip Chin-Cheung had been convicted, requires an agreement between two or more persons to commit an unlawful act with the intention of carrying it out. The Court held that there was an intention on the part of the officer to commit the offence, regardless of his motives and despite the fact that the Hong Kong authorities authorised the trafficking of the heroin to Australia. Public policy in this case, and in others like it (for example, *R* v *Latif* [1996] 1 All ER 353), favoured a traditional interpretation of the relationship between motive and intent. Divorcing the two and holding that motive is irrelevant to establishing intention enabled the conviction of a morally culpable individual involved in international drug trafficking. Departure from the orthodox rule only appears to occur when the individual's blame demands an exceptional outcome.

Recklessness: criminalising the risk-taker

Recklessness, as opposed to intention, satisfies the mens rea of some offences. The result is not intended but risk-takers show little regard for the safety of others. Public protection and deterrence can legitimise the criminalisation of reckless conduct. Nor does the criminalisation of reckless behaviour conflict with the requirement that punishment is reserved for the blameworthy as it is not unreasonable to expect individuals to act in a way which does not cause unnecessary risk to others. Recklessness is in many ways the most interesting form of criminal liability. A risk may be foreseen by an individual who then goes on to take it or the risk may be obvious to most people but was not foreseen by the individual in question. Is it fair to say that someone has acted recklessly, and is deserving of punishment, if he did not foresee the risk even if the risk would be obvious to most? The risk may not have been foreseen for a number of reasons. Some reasons why a risk was not foreseen may carry blame, such as where the individual is intoxicated. In other situations the lack of foresight does not involve blame, as, for example, where the individual is mentally impaired. The criminal law has struggled to resolve which of these positions should be adopted and a brief chronology of the leading cases demonstrates how in some situations blameless individuals could be deemed reckless, and found guilty of serious offences, due to their inability to see an **obvious risk**. Legal developments are sometimes welcome and there are few better examples of this than the way in which the House of Lords finally interpreted recklessness. Blameworthiness, and the fact that it had not always been present or deemed necessary, underpinned their reasoning as will be shown.

There have been two standard interpretations of recklessness (Williams, 1988; Norrie, 1992). The first possible interpretation is subjective and would require proof that the defendant knowingly took the unjustified risk. Even if the risk was manifest and obvious, a defendant who did not foresee it would be acquitted. The second possibility would involve an objective assessment of the risk and, crucially, would not depend on whether the defendant foresaw the risk personally. The subjective approach would protect the blameless from conviction whereas the latter approach would not, unless it is fair to say that blame attaches to the inability to see an obvious risk as well as engaging in conduct knowing it to pose a risk. One might have expected the courts to have adopted a uniform interpretation but this was not the case. Both tests were employed for some offences. One case became synonymous with each variant. *R v Cunningham* [1957] 2 QB 396 gave recklessness a subjective meaning while *R v Caldwell* [1982] AC 341 adopted an objective test. The subjective test had been in operation for 25 years prior to *Caldwell*, however as *Caldwell*, unlike *Cunningham*, was a House of Lords decision its impact was significant.

Caldwell involved damaging property with intent to endanger life or being reckless whether life would be endangered (Criminal Damage Act 1971, s1(2)) and the claim made by Caldwell was that he was drunk at the time and could not have envisaged the threat to life. This argument should have been rejected on the simple and accepted basis that voluntary intoxication cannot be used as exculpatory evidence for this offence in English law (see Chapter 6) but the Court went further and redefined recklessness so as to ensure that individuals like Caldwell could be found reckless. In criminal damage cases it was held that someone would act recklessly if '(1) he does an act which in fact creates an obvious risk that property will be destroyed or damaged and (2) when he does the act he either has not given any thought to the possibility of there being any such risk or has recognised that there was some risk involved and has none the less gone on to take it'. One wonders the extent to which this reformulation was motivated by an intrinsic sense that Caldwell was blameworthy because his inability to perceive the risk was self-induced, even though his intoxication at the time would have meant that he was criminally liable.

The position after *Caldwell* was indefensible due to its inconsistency and complexity. Both forms of recklessness endured and were employed according to the offence. A general distinction could be drawn between offences against the person which tended to follow *Cunningham* and offences involving criminal damage which used the *Caldwell* test. The obvious and fundamental objection to this approach is why two tests survived? If blameworthiness matters to recklessness then why should the defendant's perceptions or awareness remain key in some contexts but not in others? A convincing answer is hard to discern. Fires are unpredictable and potentially life-threatening so it could be that the nature of the harm influenced the House of Lords in *Caldwell*. Yet, the potential harm associated with many violent offences is equally grave rendering this reasoning flawed. Ironically the facts of *Cunningham* illustrate this: the offence with which he was charged involved unlawfully and maliciously administering to or cause to be administered to or taken by any other person any poison or other destructive or noxious thing, so as thereby to endanger the life of such person, or so as thereby to inflict on such person any grievous bodily harm (Offences Against the Person Act 1861, s23). If public protection or deterrence requires an objective approach in some contexts due to the nature of the harm, the position post-*Caldwell* only partially achieved this, not least because the subjective test was still used for violent offences.

It was not long before the ramifications of adopting an objective test emerged. In a series of criminal damage cases, individuals with limited culpability were convicted where the risk would have been 'obvious' to others (see for example, *Elliott* v *C* [1983] 1 WLR 939). The inevitably of individual injustice had been foreseen immediately by academics (for example, Williams, G, 1981) and was increasingly recognised by the judiciary. The facts of the leading case of *R* v *G* [2003] UKHL 50 illustrate the potential for injustice. Extensive damage, valued at about £1 million, had been caused by two boys aged 11 and 12 and it was accepted that they did not foresee the risk that fire would spread from newspapers that they had lit in a yard behind a shop to the shop itself and to adjoining buildings. *Caldwell* had been employed, properly given the offence, by the judge and the boys had been convicted. In the House of Lords, Lord Steyn listed the objections to *Caldwell* succinctly:

> The surest test of a new legal rule is not whether it satisfies a team of logicians but how it performs in the real world. With the benefit of hindsight the verdict must be that the rule laid down by the majority in *Caldwell* failed this test. It was severely criticized by academic lawyers of distinction. It did not command respect among practitioners and judges. Jurors found it difficult to understand; it also sometimes offended their sense of justice. Experience suggests that in *Caldwell* the law took a wrong turn. That brings me to the question whether the subjective interpretation of recklessness might allow wrongdoers who ought to be convicted of serious crimes to escape conviction. Experience before *Caldwell* did not warrant such a conclusion. (para 57)

He found that 'the case for departing from *Caldwell* has been shown to be irresistible' (para 59). Lord Bingham gave the leading judgment and his first two reasons for abandoning an objective test related specifically to blame and culpability:

[It] is a salutary principle that conviction of serious crime should depend on proof not simply that the defendant caused (by act or omission) an injurious result to another but that his state of mind when so acting was culpable... The most obviously culpable state of mind is no doubt an intention to cause the injurious result, but knowing disregard of an appreciated and unacceptable risk of causing an injurious result or a deliberate closing of the mind to such risk would be readily accepted as culpable also. It is clearly blameworthy to take an obvious and significant risk of causing injury to another. But it is not clearly blameworthy to do something involving a risk of injury to another if [for reasons other than voluntary intoxication] one genuinely does not perceive the risk. Such a person may fairly be accused of stupidity or lack of imagination, but neither of those failings should expose him to conviction of serious crime or the risk of punishment. (para 32)

At the trial both the judge and the jury thought that convicting the boys would be unfair when it was accepted that they had not foreseen the risk of the fire spreading. The judge, however, was legally bound to follow *Caldwell* and instructed the jury that the boys' lack of awareness was immaterial provided that the risk was obvious. Lord Bingham shared their 'sense of unease': 'It is neither moral nor just to convict a defendant (least of all a child) on the strength of what someone else would have apprehended if the defendant himself had no such apprehension' (para 33).

These are simple but compelling arguments. Blame is pivotal to the approach adopted: knowingly taking an unjustified risk is qualitatively and normatively different from taking an 'obvious' unjustified risk unknowingly. As Lord Bingham recognises, no culpability can fairly be attributed to those who do not perceive a risk. The unsatisfactory position of having two tests operating in parallel has been resolved in that all offences now employ a subjective test (see *Attorney-General's Reference (No 3 of 2003)* [2004] EWCA Crim 868). This test has the welcome effect of ensuring that the blameless are acquitted.

Negligence and gross negligence: criminalising the incompetent

Negligence is a civil law concept found in the law of tort which refers to situations where a defendant has a duty of care which he fails to satisfy objectively causing harm to his victim. If these criteria are satisfied, civil remedies can be awarded usually in the form of monetary damages. The criminal law sometimes criminalises negligent behaviour, most commonly in road traffic offences. Section 3 of the Road Traffic Act 1988, for example, makes it an offence to drive a mechanically propelled vehicle on a road or other public place 'without due care and attention, or without reasonable consideration for other persons using the road or place'. A definition of 'without due care and attention' is provided in s3ZA(2):

> A person is to be regarded as driving without due care and attention if (and only if) the way he drives falls below what would be expected of a competent and careful driver.

It can be seen that the test relates to his driving and it is immaterial whether the driver is aware that his driving falls short of this standard. The more serious offence of dangerous driving is found in s2 of the 1988 Act. A person is to be regarded as driving dangerously if:

(a) the way he drives falls far below what would be expected of a competent and careful driver, and
(b) it would be obvious to a competent and careful driver that driving in that way would be dangerous.

This statutory definition of dangerous driving is also objective as it relates to the perceptions of competent and careful drivers; there is no requirement that the driver was aware that his driving was dangerous. The distinction between careless driving and dangerous driving is one of degree. Whereas careless driving only requires proof that the motorist falls below the expected standard of a competent and careful driver, dangerous driving has to fall 'far below' that standard. In neither case does the driving have to result in an accident. Criminalisation is justified presumably on the potential harm that could follow driving below the standard of competent and careful drivers. It would be a rare driver who never makes a mistake, however, and it would appear likely that most motorists would technically be guilty of careless driving on a comparatively frequent basis. The offence gives police considerable discretion when dealing with incompetent drivers. In many occasions an informal warning at the roadside may suffice whereas a formal caution or prosecution may be necessary in other cases. Punishing dangerous drivers is easier to justify on utilitarian grounds as it may deter others from driving in a similar manner. Many of the activities which have been held to constitute dangerous driving, such as racing, are blameworthy and can also be justified on retributive grounds even though the offence does not require proof that the offender realised that his driving was dangerous.

Separate offences exist if the driving results in death. Death by dangerous driving is an established offence but controversy followed the passing of the new offence of causing death by careless or inconsiderate driving (s20, Road Safety Act 2006). This offence provides that a motorist who kills while driving in a way which falls below what would be expected of a competent and careful driver can be imprisoned for up to five years. As Hirst (2008) notes, this standard is unique to the motoring context and there are insufficient policy grounds to discriminate between driving and other forms of behaviour. It is a point well made.

How does the criminal law respond to deaths caused by negligence? Murder requires an intention to kill or to cause grievous bodily harm and so the negligent killer is not a murderer. Manslaughter is potentially relevant as this offence can be satisfied in a number of ways. It covers, first, offences which would have been murder but for a loss of control (which is narrowly defined) or diminished responsibility on the offender's part (see Chapter Three). As these variants would otherwise lead to a murder conviction, they are classed as voluntary manslaughter. The offence extends to some situations where the individual did not intend to kill or to cause grievous bodily harm and, because intent was lacking, these variants are termed involuntary manslaughter. Constructive or 'unlawful act' manslaughter still requires an intention on the part of the defendant to commit an offence (*Dias* [2002] Crim LR 490) which is objectively dangerous (*Watson* [1989] 1 WLR 684). As the dangerous offence is committed intentionally, there is no doubt that the individual is blameworthy and hence deserving of punishment, even though death or serious injury was not intended. The requirement that the offence is objectively dangerous helps protect individuals who kill when the risk of harm is minimal.

Murder and all of the three variants of manslaughter discussed above require an intent either to kill or to cause grievous bodily harm or to commit an offence which is objectively dangerous. There might be debate about whether it is fair that an individual who commits an offence which he does not believe to be dangerous can be convicted of manslaughter. Nonetheless, as culpability attaches to the decision to offend, the blameless are exonerated. In contrast, the final type of manslaughter, gross negligence manslaughter, allows for the conviction of the highly incompetent which raises significant issues about whether such individuals, who may have been acting to the best of their ability, should be held liable for so serious an offence. The courts recognise that negligence would be too low a standard for conviction but have argued that if recklessness was required, too many culpable individuals would escape conviction. In *Andrews* v *DPP* [1973] AC 566 Lord Atkins held that 'a very high degree of recklessness' would have to be established:

> I do not myself find the connotations of mens rea helpful in distinguishing between degrees of negligence, nor do the ideas of crime and punishment in themselves carry a jury much further in deciding whether in a particular case the degree of negligence shown is a crime and deserves punishment. But the substance of the judgment is most valuable, and in my opinion is correct...Simple lack of care such as will constitute civil liability is not enough: for purposes of the criminal law there are degrees of negligence: and a very high degree of negligence is required to be proved before the felony is established. Probably of all the epithets that can be applied 'reckless' most nearly covers the case. It is difficult to visualise a case of death caused by reckless driving in the connotation of that term in ordinary speech which would not justify a conviction for manslaughter: but it is probably not all-embracing, for 'reckless' suggests an indifference to risk whereas the accused may have appreciated the risk and intended to avoid it and yet shown such a high degree of negligence in the means adopted to avoid the risk as would justify a conviction. (p 583)

The kind of scenario in which this 'higher' form of negligence may be seen occurred in *R* v *Adomako* [1994] 3 WLR 288. A locum anaesthetist took over from a colleague during a routine operation. During the course of the operation the endotracheal tube supplying oxygen to the patient became disconnected. Adomako realised that something was wrong when an alarm sounded after 4.5 minutes, but he failed to spot the disconnection believing instead that the Dinamap machine supplying the oxygen had developed a fault. He proceeded to examine the machine and supplied the patient with atropine to raise his pulse. The patient died following a cardiac arrest nine minutes after the endotracheal tube became disconnected; it was only then that Adomako realised what had occurred. In the period between the disconnection and the cardiac arrest Adomako had allegedly missed a series of indications which should have led him to discover the problem: the patient's chest was not moving; the dials on the ventilating machine were not operating; and the patient was becoming progressively blue. It was also alleged that, despite noticing that the patient's pulse and blood pressure had dropped, he had failed to understand why. One expert witness described Adomako's standard of care as 'abysmal' while another said that a competent anaesthetist would have recognised the signs of a disconnection within 15 seconds and that his failure to do so amounted to a 'gross dereliction of care'.

His conduct was not reckless. In evidence he admitted that 'after things went wrong I think I did panic a bit'. One expert witness also testified that, once Adomako had wrongly concluded that the Dinamap machine was faulty, his actions thereafter were not unreasonable. Another expert gave evidence that it was possible that another problem may have arisen at the same time as the disconnection and that may have distracted Adomako from the fact that the tube was no longer connected. Other factors may have contributed to the accident. Gardner (1995, 26) reports that Adomako's career had consisted of a series of six-month contracts and that, at the time of the incident, he was working in one hospital during the week and another at weekends. The night before the accident he had only had 3.5 hours sleep. Finally, Adomako did not have an assistant during the operation despite this being normal practice.

Lord Mackay of Clashfern LC held that it was not necessary to prove that Adomako had been reckless and that gross negligence would suffice. What amounts to gross negligence?

> On this basis in my opinion the ordinary principles of the law of negligence apply to ascertain whether or not the defendant has been in breach of a duty of care towards the victim who has died. If such breach of duty is established the next question is whether that breach of duty caused the death of the victim. If so, the jury must go on to consider whether that breach of duty should be characterised as gross negligence and therefore as a crime. This will depend on the seriousness of the breach of duty committed by the defendant in all the circumstances in which the defendant was placed when it occurred. The jury will have to consider whether the extent to which the defendant's conduct departed from the proper standard of care incumbent on him, involving as it must have done a risk of death to the patient, was such that it should be judged criminal. (p 295)

If the jury are being asked to determine whether the defendant had been 'grossly negligent' it would appear that they are assessing his conduct rather than his state of mind. Adomako's admittance that he panicked may have given credence to his claim that he was not acting recklessly and might have helped to explain his failure to spot the disconnected tube. Potentially it may have also informed the jury's assessment of his conduct as a competent anaesthetist would not panic in such circumstances. This raises the question of whether it is necessary to have evidence of the individual's state of mind before it can be concluded that their conduct was grossly negligent. According to Rose LJ in *Attorney-General's Reference (No. 2 of 1999)* [2000] 3 All ER 182:

> Although there may be cases where the defendant's state of mind is relevant to the jury's consideration when assessing the grossness and criminality of his conduct, evidence of his state of mind is not a prerequisite to a conviction for manslaughter by gross negligence. The *Adomako* test is objective, but a defendant who is reckless…may well be the more readily found to be grossly negligent to a criminal degree. (p 186)

Evidently this offence is very fact-specific and much rests on how the jury in any case determines when negligent conduct becomes grossly negligent conduct. Whether or not the defendant's state of mind should inform their decision is left vague: it is not a prerequisite but there may be cases 'where the defendant's state of mind is relevant'.

Manslaughter can, therefore, be committed by the grossly incompetent and, as this depends on their conduct rather than their state of mind, the blameless can be convicted. Admittedly, the jury may consider the defendant's state of mind and whether he is blameworthy, but this is not mandatory. This is correct as a matter of law. Negligence relates to conduct rather than a state of mind. Why should gross negligence suffice for one of the most serious criminal offences? The harm would appear to be the sole rationale. Adomako would have been guilty of no offence if his patient had survived but had suffered brain damage. Elsewhere we have argued that the seriousness of an offence depends on both the offender's culpability and the harm caused (see Chapter Two). This would appear to be a classic case where there is significant disjuncture between harm and culpability. Not all individuals who kill, though, are guilty of a criminal offence, so culpability would appear to play some part. An accident caused by gross negligence is judged differently from other types of accident. The question then is whether any benefit accrues from this approach?

One might argue that the possibility of a criminal conviction would lead people to take greater care – an argument based on general deterrence. This may appear persuasive but the existence of an offence would have no impact in a case like *Adomako* where the individual panicked and misdiagnosed the situation. It is also difficult to see why this offence is necessary to protect society from the dangerously incompetent. Conviction follows a death and other measures could be taken, it is hoped, before their actions prove fatal, to prevent the individual from engaging in such conduct (for example professional accreditation could be removed). If recompense is paramount, civil law remedies would appear to be more appropriate. The public no doubt believe that those who cause death through gross negligence deserve punishment and we shall return to the attribution of blame and the dangers of scapegoating later in this book. For now it is sufficient to note that an individual's state of mind can have no bearing in a homicide offence with a maximum penalty of life imprisonment.

Strict liability: criminalising the blameless

There are many offences where no mental requirement or mens rea is specified in the relevant Act of Parliament (see, generally, Simester, 2005a). The legislature is at liberty to frame an offence as they see fit and so there is no constitutional objection to strict liability offences and, where parliamentary intent is clear, the courts have a duty to apply the Act. There are normative objections to strict liability offences, which will be addressed later, but the constitutional principle outlined above disguises a more complex and dynamic tension. The courts have sometimes faced enormous problems determining whether an offence is a strict liability offence due to parliament's failure either to specify mens rea explicitly or to state categorically that the offence is one of strict liability. This has forced the courts to decide the issue on an offence-specific basis and has meant that the appellate courts have had to provide more generic guidance as to how the task should be approached. It is necessary to consider the case law in some detail because the guidance provided relies on issues of blame and stigma and also because a broader assessment of the utility and efficacy of strict liability can only be undertaken meaningfully if the determinants for classification are outlined first.

Strict liability offences have a lengthy pedigree. Wilson (2011, 158) identifies two reasons for their rapid growth in the nineteenth century.

The initial impetus was industrialisation and the need for measures to protect factory workers. These offences were followed by a multitude of others concerning public safety more generally. Many of these laws were narrowly defined, carried minimal penalties and had no stated mens rea requirements. There were some early challenges. In *Cundy* v *Le Cocq* (1884) 13 QBD 207, a licensee had sold liquor to a drunken patron and had been convicted of unlawfully selling liquor to a drunken person (Licensing Act 1872, s13). The Act was silent as to whether the licensee had to be aware that the customer was drunk and Cundy appealed on the basis that he did not know the customer was intoxicated. Affirming his conviction, the Divisional Court justified imposing strict liability as they thought it right to put the onus on a licensee to determine whether a customer is sober.

The most significant challenge was brought in *Sweet* v *Parsley* [1970] AC 132, a case involving a teacher who had rented rooms to members of the 'beatnik fraternity' who proceeded to smoke cannabis on the premises. It was accepted that she had no knowledge of this even though she kept a room in the house for her own use. She was convicted of being concerned in the management of premises which were being used for the purpose of smoking cannabis (Dangerous Drugs Act 1965, s5(b)). The Act failed to specify whether awareness was a prerequisite for conviction. According to Lord Reid:

> Sometimes the words of the section which creates a particular offence make it clear that mens rea is required in one form or another. Such cases are quite frequent. But in a very large number of cases there is no clear indication either way. In such cases there has for centuries been a presumption that Parliament did not intend to make criminals of persons who were in no way blameworthy in what they did. That means that whenever a section is silent as to mens rea there is a presumption that, in order to give effect to the will of Parliament, we must read in words appropriate to require mens rea. (p 148)

The last sentence would suggest a clear and principled position: in the absence of a specific reference to strict liability, the offence should be read in such a way as to require mens rea as Parliament cannot have intended the blameless to be held criminally liable. However, this was not the case: 'It has long been the practice to recognise absolute offences in this class of quasi-criminal acts, and one can safely assume that, when Parliament is passing new legislation dealing with this class of offences, its silence as to mens rea means that the old practice is to apply' (p 149).

Creating a distinction between quasi-criminal and **criminal offences** raises concerns, the most pressing of which is whether offences can be categorised neatly along such lines. Lord Reid defined acts of a 'truly criminal character' as those which carried a stigma on conviction, a concept closely related to blame, and which would lead to public indignation if a conviction was manifestly unjust. Neither of these criteria are especially objectionable and it is obvious that an injustice is particularly acute if the consequences (whether reputational or punitive) are serious. Whether stigma attaches to those who commit a given offence is, though, subjective (what about drug possession offences?) and may change (consider public perceptions to drink driving). Perhaps a more straightforward and objective determinant was articulated by Lord Nicholls of Birkenhead in *B (A Minor)* v *Director of Public Prosecutions* [2000] 2 WLR 452 when he held that the greater the seriousness of the offence, the greater the weight that is to be given to the presumption because both the punishment and the stigma are more severe. This recognises that offences attract varying degrees of stigma which is reflected more convincingly as a continuum rather than as an absolute.

A useful summary of the present position is provided by Lord Scarman in *Gammon (Hong Kong) Ltd* v *AG of Hong Kong* [1985] 1 AC 1:

(1)   there is a presumption of law that mens rea is required before a person can be held guilty of a criminal offence;

(2)   the presumption is particularly strong where the offence is 'truly criminal' in character;

(3)   the presumption applies to statutory offences, and can be displaced only if this is clearly or by necessary implication the effect of the statute;

(4)   the only situation in which the presumption can be displaced is where the statute is concerned with an issue of social concern, and public safety is such an issue;

(5)   even where a statute is concerned with such an issue, the presumption of mens rea stands unless it can also be shown that the creation of strict liability will be effective to promote the objects of the statute by encouraging greater vigilance to prevent the commission of the prohibited act. (p 14)

Arguably the most important of these criteria is the fourth. Unless an Act of Parliament states so explicitly, the presumption can only be displaced if the statute is concerned with an 'issue of social concern' and the specific example of public safety is provided. It is easy to be glib but most criminal offences deal with issues of 'social concern' and many with 'public safety'; all violent offences could feasibly fall within this broad category, although this reading is avoided when account is taken of the second criterion as there would be little disagreement that such offences are 'truly criminal'. The utilitarian basis for the fifth criterion is also important. Even where the offence is concerned with public safety and is not 'truly criminal', strict liability will only be found where it can be shown that this is necessary to promote the aims of the statute. These would appear to be significant restrictions but many strict liability offences remain. Some are explicitly so but many are interpreted in this way by the courts. The judiciary maintain that they are engaged in an exercise which protects the blameless from social stigma and punishment by imposing mens rea requirements to 'truly criminal' acts. Yet the blameless are routinely being convicted of 'quasi-criminal' acts, and punished for them, on the assumption that little stigma attaches to such a conviction (Simons, 1997).

Conclusion

Inevitably the focus of this chapter has been on the way in which blame has informed the substantive criminal law. Yet alternative and sometimes compelling objectives exist. It is worth stepping back and starting this concluding section by considering what these alternative grounds may be and to see whether their merits are sufficient to warrant criminalisation of the blameless, at least in some instances.

One could start from the premise that the criminal law is designed to protect society from harm, whether perpetrated by individuals or corporations, and punishment is necessary to achieve this aim. If the focus is on harm, culpability is of little relevance. Objective standards of recklessness or negligence or strict liability would ease the prosecutor's burden as proving that the law has been flouted intentionally can be difficult and can lengthen trials. Recognising the task facing prosecutors is valid and, in some situations, strict liability is sensible and proportionate (Simester, 2005b), but the cost has to be recognised. Strict liability legitimates the criminalisation of conduct and the punishment of individuals whose conduct is blameless.

It is in recognition of these conflicting aims that courts have remained mindful of individual culpability. 'Quasi-crimes' and 'real crimes' are distinguished on grounds of their relative stigma and punishment. Crime control (see Chapter Two) and the need for deterrence justifies strict liability for more minor crimes. The judiciary, however, are reticent to convict the blameless of more serious offences. If deterrence is key, this position seems paradoxical as one would expect the law to prioritise those minded to commit the gravest offences. It is though a balancing act and the case law suggests that the courts value individual culpability more highly once the threshold between 'quasi-crime' and 'real crime' has been crossed. There is no reason why one aim should predominate for all offences and the probable stigma and punishment are sensible factors to take into account when deciding on prioritisation. Little sleep will be lost if a small fine is imposed on a blameless individual for an offence which carries no opprobrium whereas an obvious injustice occurs if someone is imprisoned for a serious offence when they have no personal culpability.

One theme that has proved constant throughout this chapter has been the importance of judicial interpretation. The issues discussed (motive, recklessness, negligence and strict liability) go to the heart of criminal law and yet Parliament has often left it to the courts to define these key concepts. This is not always a dereliction of duty. Parliament cannot be expected to envisage every issue that will arise once an Act is passed and some legal issues are better suited to judicial interpretation. Nonetheless, it is unsatisfactory that the courts have to guess Parliament's intent when deciding whether an offence is one of strict liability. Legislation could make this explicit and, while the classification may be objectionable as a matter of principle, at least the process would accord with democratic principles and constitutional convention. The fact that the judiciary have intervened in some cases and have imposed mens rea requirements has not influenced parliamentary practice. By implication, politicians accept the practice of the courts: interventionism has not resulted in explicitness. Could there be a tacit agreement that the balance struck by the courts is correct? The default position has been established: mens rea will be read into 'real crimes' unless parliamentary intent is clear. Parliament has accepted this which has ensured that the blameless cannot be convicted of 'real' offences unless an Act of Parliament states otherwise.

Parliament also failed to define recklessness, a term that is central to many common offences. Essentially the courts were faced with two options: imposing a subjective or an objective test. The tension is obvious. A subjective test focuses on individualistic perceptions of risk and culpability stems from a perception which is subsequently ignored. Assuming that the risk is unjustifiable, and this is largely determined on policy grounds, it is easy to construct a normative argument that deliberate risk-taking is culpable and, where the harm is sufficiently grave, criminal liability is appropriate. Conversely, recognising that individual perception is vital protects the blameless from conviction. It is indefensible to punish someone for a risk that they did not and perhaps were incapable of seeing. This argument was, according to the courts, rooted in notions of blame and helps explain the trajectory of the case law over the past 30 years.

Why did the objective test surface during this period? Perhaps the court was unduly swayed by the fact that Caldwell's lack of comprehension was caused by voluntary intoxication, which could legitimately be seen as culpable. It does not follow, however, that all failures of perception are culpable as the cases involving young offenders demonstrate. Another possibility is that the danger posed by fire influenced their reasoning, although given the multitude of dangers from which the criminal law seeks to protect society, what makes arson unique? An argument that an objective test would deter potential risk-takers is implausible. If someone could not perceive a risk they would not modify their behaviour to avoid it. The objective test both extends an argument based on culpability and introduces implicitly an additional justification. If culpability was to extend only to subjective awareness, there would be a conflict between public protection and blame. The conflict is avoided if a wider interpretation of culpability is employed. The eventual return to subjectivity demonstrates not only an awareness that deeming a failure to see a risk as culpable was unjust but suggests that an objective test was unnecessary in order to protect the public. Utilitarian aims such as public protection require an empirical basis and, when that does not materialise, its appeal becomes merely rhetorical.

If objective recklessness offends because it disregards the potential for individuals to be unable to meet a certain standard, negligence is equally problematic. A failure to satisfy a duty of care may properly give rise to civil liability and damages can have significant effects on an individual. It is far from certain that a criminal penalty will have a more severe impact than civil damages. Civil liability may also result in reputational damage, which could be significant, but there is something distinct about the stigma of a criminal conviction and the imposition of punishment which makes one wonder whether negligence is a sufficient basis for criminal liability.

It is helpful to compare negligence with strict liability. Strict liability, as we have seen, allows for the conviction of the blameless although judicial intervention has limited the possibility of this to 'quasi-crimes' unless statute is explicit. Negligence differs in so far as someone who has a duty of care only becomes liable if they breach that duty and damage ensues. Someone may breach a duty of care for various reasons some of which, like incompetence, may or may not be culpable. Individuals have diverse competencies as do those with particular duties of care. Not all drivers, for example, display the same ability and it would seem that those who breach an objective standard should not be penalised if their optimum level of ability would be insufficient. There are, though, distinctions that can be drawn with strict liability. An obvious one is that the individual assumes a duty of care willingly and ordinarily benefits from it. Why should it be objectionable to punish someone who fails if they have voluntarily taken on a duty of care? In the majority of cases one can avoid assuming a duty of care so there is a degree of freedom absent from strict liability. Another difference is that negligence has to be established whereas strict liability makes prosecution very straightforward. Using a civil standard to establish criminal liability may seem problematic but it should be viewed on its own terms as to whether it is sufficient to merit criminal liability in certain situations. In strict liability cases, the courts consider stigma and punishment in deciding whether mens rea should be read into the offence. These factors could help inform a discussion as to whether negligence is appropriate mens rea for a given offence.

The worry that a palpably culpable and incompetent individual would evade criminal liability for homicide led the courts to gross negligence manslaughter. Recklessness does not have to be proved which could be difficult as the inept often fail to foresee risks. Negligence, though, would potentially encompass too much behaviour and could deter people from assuming duties which are beneficial to society. Gross negligence effectively raises the bar by saying that the conduct has to be worse than mere negligence but whether that standard has been met is a question of fact for the jury. The objections are obvious: the test is circular and lends itself to inconsistency. Yet perhaps, by focusing on the individual's blame, juries will reserve punishment for those whose conduct can be perceived as blameworthy and acquit those whose negligence is not deemed sufficient.

What does this study of the role of blame in the criminal law tell us about blame in the criminal justice process? It was argued at the beginning of the chapter that the limits of the criminal law were vital to understanding the operation of the criminal justice process. The seemingly obvious point that the system processes people who break the criminal law is sometimes lost. The part that blame plays in the system then starts with the way in which offences are defined. If this book had failed to address some of the conceptual debates in substantive criminal law, then the picture painted would have been misleading. It has been necessary to consider these issues at a general level as the volume of offences does not allow analysis at an offence-specific level. The centrality of blame to a given offence will obviously differ but some clear conclusions can be drawn.

The first is that blame is surprisingly central to the criminal law. Objective recklessness has been abandoned. Strict liability has been reserved for 'quasi-crimes' and rejected for 'real' crimes unless Parliament has stated its intent clearly. Subjectivity demands consideration of the individual's state of mind and, where a risk is unforeseen, the defendant should be acquitted. Similarly, finding mens rea ensures that the blameless are not convicted of a strict liability offence. Had two young boys who had not been able to foresee a risk of fire or a landlady who was wholly unaware that cannabis was being smoked by her tenants been convicted, an obvious injustice would have been done. The courts have gone to considerable lengths to interpret the law in such a way that the blameless are not held criminally liable.

A second observation is that the courts' willingness to impose mens rea or adopt a subjective interpretation of the law is comparatively recent and suggests greater willingness to exonerate the blameless. It must be stressed that this trend relates to the judiciary, but they clearly perceive part of their function to be interpreting the law in a way consistent with the ideal that only the blameworthy should be liable for a criminal offence. This may be a counterbalance to popular demands that someone must be held to account in a criminal court whenever harm occurs. Similarly, the courts may be better placed than politicians to respond to cases where individual injustice could arise.

Many blameless individuals will, therefore, have been filtered out of the criminal justice process prior to conviction. Decisions regarding arrest, charge and prosecution hinge on the interpretation of the criminal law and there will be some who will be prosecuted but who are acquitted at trial as their blame could not be established. This does not imply that all those who are convicted should be regarded as morally blameworthy. Nor are all those who are acquitted morally blameless; some defendants escape justice on a legal technicality. Blame, however, plays a crucial role in the criminal law and hence in the criminal justice system.

FIVE

Blame amplification

The previous chapters have focused on situations where blame may be diminished or absent. Chapter Five is concerned with conduct that is deemed especially blameworthy. In sentencing offenders reference is regularly made to the seriousness of the offence and the degree of culpability of the offender. Under the Criminal Justice Act 2003 courts are specifically required to give consideration to the seriousness of the offence. The clear implication is that some offences are more serious than others and that it is possible to rank offences according to the degree of blameworthiness. At first sight this may appear to be unproblematic. Research which requires participants to rank offences according to seriousness generally find a measure of agreement. We would probably all agree that murder is more serious, and more blameworthy, than petty theft. In most situations we would regard violent offences as more serious than non-violent offences. Yet expressing the reasons behind our intuition may be more difficult. Is someone who murders 500 people deserving of more blame than the person who kills 10? Is someone who murders 50 people because they belong to a particular ethnic group more deserving of blame than the murderer who chooses victims at random? Orthodox criminal law jurisprudence distinguishes motive from intent (see Chapter Five) yet it is apparent that motive is not only relevant but central to the definition of some crimes. Chapter Five considers two particular aspects of blameworthiness. First, we will consider the relationship between punishment and blame within the national legal system. We will then focus discussion on the so-called **extraordinary crimes** such as genocide and crimes against humanity.

If offence-severity is a measure of harm and culpability, an incident, say criminal damage, cannot be aggravated if it is motivated on grounds of race unless the offender's culpability is greater. If it is assumed that the damage was intentional, does the specific motive of racism affect blameworthiness? When it comes to sentencing, evidence of hate is considered aggravating. Why exactly does such a motive make an offender more blameworthy and deserving of greater punishment? Genocide might be considered a particularly extreme form of hate crime. The second part of this chapter will therefore discuss those crimes which are said 'to shock the conscience of mankind'. To what extent is blame relevant when the number killed or tortured is counted in thousands?

Offence seriousness

Retributive principles have played an increasing role in the approach to sentencing in England and Wales since the late 1980s. The Criminal Justice Act 1991 was underpinned by concepts of **just desert** and retribution. The Criminal Justice Act 2003 continued to promote retributive principles although s142 acknowledged other, possibly contradictory, purposes of sentencing. Von Hirsch et al (2009) indicates that criminological interest in retribution and desert dates from the mid-1970s. The interest was partly generated by the post Second World War boom in the literature of analytical moral philosophy. It was also partly a reaction to mounting criticism of the focus on rehabilitation in many criminal justice systems during the 1960s. Criticism of rehabilitation in turn was partly based on a growing scepticism about its effectiveness. It was also connected to a growing interest in Kantian ideas and particularly Kant's view that: 'Juridical punishment can never be administered merely as a means for promoting another good either with regard to the criminal himself or to civil society, but must in all cases be imposed only because the individual on whom it is inflicted has committed a crime' (quoted in von Hirsch, 1992, 60).

Von Hirsch identifies the publication of the American Friend Service Committee report, Struggle for Justice in 1971 as being a pivotal moment. The report argued in favour of proportionate sentences and against sentencing based on rehabilitative grounds. At the heart of the AFSC report was the idea that fairness in sentencing required punishments to reflect the seriousness of the offence rather than the likelihood of the offender re-offending or the ability of the offender to reform.

For von Hirsch:

> Desert theories for sentencing have had the attraction that they purport to be about just outcomes: the emphasis is on what the offender should fairly receive for his crime, rather than how his punishment might affect his future behaviour or that of others. It also seems capable of providing more guidance: the sentencer, instead of having to address elusive empirical questions of the crime-preventative effect of the sentence, can address matters more within his or her ken, concerning the seriousness of the criminal offence – how

harmful the conduct typically is, how culpable the offender was in committing it. (Von Hirsch et al, 2009, 116)

We comment elsewhere in this book on the extent to which assessing blame is any less elusive than questions of crime-preventative effectiveness. Here we wish to focus on the link between punishment and blame. Von Hirsch places blame at the centre of punishment: 'The criminal sanction conveys censure' (p 116). According to von Hirsch, developing ideas first expressed by Kant:

> Any human actor...should be treated as a moral agent, having the capacity (unless clearly incompetent) of evaluating others' assessment of their conduct. A response to criminal wrongdoing that conveys blame gives the individual the opportunity to respond in ways that are typically those of an agent capable of moral deliberation: to recognise the wrongfulness of action; to feel remorse; to make efforts to desist in the future – or to give reasons why the conduct was not actually wrong. What a purely 'neutral' sanction not embodying blame would deny, even if no less effective in preventing crime, is precisely this recognition of a person's status as a moral agent. (pp 116–17)

Von Hirsch identifies two accounts of retributive justice. The **benefits and burdens theory** associated with Herbert Morris (1968) and Jeffrie Murphy (1973) justifies punishment on the basis that it offsets the advantage law-breakers gain through their offending. Laws benefit us all by restraining predatory conduct: others benefit from my self-restraint and I benefit from the restraint of others. The offender continues to gain the benefit of others' restraint without exercising self-restraint. The theory may be criticised on the basis that it over-emphasises the extent to which we benefit from the law abiding behaviour of others. A more fundamental criticism is that the theory provides little assistance in deciding the level of punishment. The seriousness of an offence does not always depend on the tangible benefit gained. Even if one considers benefit in a more abstract sense it is difficult to compare and rank different offences. Von Hirsch offers tax evasion as an offence which might be explained in terms of unjustified advantage:

> [The] tax evader refuses to pay his or her own tax, yet benefits from others' payments through the services he or she receives. Tax evasion, however, is scarcely the paradigm

criminal offense, and it is straining to try to assess the heinousness of common offenses such as robbery in similar fashion. (Von Hirsch, 1992, 62)

The alternative account, the 'expressive' theory, provides that: 'Punishing someone consists of doing something painful or unpleasant to him, because he has committed a wrong, under circumstances and in a manner that conveys disapprobation of the offender for his wrong' (p 66).

The advantage of this account is that it does not rely on an idealised view of society based on mutual benefit. It is also suggested that it provides a better basis for deciding on levels of punishment:

> If punishment is seen as an expression of blame for reprehensible conduct, then the quantum of punishment should depend on how reprehensible the conduct is. The punishment for typical victimizing crimes would depend on how much harm the conduct does, and how culpable the actor is for the harm – and no longer on how much extra freedom of action the actor has arrogated to himself vis-à-vis third parties. (p 67)

To arrive at just and proportionate sentences it is necessary to consider both ordinal and cardinal proportionality. Ordinal, or relative, proportionality dictates that individuals convicted of crimes of similar seriousness should receive comparable punishment; more serious offences should attract greater punishment than less serious ones. Ordinal proportionality provides no guide to the absolute level of punishment: the most serious offence might be punished with the death penalty or with a small fine; provided lesser offences are punished less severely, principles of ordinal proportionality are satisfied. The overall level of punishment is determined by cardinal proportionality which sets limits on the overall severity of available sentences.

It seems widely accepted that the seriousness of offence depends on a combination of the harm caused or intended and the culpability of the offender. This view is reflected in s143 of the Criminal Justice Act 2003. At first glance, grading offence severity may appear to be relatively unproblematic. The Minnesota Sentencing Guidelines Commission, for example, has produced a sentencing guidelines grid which ranks offences according to seriousness and it appears there was little disagreement on the underlying assessments of seriousness. Research into public attitudes to sentencing similarly seems to suggest a broad level of agreement when it comes to ranking the seriousness of offences. For example, research commissioned by the Sentencing Council on public attitudes to the sentencing of sexual offences revealed a broad level of agreement among the public on factors affecting seriousness (Sentencing Council, 2012b). The research, however, did reveal differing attitudes to offence seriousness when the views of victims/survivors were compared to the public. Interestingly, bearing in mind the discussions on juvenile offending in Chapter Three, both victim/survivors and the public took the view that the age of the offender should not affect culpability.

During the research, comparisons were invited between rape and other offences. The public saw rape as more serious than grievous bodily harm or supplying class A drugs (Sentencing Council, 2012b, para 5.2) although selling heroin was seen as 'almost as serious as rape' as were random, potentially life threatening attacks by strangers. Victims/survivors tended to see only homicide as more serious than rape and even then suggested that homicide 'at least meant the victim no longer experienced the pain and aftermath of the offence' (para 5.2). The aggravating factors identified by the research were:

- premeditation or planning
- sustained or repeated offences
- multiple offenders
- previous offending
- age and vulnerability of the victim
- use of violence, torture or weapons
- abduction and detention
- transmission of a sexually transmitted infection
- production and distribution of images.

The participants in the research were also asked to consider the defendant's character and what impact, if any, it should have on the seriousness of the offence. On balance it was felt that previous good character should not be taken into account:

> Indeed the participants could report 'good character' to be an aggravating factor because the offender had essentially been in a position of trust and also let down their own family and community to a greater extent by committing a sexual offence. It was also felt this may indicate greater culpability as they were hiding behind a 'cloak of respectability' but knew the offence was wrong. (para 6.3)

The views of the public on sentencing sexual offences are broadly in line with the guidelines on seriousness produced by the Sentencing Council (Sentencing Guidelines Council, 2004).

The factors indicating higher culpability include (the order has been changed from that in the Guidelines):

- offence committed while on bail for other offences;
- failure to respond to previous sentences;
- previous conviction(s), particularly where a pattern of repeat offending is disclosed;
- failure to respond to warnings or concerns expressed by others about the offender's behaviour;
- offence committed while on licence;
- offence was racially or religiously aggravated;
- offence motivated by, or demonstrating, hostility to the victim based on his or her sexual orientation (or presumed sexual orientation);
- offence motivated by, or demonstrating, hostility based on the victim's disability (or presumed disability);
- offence motivated by hostility towards a minority group, or a member or members of it;
- deliberate targeting of vulnerable victim(s);
- commission of the offence for financial gain (where this is not inherent in the offence itself);
- high level of profit from the offence;
- planning of an offence;
- 'professional' offending;
- offenders operating in groups or gangs;
- an intention to commit more serious harm than actually resulted from the offence;
- use of a weapon to frighten or injure victim;
- deliberate and gratuitous violence or damage to property, over and above what is needed to carry out the offence;
- abuse of power;
- abuse of a position of trust;
- an attempt to conceal or dispose of evidence;
- commission of an offence while under the influence of alcohol or drugs.

These aggravating factors can be seen to fall into a number of separate categories. The first five indicate that a failure to respond to earlier warnings will result in greater culpability. It seems intuitively right that if I have been told before not to do something my level of blame will be higher if I then proceed to do the thing. Release on bail, previous convictions and prior warnings all suggest that an offender is aware of his or her actions and the possible consequences. Of course, one might argue that there should be little difference in culpability between the offender who has offended repeatedly in the past without being discovered and the persistently unsuccessful criminal. Here again one encounters the problem of moral luck.

The second group of factors relate to the victim: hate crimes and targeting of the vulnerable increase the level of culpability. Clearly discrimination on grounds of ethnicity, religion, sexual orientation or disability is morally reprehensible and therefore blameworthy. Interestingly, offences motivated by hostility to the victim's gender or age are not listed, although there seems little reason why it is not as morally reprehensible to set out deliberately to target the elderly, or women as it is to target homosexuals or Jews. Hostility towards minority groups is identified as an aggravating factor but not hostility towards majority groups although the degree of culpability would logically seem to be the same. Perhaps the identification of the targeting of vulnerable victims raises the biggest problem. Arguably, many rational offenders may seek to target the vulnerable: it is easier to burgle an unlocked than a locked house. In some cases it may be difficult to see why the deliberate targeting of the vulnerable should actually increase culpability. It may also be difficult to assess levels of vulnerability: is an 85-year-old person inherently more vulnerable than one who is 65 years old? There is a problem also with the extent to which motivation can be readily identified. The Sentencing Council identify two other motivational factors relating to financial gain and profit. It can be accepted that stealing £1,000 is likely to be regarded as more serious than stealing £10 but this surely has more to do with levels of harm than levels of culpability.

The third group of factors are concerned more with the mode and method of offending. There seems to be a widespread view that premeditation or planning increases culpability and there are parallels here with the defence of loss of control discussed in Chapter Three. Diminished levels of self-control might also be a factor, mitigating sentences imposed on juvenile offenders. **Professional offending** might be considered to be linked to planning and premeditation. Identifying group offending as a factor is perhaps more problematic. Social psychology might suggest that we are more susceptible to loss of self-control when acting within a group. Arguably too, groups are more likely to act with hostility to those 'outside the group'. One can understand that it may be more frightening to be attacked by a group than by an individual but this surely goes to the extent of harm rather than the level of culpability. Deliberate and gratuitous harm and violence or damage to property might be more readily accepted as increasing culpability as might the abuse of power or trust. The attitude to previous good character in relation to sentencing sexual offences is relevant here in the sense that previous good character might itself contribute to placing an individual in a position of trust.

The effect of alcohol and drugs on culpability is discussed in Chapter Six. In regard to 'attempts to conceal or dispose of evidence' again it is to be wondered why this might increase culpability. It is true that the wrongdoer who, on realising what she or he has done, immediately gives themselves up and expresses remorse might be regarded as deserving less blame then the wrongdoer who lays low and says nothing. Yet if we imagine that Ann uses a kitchen knife to stab and kill Ben, is Ann really more culpable if she hides or destroys the knife than if she simply returns the bloodied knife to the kitchen and continues with her life?

Von Hirsh seems to suggest that assessing culpability is less puzzling than assessing harm:

> Culpability can be gauged with the aid of clues from substantive criminal law. The substantive law already distinguishes intentional conduct from reckless and from criminally negligent behaviour. It should be possible in principle to develop, for sentencing doctrine, more refined distinctions concerning the degree of purposefulness, indifference to consequences, or carelessness in criminal conduct. The doctrines of excuse in the substantive criminal law could also be drawn on to develop theories of partial excuse – for example, of partial duress and diminished capacity. (Von Hirsh et al, 2009, 4–5)

While it may well be **possible in principle** to develop more sophisticated measures to gauge culpability the fact remains that little development work has actually been done.

Robinson and Darley (2007) point out that it is common for us to think that our assessments about culpability and judgements about punishment are entirely reasoned in the same way we regard most judgements we make about our daily lives, but social science evidence suggests that judgements about justice, especially for violations that might be called the core of criminal wrongdoing, are more the product of intuition than reasoning. Their intuitional nature means, among other things, that they are judgements quickly arrived at, even by people with little education or life experience, that they frequently are held with strong feelings of certainty, and that the reasons we reach such judgements with such certainty are generally inaccessible to us.

Robinson and Darley (2007) refer to the research by Tversky and Kahneman which suggests that people frequently use intuitive, short-cut methods to reach decisions and then go on to act on them. Kahneman further suggests that: 'The evidence, both behavioural... and neurophysiological...is consistent with the idea that the assessment of whether objects are good (and should be approached) or bad (and should be avoided) is carried out quickly and efficiently by specialized neural circuitry' (Kahneman, 2003, 701).

Similarly Jonathan Haidt found that people report strong intuitions about things that are morally wrong, but are unable to provide a principled explanation for their judgements (Haidt, 2001). Having reviewed the relevant literature, Robinson and Darley conclude:

> In sum, there is at least some degree of consensus that many moral judgments are made by a deeply intuitive system. If such judgments were the product of a set of principles of morality learned from others, it would seem to be a straightforward matter to derive the 'wrongness' of acts from these principles, just as mathematical inferences can be made from a set of axioms and subsequently explained with reference to them. Moral dumbfounding and related effects in the psychological literature suggest that this is not how these judgments are made.
>
> To summarize, we are suggesting that the belief that serious wrongdoing should be punished and the culturally shared judgments of the relative blameworthiness of different acts of wrongdoing are commonly intuitive rather than reasoned judgments. This being so, these judgments come quickly to mind and are accompanied by strong feelings of certainty. The fact that these intuitions are the product of interpretative habits is obscured to the person because the processes that produce them are automatic and rapid, and leave no 'mental traces'. (Robinson and Darley, 2007, 8)

These findings have important implications for the retributive project. As we have seen already, an assessment of the measure of blame is central to the proportionality of punishment. The impression might be gained that blameworthiness can be scientifically and objectively assessed by weighing in aggravating and mitigating factors. Current social science research paints a very different picture.

Shocking and extraordinary crimes

In 1994 the population of Rwanda was approximately 7 million and was divided into three ethnic groups: the Hutu (85%), the Tutsi (14%) and the Twa (1%). According to the independent report commissioned by the Secretary General of the United Nations, during a 100-day period between April and July 1994 approximately 800,000 people were killed. Most of those killed were Tutsis. An estimated 200,000 women were raped and other appalling atrocities were carried out (United Nations, 1999). In its 2012 report Genocide Watch identified nine countries where genocide was taking place and a further 11 countries at the 'preparation for genocide' stage. According to Genocide Watch, at the preparation stage:

> Victims are identified and separated out because of their ethnic or religious identity. Death lists are drawn up. Members of victim groups are forced to wear identifying symbols. Their property is expropriated. They are often segregated into ghettoes, deported into concentration camps, or confined to a famine-struck region and starved. (Genocide Watch, 2012, 5)

In recent years it seems as if genocide, mass killings, war crimes and crimes against humanity have increased to such an extent that they may no longer be considered **extraordinary crimes**. At the same time 'Since 1989, the use of international judicial institutions to hold accountable those who are accused of perpetrating atrocities have burgeoned' (Schabas, 2012, 2).

On 29 November 1864 members of the Third Colarado Volunteer Cavalry Regiment under the command of Colonel John Milton Chivington carried out an attack on an unarmed, Indian settlement at Sand Creek. There were about 500 Southern Cheyenne and Arapaho living in the settlement, two-thirds of whom were women and children. Chivington ordered his men to 'Kill and scalp all, little and big...Nits make lice'. Eye witness accounts reported mutilations, killing of young children and final estimates of the number killed number 150 with many others seriously wounded. The massacre at Sand Creek was sadly not an isolated incident during the nineteenth century expansion of the

United States westwards (see Waller, 2007, 26). Neither Chivington nor any of the others involved in the massacre were ever prosecuted.

On 13 July 1942 members of Reserve Police Battalion 101 assembled outside the Polish village of Jozefow. They were middle-aged men considered to be too old to serve in the German army and had only arrived in Poland less than three weeks earlier. Their commander was Major Wilhelm Trapp, a 53-year-old career policeman. With the men assembled Trapp announced that the battalion had been ordered to round up the 1,800 Jews that lived in the village. Males of working age would be transferred to a work camp; the remaining Jews were to be shot on the spot. Trapp indicated that he was not happy about the assignment, but that those were his orders. He indicated, however, that any of the men who did not wish to participate in the shooting could choose not to participate in the massacre. Out of nearly 500 men only 12 declared themselves unwilling to shoot. The incident is explored in detail in Christopher R Browning's *Ordinary men* (2001).

It is tempting to believe that atrocities and other evil acts are carried out by evil people. We prefer to believe there was something inherently evil in Colonel Chivington, even if he had formerly been a Methodist minister. We like to think that we would join the 12 police reservists who refused to participate in the massacre at Jozefow. Phillip Zimbardo suggests that the idea that there is a clear distinction separating good people from bad people gives us comfort for at least two reasons:

> First, it creates a binary logic, in which Evil is essentialized. Most of us perceive Evil as an entity, a quality that is inherent in some people and not in others…it also takes 'good people' off the responsibility hook. They are freed from even considering their possible role in creating, sustaining, perpetuating, or conceding to the conditions that contribute to delinquency, crime, vandalism, teasing, bullying, rape, torture, terror and violence. 'It's the way of the world, and there's not much that can be done to change it, certainly not by me.' (Zimbardo, 2007, 7)

A series of experiments were conducted at Yale University in 1961–62 by Stanley Milgram. He found that almost two-thirds of participants, ordinary Connecticut residents, were willing to give apparently harmful electric shocks – up to 450 volts – to a pitifully protesting victim, simply because a scientific authority commanded them to, and in spite of the fact that the victim did not do anything to deserve such punishment. Following the experiment Milgram commented:

Many people, not knowing much about the experiment claim that subjects who go to the end of the board are sadistic. Nothing could be more foolish than an overall characterization of these persons. It is like saying that a person thrown into a swift-flowing stream is necessarily a fast swimmer, or that he has great stamina because he moves so rapidly relative to the bank. The context of action must always be considered. The individual, on entering the laboratory, becomes integrated into a situation that carries its own momentum. (Milgram, 1977, 118)

Some 10 years later, in August 1971, Phillip Zimbardo began an experiment aimed at discovering what went into the making of a prison guard. Zimbardo recruited a number of Stanford university students and some Palo Alto police officers to participate in the experiment. A mock prison was set up and roles as prisoners and guards were randomly assigned. The experiment was scheduled to run for two weeks but had to be abandoned after only six days because the guards became increasingly abusive and the prisoners dangerously stressed:

[All the participants] began the experience as seemingly good people. Those who were guards knew that but for the random flick of a coin they could have been wearing the prisoners' smocks and been controlled by those they were now abusing. They also knew that the prisoners had done nothing criminally wrong to deserve their lowly status. Yet, some guards have transformed into perpetrators of evil, and other guards have become passive contributors to evil through their inaction. Still other normal, healthy young men as prisoners have broken down under the situational pressures, while the remaining prisoners have become zombie-like followers. (Zimbardo, 2007, 172)

Over 30 years after the Stanford Prison Experiment reports of the abuse of detainees in Abu Ghraib prison in Iraq by US Army Reservists showed disturbing similarities.

We saw earlier in the chapter that deliberate targeting of particular victims is seen as a factor increasing culpability. Genocide might be regarded as the most serious of all hate crimes. Yet the evidence from social psychology is that genocide does not occur outside a particular social context. Colonel Chivington's reference to the Indians as 'lice' and 'nits' is pertinent here and in most situations where genocide occurs there are sustained attempts to dehumanise the targeted group. The members of Reserve Police Battalion 101 and the participants in Milgram's and Zimbardo's experiments were just ordinary human beings like any of us. Yet, in a particular set of circumstances, they were capable of acts of which most of us would strongly disapprove. The question of the extent to which they should be 'blamed' for their actions is less easy to answer. It may be a comfort to blame them because by blaming them we are saying, in a similar situation, we would have acted differently. The disturbing finding of Zimbardo's, and Milgram's and others' work is that there is no evidence that we would.

In Chapter Seven there is some discussion of international criminal law and the work of the international criminal tribunals. The issue of quantifying blame and ranking offence seriousness was raised particularly starkly by the International Tribunal for Rwanda (ICTR). The tribunal had been established by the United Nations Security Council and the maximum punishment the court could impose was a sentence of imprisonment. For a period of time while the court was hearing cases, the Rwandan courts still had the power to impose the death penalty. There was therefore the possibility that an individual convicted of murdering a shopkeeper might face the death penalty in the Rwandan courts while an individual convicted of murdering hundreds of shopkeepers would receive a sentence of imprisonment from the ICTR. This point did, to some extent, undermine the credibility of the ICTR in Rwanda, but raises a fundamental question: to what extent is carrying out multiple murders more blameworthy than carrying out a single murder? Is blame something tangible that can be quantified exactly: one murder = one unit of 'murder' blame, 10 murders = 10 units of 'murder' blame? The links between blame, retribution and punishment seem to suggest blame can be so quantified. Yet there appears to be little scientific evidence to support this view.

SIX

Putting oneself in harm's way

It is an everyday occurrence: people put themselves into positions where it becomes far more likely that they will offend. These actions constitute a continuum of conduct which range from putting oneself in a situation that makes offending virtually certain, through conduct where offending is a probable consequence, to situations where the causal link is far weaker. In all cases, the initial decision does not remove all later choice, although it may severely restrict the options available or may impair the individual's ability to act rationally. As the initial conduct is usually voluntary, it may reasonably be regarded as blameworthy but that does not mean that the process of causation and attribution is straightforward. The overarching concern is whether the precursory conduct aggravates any future offence or merely provides the context and whether it should even serve as mitigation. The allied question of policy is how the criminal law should rely on blame when determining how to respond to these cases when other factors such as deterrence appear of relevance. For the purposes of this chapter, the discussion concerns *deliberate* decisions which increase the likelihood of offending. **Putting oneself in harm's way** encapsulates the voluntariness of this behaviour. Other factors, such as socio-economic deprivation, may also be **criminogenic**, but these factors will be discussed elsewhere on the basis that the conduct is not (we would argue) voluntary and, even if this were the case, it could not sensibly be regarded as a decision to engage in behaviour which heightens the risk of offending.

Criminologists have largely ignored this phenomenon for understandable reasons. Studies into behaviour prior to the offence have often focused not on the actions of offenders, but on the actions of victims. Attempts to reduce crime victimisation are welcome but there is a danger that victims who are seen to have acted 'imprudently' are judged to be in some way to blame for the crime. Victim-blaming is highly context-specific. Despite well-publicised campaigns warning of the dangers of leaving valuables unattended in cars, for example, victims are not castigated if the contents of a car parked in a vulnerable location are stolen. Compare that with victims of sexual violence who are routinely subjected to claims that they in some way 'provoked' the offence by, for example, dressing in a certain way (Walklate, 2009, 231).

This chapter does not consider the actions of victims but it is important to recognise why this wariness exists. This neglect is regrettable as this chapter demonstrates the multitude of issues at stake and the practical ramifications that arise as a consequence. Not all of these issues have previously been identified, let alone analysed, and so this chapter serves as an attempt to map new terrain.

Returning to the continuum above, it would appear that there is some inverse correlation between the certainty of the future offence and the frequency with which the issue arises. Only rarely are the courts faced with situations where someone acted in such a way that offending was virtually certain. More commonplace scenarios, where the likelihood is more remote, cause particular problems: the frequency supports calls for a deterrent response but the weaker causal link suggests less blame. In order to consider these issues, the chapter will consider four scenarios in turn, each of which exemplify different points on the continuum: joining criminal or paramilitary organisations; becoming **associated** with the drug trade; offending to feed an existing drug habit; and offending after becoming voluntarily intoxicated. There are commonalities but it is equally apparent that significant differences exist. Blame helps link these scenarios but equally it helps to expose the distinctions.

Blame, gang membership and paramilitary involvement

Those who join criminal gangs or paramilitary organisations do so with the expectation (and quite possibly the hope) of offending. (We are ignoring situations where mere membership of the organisation is a criminal offence.) Recruits to paramilitary and terrorist organisations are aware that members engage in serious, violent criminality. Funding is often secured through other illegal activity such as drug dealing, prostitution and extortion. Non-compliance is likely to be met with violence, a fact of which members will no doubt be acutely aware. There is no difficulty establishing a link between the decision to join and the offence. The issue in such cases relates to situations where, after joining an organisation known to offend, the individual offends but claims that he did not want to but did so under duress. Voluntariness and blame evidently attach to the original decision to join, causality may be obvious, but, assuming the veracity of the individual's account, does blame attach to the offence committed under duress? Duress may well have been applied given the nature of the organisation. Nevertheless, the certainty of offending and the likelihood of violent compulsion would surely have been foreseeable and the essence of duress is that there is a lack of blameworthiness on the individual's part. One could legitimately question whether that is the case here. Refusing to recognise the duress, though, is problematic. Excluding such an argument would mean that an individual's initial decision to participate would make him liable for all ensuing criminal activity, or at least all foreseeable criminal activity, even if he was forced to commit it. Young, naive or vulnerable recruits would be offered no protection from violent coercion.

Instinct might suggest that the availability of such a defence is most pressing for serious crimes. The severity of the crime, however, partly determines the availability of the defence. Duress is not available as a defence to the very gravest crimes in most domestic legal systems or to the most serious crimes in international criminal law. This absolute position gives rise to some fundamental, and potentially uncomfortable, questions about blame. In the infamous case of *Erdemović* (IT-96-22-A) a young soldier refused to obey an order to execute a group of about 70 civilians. He was told that if he had sympathy for the victims he should join them, at which point he carried out the order. At his trial he pleaded guilty, but claimed that he had shot the civilians under duress. A majority of the Appeal Chamber held that duress could not be used as a defence to war crimes or crimes against humanity. In this case the execution of numerous civilians was exceptionally grave, but one cannot ignore the abnormally severe pressure he faced. Perhaps it is also worth noting that Erdemović had not joined a paramilitary or a criminal organisation, but, rather, was a member of an army and had not joined with the expectation that he would be a party to the massacre of civilians. For present purposes, the dissenting judgment of Judge Stephen is of particular relevance. Judge Stephen reviewed the principles of the common law and argued that duress existed as a defence because the defendant's actions were not blameworthy and it would be unjust to punish him for his actions. He noted that duress was not available as a defence to murder in the common law (see below) but could find no compelling reason why this was the case. A possible answer was provided by Judges McDonald and Vohrah. They also accepted that the basis for the defence was a lack of blameworthiness, but they held that murder could be distinguished from other offences due to the sanctity of innocent life.

The leading English case, *Howe* [1987] 1 All ER 771, did establish that duress cannot act as a defence to murder, but it is unfair to say that the judges failed to articulate a convincing rationale for this rule. Recognising that 'the overriding objects of the criminal law must be to protect innocent lives and to set a standard of conduct which ordinary men and women are expected to observe', Lord Hailsham LC held that:

> Other considerations necessarily arise where the choice is between the threat of death or *a fortiori* of serious injury and deliberately taking an innocent life. In such a case a reasonable man might reflect that one innocent human life is at least as valuable as his own or that of his loved one. In such a case a man cannot claim that he is choosing the lesser of two evils. Instead he is embracing the cognate but morally disreputable principle that the end justifies the means. (p 780)

At first glance this appears to be an argument based on the sanctity of life, but it is in fact an argument about blame. By finding that the defendant had embraced 'the cognate but morally disreputable principle that the end justifies the means', Lord Hailsham is attaching blame to the defendant's actions. The argument does rest on the sanctity of life in that someone who commits a lesser harm does not make such a calculation and hence lacks blame. How convincing is this argument? What if someone was forced to decide whether to kill one person when the threat relates to the lives of several? Having an absolute rule would mean that he would be guilty of murder even if his actions paradoxically saved lives. Lord Hailsham was sensitive to this possibility, believing that it could be dealt with appropriately at the prosecutorial or sentencing stage.

These cases establish that no-one can rely on duress as a defence to murder, so those who join a paramilitary or criminal organisation and who kill under duress are treated no differently from a random individual placed in this invidious position. Yet the blame appears markedly different. A paramilitary or someone who joins a violent criminal gang exposes himself to such a risk and the decision to join the organisation introduces an element of blame which is not present in a case involving a random individual. If Lord Hailsham is correct, the blame attaches equally in that both adopted a 'morally disreputable principle'. The fact that both individuals may have acted in such a way, though, does not mean that there is equivalence. Surely the paramilitary was engaged in disreputable conduct beforehand *and* there was a factual link between this and the subsequent (and 'morally disreputable') 'decision' to offend? The other individual found himself in this position by chance.

The law does distinguish between the paramilitary or gang member and the 'innocent' person in cases involving lesser crimes. Duress exists as a potential defence to most offences, although the law is complex as there are obvious policy reasons favouring a restrictive approach. This complexity means that a general account of the law is beyond the scope of this work especially as in-depth analyses can be found elsewhere (Ashworth, 2009; Ormerod, 2011; Simester et al, 2010). One such restriction is that the defence is forfeited if 'a person has voluntarily, and with knowledge of its nature, joined a criminal organisation or gang which he knew might bring pressure on him to commit an offence and was an active member when he was put under such pressure' (*Sharpe* [1987] 1 QB 853 at 861). This case involved an armed robber who was denied the opportunity to plead duress following the shooting of a post office employee, despite a claim that his participation had only been secured at gun point.

If policy dictates a generally restrictive approach to duress, removing the defence in this situation can be justified on similar grounds:

> The policy of the law must be to discourage association with known criminals, and it should be slow to excuse the criminal conduct of those who do so. If a person voluntarily becomes or remains associated with others engaged in criminal activity in a situation where he knows or ought reasonably to know that he may be subject to compulsion by them or their associates, he cannot rely on the defence of duress to excuse any act which he is thereafter compelled to do by them. (*Hasan* [2005] UKHL 22 at para 38)

Although this might appear to be an absolute bar to pleading duress after becoming involved with paramilitary or criminal enterprises, it does not appear that the initial decision to join the organisation precludes any later reliance on duress. The bar would appear to demand continuing association with the organisation or gang which presumably could be terminated.

Despite this, *Hasan* places a broad restriction on pleading duress in two ways. Most notably, the quotation from the judgment shows that the test is objective: it is not necessary for the individual to be aware that his voluntary association may subject him to compulsion if he 'ought reasonably' to have known this. A subsequent Court of Appeal decision recognised that this ruling could remove the possibility of duress from someone who knew that an associate carried a knife and with whom others had warned him not to associate (*Ali* [2008] EWCA Crim 716).

Imposing an objective test as opposed to a subjective one has implications for this study. It is, at least theoretically, possible to envisage a scenario where someone ought to have seen the risk of compulsion but failed to do so (examples certainly abound in other areas of the criminal law when an objective test is adopted). Naive individuals may well be vulnerable to approaches from such organisations. Should such a person be treated in the same manner as someone who knowingly embraced the risk? If blame is relevant to criminal liability or punishment, can an objective approach be defended? The distinction may be academic (in *Hasan* it was argued that a jury would be unlikely to conclude that a defendant failed to see a reasonable risk) but the policy is deliberate. The quote from the judgment shows that the policy rests on the idea that individuals should be discouraged from associating with criminals. Blame is not the issue but deterrence, and that objective does not demand blameworthy conduct on the part of the defendant.

The second restriction, which is of greater practical significance, relates to the phrase 'association with known criminals', a construction that would appear to go beyond actively joining criminal enterprises. *Ali* [2008] EWCA Crim 716 provided the example of an individual who knew that an associate carried a knife and had been warned by others of the dangers of associating with him. Drawing the boundary in this manner expands massively the number of people potentially affected by this ruling. It has particular ramifications for drug users. On the vast number of occasions when drugs are purchased, the buyer knowingly associates with dealers who are, by definition, criminals. One might have had more sympathy for the restriction in that it would have applied to a comparatively small number of people who had made the decision to join groups whose mission was to offend if *Hasan* had adopted a narrower formulation. A justification could have been found which relied on both blame and deterrence if a subjective test had been applied. Other than a crude recourse to deterrence, it is difficult to see how one can support this broader interpretation.

Purchasing drugs, 'associating with criminals' and expanding the 'blameworthy'

It is trite but true that every drug deal represents an association with a known criminal. It is also well known that the drug trade is brutal with debts frequently enforced by violence (Brownstein et al, 2000; Curtis and Wendel, 2007; Goldstein, 1985). Debtors may, though, be pressurised into offending in lieu of a debt, for example by drug trafficking, raising issues similar to those discussed in the preceding section. There is, it is submitted, one key distinction. A gang member or a paramilitary can expect to offend and can reasonably foresee that refusal will be met with violence. Those in debt to a drug dealer may expect violence, however it is unlikely that they would have envisaged pressure to offend.

Although the English courts have treated the relationship between user and dealer as a criminal association, we would argue that there is a difference between those who purchase drugs and those who join a criminal or paramilitary organisation: the former involves contact with and, in the broadest sense, participation with criminals while membership makes one part of the criminal enterprise. Users may be said to *enable* the enterprise but they do not *belong* to it. The enterprise may not exist without users but one should be wary of finding moral equivalence between an enabler and a participant via association.

Statistically, drug users may be more likely to find themselves in a situation where they offend under duress than non-users, though that risk is obviously less overt and less foreseeable than for someone joining a criminal enterprise. The courts have argued that these distinctions are meaningless by prescribing so wide a definition of association. The leading case of *Hasan* [2005] UKHL 22, discussed in the preceding section, does in fact allow for a situation where duress may be allowed more readily in a case involving a drug user. It will be recalled that duress will not be available to someone who voluntarily becomes or remains associated with others engaged in criminal activity in a situation where he knows or ought reasonably to know that he may be subject to compulsion. A jury may be more willing to say that a drug user could not reasonably envisage being compelled to offend compared to someone who joins a criminal organisation. Case law suggests that the courts take a hard line. The accused in *Heath* [2000] Crim LR 109 was charged with possessing a Class B drug with intent to supply and maintained that he had done so after serious threats were made by a dealer to whom he owed money. Heath acknowledged the reality of his situation, stating that 'people collect their debts in one way'. His defence of duress was excluded as the risk of duress was freely undertaken. It seems odd that reliance was made of Heath's comment when the more obvious and natural interpretation would be that violent retaliation was likely.

Drug misuse and crime

It is well-documented that drug-users commit a disproportionate amount of crime. A meta-analysis of 30 studies undertaken by Bennett et al (2008) reported that users were three to four times more likely to commit a variety of offences than non-users. It has been estimated that up to half of all property crime in England is drug-related and that the market value of the property stolen could be £2.5 billion a year (DrugScope, 2013). Even though the correlation between drug use and crime is beyond dispute, this does not prove that there is a direct causal link. Those who are both drug-users and offenders are not a homogenous group:

> [There] are some individuals for whom the acute, and possibly chronic, cognitive effects of some drugs, such as alcohol, increase the propensity toward criminal behaviors. For others, involvement in deviant behavior weakens bonds to conventional norms and increases involvement in deviant subcultures (including the illicit drug market) that provides opportunities and reinforcement for increased deviant behavior, including drug use. Finally, for others, probably a majority, biopsychological factors (for example, temperament) and early parent–child interactions, in combination with socioenvironmental factors increase the risk for involvement in all types of deviant behavior. (White and Gorman, 2000, 195)

Research suggests that criminal behaviour usually pre-dates drug use, a finding which challenges the popular belief that people offend in order to fund a pre-existing drug habit (Menard et al, 2001). The authors of this study, however, found that once offenders start using drugs, each behaviour increases the likelihood of the other, leading the authors to conclude that, by this stage, crime affects drug use and drug use affects crime. Ford (2005) also found significant indirect connections in the relationship between drug use and delinquency. His primary contention was that both drug use and delinquency weakened the social bond which increased the risk of both behaviours continuing.

How do these findings inform a discussion of blame in the criminal process? First, early initial forays into criminality may be wholly unrelated to subsequent drug use: the offender might not heighten his risk of offending by taking drugs, but may heighten his risk of drug taking by offending. In terms, then, of apportioning blame, it would appear appropriate to treat such an offender in the same way as any other first-time offender. If, as Menard et al (2001) suggest, crime pre-dates drug use, the situation thereafter becomes complex. Both the early offences and the initial drug use were (probably) voluntary and both may well be precursors to later crime. Accordingly, there would appear to be two possible departure points and both would support a claim that the offender had deliberately increased the likelihood of offending. In fact, the attribution of blame appears far less problematic than if there was a direct causal link between drug taking and crime. In the last scenario, one would have to find that someone using drugs did so in the knowledge that there was an increased risk of offending. Presumably few individuals start using drugs with this in mind. Consequently, the fact that the two activities are commonly entwined may be less problematic than supposed. What, however, if drug use and criminality are in fact linked to another common factor such as a risk-seeking personality?

In such cases it seems reasonable to ask two questions: to what extent does that trait explain the offending behaviour and to what extent does that trait affect blame? There are many people with risk-seeking personalities, and such people may be more likely to offend or use drugs, but others channel this by, for example, participating in extreme sports. The quantification of blame should then encompass more than the fact that the offender was a drug user. Recognition must be given to the variety of ways in which drug use can feature in an offender's life at any particular point; research suggests that the relationship is fluid and becomes more prominent as criminality becomes entrenched (Menard et al, 2001). It may also be appropriate to recognise the fact that an offender is trying to address a drug habit and is taking positive steps to reduce the risk of recidivism. This could even be regarded as an attempt to put oneself out of harm's way.

The impact of blame is important for another reason with this type of offender. Drug users in treatment frequently report stigmatisation or self-stigmatisation and this in turn is likely to undermine the effectiveness of treatment (Room, 2005). Blame could then have a negative effect when it comes to rehabilitating offenders with substance abuse problems. Luoma et al (2007), however, found that substance abusers receiving treatment who were also involved in the criminal justice system reported less stigma than other service users. This is an intriguing finding. Perhaps drug users who are not involved in crime feel that they suffer because of the common assumption that users offend in order to feed their habit. In this context, the stigma flows from an overly-simplistic, but widely-held, view of causality. The divergence between popular assumption and empirical evidence creates problems for policy-makers, particularly those dependent on electoral support. Responding to the public mood may lead to political success, but it is unlikely to have a positive impact on the underlying problem. Indeed, it may exacerbate it, as is the case when aggressive enforcement of drug laws have been shown to drive up the price of drugs leading to increases in crime (Quinn and Sneed, 2008). Evidence-based policy may dispel some myths, or, at least, demonstrate that the reality is more complex than commonly understood. Attempts to explore crime, and even more so to explain it, can be seen by some as an attempt to excuse it. By simplifying the causal connection between drug use and crime, the popular view is that the offender is to blame for his predicament and that this should be reflected in how the criminal justice system responds. In certain cases, such a conclusion may be warranted but, due to the evidence offered above, it is clear that such a finding should not be universal.

Blame, intoxication and alcohol-related offending

The last scenario to be considered is by far the most common – offences committed by those who had been drinking alcohol. There would appear to be correlation between intoxication and offending (Aldridge et al, 2011, 13–15). According to the British crime statistics, 44% of those who reported that they had been the victim of violence said that the attacker had been 'under the influence of alcohol at the time' (Home Office, 2011, table 7.10). Research has also found a causal association between alcohol abuse/dependence and several classifications of offending in a New Zealand birth cohort (Boden et al, 2013). The relationship was particularly marked for violent offences (Boden et al, 2012). Finding a direct causal link between intoxication and violence is notoriously problematic (Dingwall, 2006); evidently the majority of those who become intoxicated do not then offend. Nonetheless, one cannot sensibly disregard the fact that a very high proportion of violent crime is committed by those who are drunk, nor can one ignore the reality that most of these individuals put themselves in such a state voluntarily.

Alcohol is used in many contexts as an explanation and as a justification for atypical behaviour, so it should come as no surprise that offenders often blame alcohol use for their criminal conduct. Despite this, most studies show that offenders do not see a simple causal link and that the explanations offered are complex and nuanced. When McMurran and Hollin (1989) asked 100 young offenders, all of whom were moderate or heavy drinkers, whether they saw a link between their drinking and their offending, 55.7% said, initially, that they did not. Yet, when the offenders were then presented with a sample of cue cards, many did identify a link. Some of these links amount to a decision to put oneself in harm's way: most notably, 37.5% stated that they did things that they would not do if they had not been drinking. Parker (1996) similarly found that his sample identified a variety of links. Three of the most common again suggest a decision to put oneself in harm's way: drinking made them impulsive and then they offended; drinking caused problems which led them to offend; and the places where they drank led them to offend.

More recent research by Newbury and Dingwall (2013) considered the perceptions of correlation between drunkenness and offending offered by a sample of young females who had offended, sometimes seriously, after binge drinking. The sample was drawn from a larger research project (Newbury, 2011) concerned with young offenders, the majority of whose offences were not related to alcohol. This meant that the interviewees were asked no specific questions about alcohol use nor were they presented with cue cards as in the studies above. Although the sample often expressed extreme remorse, they also stated that alcohol was the direct cause of their offending as it had a detrimental effect on their personality. Newbury and Dingwall's study shows that attributing blame to their sample is problematic. Many interviewees had experience of previous episodes where binge drinking had led to harm yet had not modified their drinking behaviour as a result. At the same time, one of the study's key findings was that most of those interviewed displayed genuine, and at times frightening, ignorance about safe alcohol consumption.

The situation is, therefore, complex: direct causation between intoxication and offending is hard to find; a high proportion of violent crime is committed by those who are intoxicated; most of these people drank voluntarily; people no doubt believe that there is some link and therefore few would be easy with the idea that individuals should escape any form of criminal liability on the grounds of being voluntarily intoxicated at the time. How should an intoxicated person who subsequently offends be treated?

One could start from a position that an individual should gain no benefit from getting intoxicated voluntarily. This was the original common law stance (McCord, 1992) and still represents the position in Scotland (*HM Advocate* v *Savage* [1923] JC 49) and in several states in the USA (*Montana* v *Egelhoff* 518 US 37 (1996)). The effect of this is that an intention to become intoxicated is regarded as an alternative to an intention to commit the offence in question. Difficult questions of relative blame arise. It would not be implausible to construct a normative argument that the blame associated with voluntarily getting intoxicated equates to that of committing a crime. The task, though, would be daunting; not least as it would entail showing that the blame associated with getting intoxicated corresponded to the blame associated with committing the actual offence in question. Surely, though, the blame in getting intoxicated remains constant, whereas the blame associated with offending depends on the seriousness of the offence? It cannot be the case, for example, that the blame associated with intoxication equates to both the blame associated with criminal damage and the blame associated with murder. Perhaps it would be more intellectually honest to justify this stance explicitly on the grounds of public policy, although one should be wary of accepting that such a policy would have any real deterrent effect.

Some Commonwealth countries adopt an opposite position whereby evidence of intoxication is seen as a relevant factor in determining whether an individual satisfied the requirements of the offence. This does not lead to an automatic acquittal although it allows for this possibility. This may appear paradoxical in that someone who is so intoxicated that he could not have intended to commit the offence escapes liability while someone less intoxicated who nevertheless intended to do so is convicted, but the position accords with standard criminal law doctrine which requires the prosecution to prove all of the constituent elements of an offence including intention where relevant. Another interpretation of this approach is that it allows a distinction to be drawn between the blame associated with intending to become intoxicated and the blame associated with intending to commit the offence. Society may well believe that an intoxicated person who stabs someone is blameworthy, but the better question is whether that person is as blameworthy as a sober individual who intentionally stabs the victim. This is further complicated when one remembers that becoming intoxicated is not of itself criminal and there would be debate about whether it should be regarded as blameworthy at all.

Perceptions of blame help explain the popular reaction to certain cases where intoxicated individuals have been acquitted in these jurisdictions. *Daviault* (1994) 93 CCC (3d) 21, a particularly infamous Canadian case, involved a chronic alcoholic who sexually assaulted an elderly disabled woman after consuming a vast quantity of beer and brandy. The Canadian Supreme Court held that it was incumbent on the prosecution to prove that Daviault satisfied all of the requirements of the offence. His extreme intoxication at the time meant that this was impossible. The media incredulity following his release led to rapid legislative changes designed to ensure that those facing trial for violent or sexual offences could not escape conviction on similar grounds. The outrage is, of course, understandable and no doubt reflected a widely-held view that considerable blame attached to Daviault's conduct. It was this disjuncture between a judicial outcome and popular belief that led Parliament to reform the law. It is worth reflecting further on the reaction. First, there is no way of knowing whether the public felt that Daviault's blame was identical to that of a sober offender. There was outrage, but that may have been because he was not held to account in any way for his conduct; we have no way of gauging whether or not his alcoholism would have affected the public's perceptions of his blame. Second, a binary position had to be adopted: Daviault's intoxication was or was not relevant. When faced with a stark choice, the reaction would suggest that the public would have arrived at the opposite conclusion to the Supreme Court, although it is worth remembering that the public's knowledge of the facts of the case would have been partial and that the Supreme Court was determining a point of law and not acting as a moral arbiter.

Alternative approaches exist which allow for greater nuance. One could, for example, distinguish between different offences, as in England and Wales, where intoxication is potentially relevant for some offences but is irrelevant for others. Such an approach may appear to have little to commend it: blameworthy individuals will escape liability for some crimes while others are convicted despite failing to satisfy the requirements of the offence. Yet this approach, confirmed by the House of Lords in *Majewski* [1977] AC 443, is more logical than is sometimes supposed. Offences requiring intention are classified as specific intent offences and evidence of intoxication can be considered. An acquittal can follow, although, if the offence can be committed without intent, usually recklessly, evidence of intoxication must be excluded.

Commentators have generally found flaws with this approach (for example, Cavender, 1989; Farrier, 1976; Smith, 1976; Virgo, 1993). Everything rests on how an offence is classified, yet this is far from settled and there are theoretical disputes about whether existing classifications are correct (Williams, 1983). Recklessness is also found too readily. English law defines recklessness as the conscious taking of an unjustified risk (*R v G* [2004] 1 AC 1034). The risk relates to a specified harm. Yet, the sense in which recklessness is used here is more generic and appears to relate to consciously getting intoxicated, with the attendant risk that one might then offend in an unspecified manner. The blame shifts from an intent or recklessness about causing a particular harm to that generally associated with becoming intoxicated.

If blame attaches to intoxication then why not make that a distinct offence? Germany, for example, has an offence of **total intoxication**:

> Whoever intentionally or negligently get [sic] intoxicated with alcoholic beverages or other intoxicants, shall be punished with imprisonment for not more than five years or a fine, if he commits an unlawful act while in this condition and may not be punished because of it because he lacked the capacity to be adjudged guilty due to the intoxication, or this cannot be excluded. (Strafgesetzbuch StGB, Section 323a)

One of the present authors has advocated this approach before (Dingwall, 2006) on the basis that it balances the need to deter alcohol-related crime while ensuring that the fundamental principles of criminal liability are respected. Central to his argument is that the German offence recognises that those who offend while intoxicated deserve punishment and that the offence identifies the blameworthy conduct, that is, the voluntary intoxication and not the subsequent offence. Not everyone accepts that the locus of the blame relates to the intoxication. The New South Wales Sentencing Council (2009) rejected the creation of an offence of this nature on a number of grounds including:

> The creation of a special offence that includes intoxication either as an element, or as an aggravating element, risks punishing the offender for being intoxicated or for their moral irresponsibility, while the true focus of sentencing should be on the act committed by the offender while intoxicated. (New South Wales Sentencing Council, 2009, 103)

Two other objections can be raised, one practical and one theoretical. Although such an offence might best reflect the offender's blame, would it accord with the public's sense of justice? If Daviault had been convicted of this offence, would the popular reaction have been any more muted? If the maximum sentence is five years imprisonment, only those threatened with longer terms would want to be convicted of this 'lesser' offence. Discontent may be fuelled if all of those convicted of the offence had committed grave acts. Second, this approach still depends on a criminal harm occurring. In terms of blame, however, can a distinction be drawn between an intention to get intoxicated and an intention to get intoxicated which leads to a criminal harm occurring? Although this offence ostensibly punishes the earlier conduct which puts the offender in harm's way, it remains completely dependent on an ensuing harm which, according to the offence definition, was neither intentional nor reckless. Here moral luck enters the equation (see Chapter Three). If getting intoxicated is the blameworthy activity in such cases, it begs the question of whether existing drunkenness offences provide the remedy even if these typically attract minor penalties and have to be enforced selectively? It is suggested that they cannot perform this function. The penalty level would lead to outrage if serious harm was caused; and, despite the number of drunkenness offences that exist, many scenarios, including that in the *Daviault* case, would not be covered.

Conclusion: voluntarily heightening the risk of offending

It has been pre-supposed that blame attaches to the activities referred to above (joining criminal organisations, using illegal drugs, voluntary intoxication) and that, if these activities then lead to an offence occurring, it is appropriate and just for the law to take account of the earlier behaviour. Even if blame links these behaviours, however, there is no reason why policy dictates a uniform response. Joining a terrorist group, for example, exposes an individual to a far greater risk of offending than consuming alcohol.

Policy may favour a robust response which ignores such variables. Society has strong reasons for wanting to deter behaviour which, although not necessarily criminal in itself, may act as a precursor to crime. The policy of not allowing drug users to plead duress can be seen as an obvious example of a failure to distinguish between different factual scenarios and a willingness to apply a far-reaching definition of blame in order to justify the removal of a potential defence. Deterrence cannot, though, fully explain criminal justice policy in this area. Were this the case, the obvious response to alcohol-related offending would be to say that, provided the drinking was voluntary, the use of alcohol would be ignored when determining liability or sentence. Most jurisdictions, as has been seen, do not adopt such an approach. Instead, other factors are recognised as being important determinants of liability and these either override or limit deterrent concerns. Intoxication challenges common legal requirements that an offender either intended to commit a crime or was reckless about its commission. This, too, is an argument about blame; the offender may be blameworthy but to what does that blame attach? This is a common thread to all of the scenarios considered in this chapter. In each case one has to try and determine whether blame attaches to the earlier conduct or to the subsequent offence. Put thus, this seems a binary decision, but that has the potential to mislead. Arguably blame could attach to neither, one or both of the incidents. Returning to the intoxicated offender, one could hold the view that intoxication is not blameworthy and that it would be inappropriate to hold an intoxicated person liable for an offence that he did not intend to commit. It would be equally plausible to argue that intoxication is blameworthy and that offences committed in that state should be similarly regarded or that, while intoxication is indeed blameworthy, no blame should attach to an offence committed in that state.

If the assessment of blame is complicated by the fact that both the precursory conduct and the crime could be deemed blameworthy, there is also the question of the degree of blame. It is possible to accept that a drug addict who offends to feed his or her habit is to blame both for the initial habit and for the theft, but does that habit affect the blame that attaches to the theft? Determinations of where blame lies may best be a question of whether criminalisation is warranted and, just as crucially, what conduct should be criminalised. Questions relating to degrees of culpability are more commonly relevant at the sentencing stage, particularly if proportionality is a relevant determinant. Retributive notions of justice depend on the gravity of the offence which is usually taken to include both an assessment of the harm caused or intended and of the individual's personal culpability (see, further, Chapter Five). Offence-gravity is difficult to quantify objectively and the scenarios in this chapter further complicate this assessment. The prior use of alcohol and drugs provides a useful example. Australian research (Potas, 1994) has shown that sentencers faced with identical factual scenarios treated evidence of intoxication very differently with the result that individual outcomes varied markedly. This research probably reflects broader discrepancies about how society regards intoxication. The traditional position in England and Wales was that sentences would not be affected by evidence of intoxication (*Bradley* (1980) 2 Cr App Rep ((S) 12; *Parkhouse* [1999] 2 Cr App Rep ((S) 208); however, examples can be found of 'exceptional' cases where, presumably, less blame was seen to attach. These cases fall into two general categories, both of which are revealing: the first concerns men of previous good character who committed sexual offences (*Spence* (1982) 4 Cr App Rep ((S) 175), the second, incidents best described as drunken 'frolics' (*Abrahams*

(1980) 2 Cr App Rep ((S) 10). Drunken 'frolics' may perhaps deserve sympathy, but it is far from obvious why a distinction can be drawn between sexual offences and other offences.

The most clearly articulated case law comes from New South Wales. As a general principle:

> The degree of deliberation shown by an offender is usually a matter to be taken into account; such intoxication would therefore be relevant in determining the degree of deliberation involved in the offender's breach of the law. In some circumstances, it may aggravate the crime because of the recklessness with which the offender became intoxicated; in other circumstances, it may mitigate the crime because the offender has by reason of that intoxication acted out of character. (*Coleman* v *The Queen* (1990) 47 A Crim R 306 at 327)

Further guidance was provided about when mitigation was appropriate:

> The fact that an offender was intoxicated at the time of committing an offence is not of itself a reason for mitigating the sentence which should be imposed on the offender. However, the fact that an offender was intoxicated at the time of committing the offence may be taken into account as mitigating the objective criminality of the offence, insofar as it indicates that the offence was impulsive and unplanned and that the offender's capacity to exercise judgement was impaired. (*Walters* v *The Queen* [2007] NSWCCA 219 at [38])

Sentencing remains under-researched and this restricts the discussion here in two ways. First, there is a lack of a meaningful evidence base from which to determine policy. Second, contentious policy decisions can go unchallenged leading to an erroneous belief that the policy commands universal support. The Sentencing Guidelines Council (2004, para 1.22) determined in a guideline on offence-severity that intoxication by alcohol or drugs should aggravate a sentence. This does not provide empirical proof that sentences are being increased in such cases despite statutory requirements that guidelines must be followed unless it is contrary to the interests of justice (Coroners and Justice Act 2009, s125). Nonetheless, the guideline deserves comment as the descriptive nature and practical utility of a sentencing guideline means that a considered normative analysis is lacking. For example, it is unclear whether the decision is based on blame or whether deterrence was the determining factor.

Guidelines are designed to ensure greater uniformity of approach which, when one considers Potas' findings, appears laudable. A standard approach to such cases, however, presupposes that all offenders who were intoxicated at the time of the offence deserve identical treatment. Padfield (2011), an academic who also sits as a judge, disputes this, arguing that sentencers need to retain discretion in such cases, as intoxication can have an impact on culpability in different ways. This stance was also taken by the New South Wales Sentencing Council (2009, 113) Padfield's argument was in part a response to an article by Dingwall and Koffman (2008) who suggested a uniform approach, but one that differed significantly from the sentencing guideline. The authors contended that sentencing disparity resulted from the absence of an agreed policy for sentencing intoxicated offenders and that this disparity led to individual injustice. They rejected the argument, however, that sentences should be increased on the basis of intoxication and suggested instead an approach allowing mitigation if it was a first offence, thereafter intoxication would not influence sentence. Dingwall and Koffman's model was situated in a retributive sentencing framework so it excluded other policy objectives such as deterrence or public protection, both of which may favour treating intoxication as an aggravating factor. By adopting a retributive approach, however, blame featured large in their analysis and led to the distinction being drawn between first time offenders and recidivists. An offender of previous good character who offended while intoxicated was seen as less blameworthy than a sober offender. An individual who had previously offended while intoxicated, though, deserved no credit as he had failed to alter his behaviour. This conclusion raises another question of relative blame which the authors do not address: can one infer that a decision to become intoxicated having previously offended in that condition equates to a decision to offend while sober? Are they not qualitatively different?

What is important here is that all of these approaches are directly concerned with blame. What differs is how assessments of blame are best calculated. Recognising variety in circumstance and using this as a justification for discretion, Padfield's (2011) argument implies that blame is not uniform in such cases. Dingwall and Koffman (2008) also reject such a notion by distinguishing between first time offenders and repeat offenders but, within these categories, there is less room for manoeuvre as intoxication is irrelevant for all but first time offenders.

Their approach does not wholly disregard discretion in that judges dealing with first time offenders would still have to decide how much mitigation is appropriate and this decision depends, at least in part, on blame. Meanwhile the Sentencing Guidelines Council (2004) deems intoxication to be an aggravating factor, a conclusion that clearly relates to blame.

This chapter represents the first attempt to tie together four diverse areas of criminal justice policy. All raise both practical and theoretical issues of concern. Frequently, legal intervention relies on claims that the earlier conduct was blameworthy and that this justifies departure from standard requirements of the criminal law (as is the case with intoxication) or the removal of a potential defence (as is the case with those who 'associate' with criminals). The methods employed to allow these outcomes are often tortuous and contestable, even where the policy objective is sound. Perhaps it would be better to focus on the initial blameworthy conduct and seek an appropriate way of responding to it. This may well involve creating specific offences (such as those prohibiting membership of prescribed organisations) or of reviewing the enforcement of existing offences (such as drunkenness offences). One must be wary of presupposing that criminalisation provides the remedy (see Chapter Seven); there is a clear danger of 'net-widening' when one is attempting to curb behaviour which may well lead to significant harm. Where the potential harm is grave and the earlier conduct blameworthy, however, recourse to the criminal law may be appropriate. The dangers of 'net-widening' should make one wary of extending the reach of the criminal law but it should not exclude intervention where necessary.

Blame may provide a valuable mechanism for considering these types of case, but it is important to remember that other policy drivers operate. Deterrence may lack the empirical support that is commonly supposed (Von Hirsch et al, 1999), yet combating earlier decisions which heighten the risk of offending might feasibly reduce their occurrence. The offences in question are also often comparatively serious and the public rightly expect protection from the criminal justice system. These concerns validate an approach which treats behaviour which increases the risk of offending as aggravation.

Compelling as this may sound, blame is more complex and may support an alternative conclusion, at least in some instances. While the preliminary conduct may properly be regarded as blameworthy, the impact that it had on subsequent events may have reduced the blame that can fairly be attached to the offence. In all cases, should the offender be judged as harshly as an individual committing the offence without that background? To reverse the proposition, if someone commits an act of violence while they are sober are they really *less* blameworthy that an intoxicated assailant? Fairness might demand sympathising with individuals who have made poor earlier choices which can rightly be considered blameworthy.

What is apparent from the survey provided in this chapter is that the way in which the criminal justice system responds to those who put themselves in harm's way is inconsistent, though there is perhaps an increasing readiness to treat such individuals unsympathetically. Inconsistency can perhaps be explained on two grounds. The first is that there can be legitimate disagreement about whether prior conduct mitigates or aggravates a subsequent offence. Uniformity of approach avoids inconsistent outcomes (theoretically) but it masks the debate by categorising crudely. Retaining discretion also tends to mask the debate as judges are free within reason to apply the law in what they see as a fair manner. The second explanation for inconsistency is that policy is driven not just with reference to blame. Our review is limited as a result as we cannot know the extent to which blame is central, marginal or irrelevant to policy in practice. This is true even where it is a stated justification.

The final claim made in this chapter is that, whatever the motive, there is evidence to suggest that there is an increasing trend among legislators and judges to treat decisions to put oneself in harm's way as an aggravating factor. Obvious examples include the way in which the courts in England and Wales have extended the concept of associating with criminals to encompass drug users and the decision taken by the Sentencing Guidelines Council to treat intoxication as an aggravating factor. Indeed, none of the scenarios that were considered in this chapter showed any signs, in any jurisdiction, of greater leniency. This conclusion supports one of the book's broader conclusions, namely that blame is increasingly being used to justify reactive criminal justice interventions. The next chapter addresses this theme.

SEVEN

Blame, punitiveness and criminalisation

The growth of blame culture and the need for scapegoats

> We live in a world that is said to be full of risk, danger and threat. Every day, a new social issue emerges to assail our sensibilities, often accompanied by the cry: What's to be done? Who's to blame? On each occasion, there is an assumption that things are getting worse: that our society, communities and very lives are becoming more risky and more dangerous. In the 1980s and 1990s, panics focused on issues such as dangerous dogs, mugging, video games, satanic abuse and child sexual abuse. More recently, they have centred on elder abuse, people trafficking, the internet and welfare scroungers. In the midst of this, claims of historical sexual and physical abuse have taken centre-stage. (Cree et al, 2014)

In September 2013 the findings of two Serious Case Reviews were published. Serious Case Reviews are undertaken by Local Safeguarding Children Boards in cases where a child has died or suffered serious harm as a result of suspected abuse or neglect. They are governed by the Local Safeguarding Children Boards Regulations 2006 made by the Secretary of State under the provisions of the Children Act 2004. The stated purpose of such reviews is to ascertain what lessons can be learned to inform future practice of all those with responsibility for safeguarding children. Inevitably, however, the reports, and others like them, are often seen more as an official attempt to find scapegoats and allocate blame. On 9 January 2011 two-year-old Keanu Williams died in Birmingham as a result of multiple injuries arising from separate incidents. In June 2013 Keanu's mother was convicted of his murder and her partner was convicted on charges of child cruelty (Birmingham Safeguarding Children Board, 2013). On 3 March 2012 four-year-old Daniel Pelka died in Coventry as a result of persistent abuse and neglect.

On 31 July 2013 Daniel's mother and stepfather were convicted of his murder (Coventry Safeguarding Children Board, 2013).

The Birmingham Safeguarding Children Board review was reported by the *Daily Mail* with the headline: 'The four missed chances to save Keanu: How social services failed two-year-old boy beaten to death by his mother as it's revealed even SHE was surprised he wasn't taken into care' (*Daily Mail*, 3 October 2013). The *Guardian's* headline was slightly more measured: 'Professionals failed to prevent toddler Keanu Williams' death, report finds' (*Guardian*, 3 October 2013). Similarly, the headlines announcing the Coventry review read: 'Everyone to blame but no one punished: Teachers, doctors, the police and social workers escape justice after missing 27 chances to save tragic Daniel Pelka' (*Daily Mail*, 17 September 2013). Although the review into child protection commissioned by the Department for Education and undertaken by Professor Munro (DfE, 2011) stressed the need to value professional expertise and hinted at learning more and blaming less, the focus continues to be on blame and scapegoating.

It is clearly vitally important that we do learn from tragedies and disasters to try to prevent them occurring in the future. Professor Munro was right to stress the need to create and develop a learning system, although, in practice, inquiries such as the Serious Case Reviews often do little more than feed a blame culture. According to the *Guardian* (8 October 2013) there are about four such reviews published each week. With the length of the average review being in the region of 500 pages, reading the full report becomes a practical impossibility and it becomes inevitable that the focus is on the headlines. The current situation is neatly summed up by Ray Jones in the *Guardian*:

> Of course it is crucial to review locally what happened when something awful occurs and to take necessary actions. But I cannot imagine what new general learning will come from more and more serious case reviews. Instead they have become a tool for apportioning and allocating accountability. This is now explicit in the government's description of them. They feed the blame culture. They are also costly and a major distraction from focusing on current practice as resources and management attention are heavily deployed. (*Guardian*, 8 October 2013)

Between July 1963 and October 1965 five children between the ages of 10 and 17 were murdered. At least four of them had been sexually assaulted before they were killed. In 1966 Ian Brady and Myra Hindley were convicted of their murders and sentenced to life imprisonment. There were no public inquiries, no investigations into why the police had taken so long to discover and investigate the earlier murders, there was no effort to spread the blame wider than the two individuals who had carried out the killings. It is difficult to imagine the same reaction today. The desire to minimise risk, to prevent such things happening again seems to lead inexorably to a search for scapegoats.

The reaction to the publication of allegations against Jimmy Savile in October 2012 is indicative of the modern preoccupation with blame. Following the broadcast of a television documentary, *Exposure: the other side of Jimmy Savile*, by ITV on 3 October 2012 the Association of Chief Police Officers requested that the Metropolitan Police Service (MPS) assess the claims made in the programme. On 9 October 2012 the MPS announced that the investigation would be entitled Operation Yewtree and would be carried out in association with the NSPCC and the National Association for People Abused in Childhood. In January 2013 'Giving Victims a Voice', a joint MPS and NSPCC report into allegations of sexual abuse made against Jimmy Savile under Operation Yewtree was published (NSPCC, 2013). Jimmy Savile had died in October 2011 so there was no possibility of criminal proceedings against him. This lack of criminal proceedings was part of the justification for the publication of the report. Operation Yewtree had a wider remit than simply investigating allegation made against Jimmy Savile. It consisted of three strands:

> The first strand is offences believed to have been committed by Jimmy Savile on his own; the second is where victims have said there were other people around Savile who they believe were involved in offending; the third strand involves accounts from people who have come forward as a result of the publicity about Jimmy Savile but who have said they were sexually assaulted by people unconnected to him. (NSPCC, 2013, para 2.2)

As with Serious Case Reviews, Operation Yewtree was keen to learn lessons for the future: 'By drawing on the experiences of victims we can begin to explore how police and other bodies can learn to be more effective in the resolution and prevention of serious crime relating to predatory abusive behaviour' (para 3.5).

Yet blame remains central to the investigations and publicity surrounding the allegations:

> Central to the many questions being posed by both his
> victims and others are why did it happen and why was it
> not noticed and stopped by police, health, education or
> social services professionals, people at the BBC or other
> media, parents or carers, politicians or even 'society in
> general'? (para 3.6)

As was discussed in Chapter One, modern society increasingly seems
perturbed by seemingly uncontrolled events and this apparent lack of
control leads to a desire for blame: we couldn't prevent it – it must be
somebody's fault! As a result of Operation Yewtree more than 10 public
figures have been investigated by the police in relation to allegations
of sexual abuse. Of course it is right that allegations of abuse are
properly investigated and that criminal proceedings are taken against
those directly responsible. Yet the search for scapegoats goes beyond
those who are directly responsible to include the BBC, a number of
care homes, schools and NHS institutions.

From civil liability to criminal liability

An allied trend is that, when a supposedly blameworthy party is
identified, justice is seen increasingly to demand punishment in the
criminal courts rather than recompense in the civil courts. It is difficult
to establish whether this is a gradual on-going process where less
tolerance is shown over a lengthy timeframe, possibly due to a realisation
that the existing process fails to deliver on expectations, or whether
this exasperation with civil remedies is a more recent development. If
there is a perception that civil remedies are inadequate, one needs to
question why as well as attempt to explain why punishment is seen
as necessary. One concern may be that a reliance on the civil law has
failed to prevent harm from occurring as its focus is on remedying
damage that has already been caused. The threat of punishment by
way of contrast might deter people from engaging in conduct which
could be harmful. The public have an enduring faith that deterrence
does lead to a modification of behaviour, a conclusion that is not borne
out by the extensive empirical literature in this area (Von Hirsch et al,
1999). The disjuncture between the intuitive logic of deterrence and
the reality can probably be explained on the basis that individuals have
limited knowledge of the likely consequences of breaking the law and
fail to act with the rationality that is often supposed.

Another justification for adopting the criminal justice system
would be that punishment is necessary to reflect the individual's

blameworthiness. Unlike the recourse to deterrence, this is not an argument based on the avoidance of future harm but is essentially a retributive claim. Proportionality is usually used by penologists to quantify the punishment that an offender deserves. It could also be used more widely to gauge which forms of blameworthy conduct should result in criminal rather than civil liability. Evidently, there are recent examples of very serious conduct which escapes criminal censure while other obviously more trivial varieties do not. Some of the behaviours which have become criminalised are serious, most notably corporate manslaughter; in these cases using criminal rather than civil processes could perhaps be viewed as a welcome redressing of the balance. There is, however, no overall coherence to the behaviours that have been criminalised in recent years. Some conduct, in particular anti-social behaviour, appears comparatively minor. The trend then has been general and has encompassed areas that probably should have been criminalised in the past as well as behaviour previously seen as too trivial or otherwise undeserving of criminal liability.

The political background is crucial to understanding this trend as it reached its zenith during the period of office of the last Labour government (1997–2010). Tony Blair, who held the Shadow Home Affairs brief prior to becoming party leader, recognised that the party's previous criminal justice policies had been perceived as unduly lenient and had become an electoral liability. He also saw that those living in disadvantaged communities were disproportionately affected by crime and that Labour had failed to grasp the significance of this to its traditional core support. A radical change occurred in the mid-1990s when Labour started to challenge the Conservative government's record and proposals on the basis that they were insufficiently severe rather than overtly punitive and regressive. Despite vocal debate, there was in fact a tacit agreement that greater use of the criminal law in combination with increased penalties was necessary. This stance was intriguing as it came at a time when crime rates were falling, but it can be understood when one considers the respective positions of the two major parties: Labour, in essence, were trying to plug a perceived weakness while the Conservatives, conscious that electoral support was fast evaporating, sought to cling on to their advantage in a vital area of policy. After Labour won the 1997 election they were true to their mantra that they would be 'tough on crime, tough on the causes of crime'. It is well known that sentences increased and the prison population expanded massively during Labour's period in office. Less attention has been given to the way in which the government created a vast number of new offences, helped in part by the size of their parliamentary majority.

For a supposedly progressive party, Labour presided over a period of sustained and substantial expansion to the criminal law.

Labour's agenda, though, was more ambitious as it sought to tackle not only crime but anti-social behaviour which also tends to affect the disadvantaged disproportionately. There is no doubt that to those on the receiving end of such conduct the distinction between criminal and lawful behaviour is academic. Yet there was no evidence to suggest that there had been a surge in anti-social behaviour nor was there an obvious popular outcry for new legal powers. (Although there may well have been support for greater enforcement of minor offences that affect quality of life.) Conceptually, however, anti-social behaviour encompasses a broad range of activity, much of which is lawful. The challenge for policy makers was how to regulate lawful conduct which had an adverse impact on others.

A novel legal structure was devised which created a hybrid of civil and criminal law: a civil order would be issued prohibiting the individual from engaging in specified behaviours and an offence would be committed if the recipient breached the terms of the order. Research has shown that the vast majority of applications for Anti-Social Behaviour Orders (ASBOs) are granted, but there is marked geographical disparity in their use. The fact that the bulk of applications are successful might suggest that only worthy cases, supported by compelling evidence, are pursued, but an alternative possibility is that the courts are lax in challenging the cases brought. If applications tend to succeed, the longer-term benefit appears marginal as the majority of ASBOs are breached with the consequence that the individual is liable for punishment and possibly imprisonment. The rate of non-compliance shows that ASBOs fail to deter those minded to act in an anti-social manner, indeed there are anecdotal claims that some view an ASBO as a badge of honour. In March 2014 the Anti-Social Behaviour, Crime and Policing Act received the Royal Assent. The Act abolishes ASBOs, the coalition government partly justifying abolition on the grounds of the rate of non-compliance, but replaces them with 'injunctions to prevent nuisance and annoyance'.

For once, the media criticism did not contend that ASBOs were insufficiently severe, instead they were portrayed as faintly ludicrous; stories about pensioners receiving ASBOs for swearing and neighbours being issued with ASBOs for failing to prevent livestock entering adjoining gardens were reported. Cases of this sort did arise very infrequently but the missed story related not to the atypical but to the typical. Research by Koffman (2006b) found that ASBOs were most commonly issued for behaviour that was criminal suggesting that

ASBOs were being used as an alternative to prosecution, a strategy which carried an attraction for the authorities as the standard of proof for an ASBO is lower than that for a criminal conviction. Given the fact that the conduct which usually attracts an ASBO is criminal, there is an argument that the process could usefully be viewed as a form of pre-trial diversion (see, further, Chapter Two) and many of the concerns about the lack of due process safeguards commonly associated with diversionary strategies apply here.

The criminalisation of anti-social behaviour is unusual for a number of reasons. First, although many suffer from this conduct the problem was not getting appreciably worse. Second, neither the public nor the media demanded criminalisation; if anything, the media ridiculed the response by publicising absurd cases. Third, the impetus came from a supposedly progressive government who wanted to demonstrate a resolute and punitive response to minor deviancy. The government cannot be faulted for recognising the plight of those faced with anti-social behaviour but failed to appreciate that there was no popular appetite for ASBOs. Finally, the legal structure was novel in that it combined elements of civil and criminal law. The offence, speaking strictly, related not to the anti-social behaviour but to the breach of the civil order. Yet what emerged was that this system was often employed as an alternative not only to the civil procedure (as intended) but, more frequently, as an alternative to the criminal procedure. Reducing the standard of proof meant that ASBOs were easier to secure than convictions, so the net widened to capture not only those originally envisaged (the serially anti-social), but those whose allegedly criminal conduct would not ordinarily have resulted in conviction.

Death caused by corporations may appear to represent a very different harm to anti-social behaviour, but there are surprising similarities. The first is that this was far from a novel problem and, while there were a number of high-profile incidents which cost lives, earlier tragedies were often 'resolved' successfully in the civil courts. Litigation was often pursued in tandem with an official enquiry which sought to identify blame so that lessons could be learnt which would improve safety in the future. A second similarity is that, with the exception of some immediate victims, the public did not demand that company directors or employees should be punished when a death occurred. Media support was also limited. Finally, experience had demonstrated that there were both conceptual and practical problems associated with criminalising corporate (mis)conduct. The most fundamental of which was who should be held criminally liable if a death arose? Often this would be far from obvious given the size and complexity of many companies: an individual employee, for example, may have failed to maintain a section of railway line, but if he was inadequately supervised and over-stretched it would appear harsh to hold him wholly or possibly even partially to blame in a criminal court. There is also the question of how a corporation should be punished. Would it be appropriate to imprison those who are identified as having been at fault? In the example above, should that include the individual who failed to provide adequate resources and supervision? Problems remain if a financial penalty is seen as more acceptable. Consumers, employees and shareholders could suffer if a company is forced to raise the necessary funds even though they bear no responsibility for the death. Moreover, once a decision has been taken to criminalise corporate manslaughter, the imposition of a fine seems an inadequate response given the harm caused and leads to an impression that homicide in this context is far less serious than is ordinarily the case. If the punishment is perceived as unduly lenient, there is a danger that criminalisation will paradoxically trivialise the harm in the eyes of victims, although there is the real possibility of scapegoating if lengthy prison terms are imposed.

Prior to the Corporate Manslaughter and Corporate Homicide Act 2007 coming into force on 6 April 2008, corporate entities could be prosecuted for a range of criminal offences including gross negligence manslaughter (see Chapter Four). Yet it was difficult to convict corporations as it had to be proved that a senior individual who could be seen as a 'controlling mind' or embodying the company was guilty of the offence. The new Act allows conviction if it can be shown that there was a gross breach of a duty of care by 'senior management' rather than by one individual. Although the offence refers to 'senior management', it is important to stress that the offence is concerned with corporate liability and does not apply to senior personnel within the organisation. Individuals, though, can still be charged with gross negligence manslaughter in appropriate cases. The penalties that can be imposed include unlimited fines, remedial orders and publicity orders.

This Act supplements gross negligence manslaughter, an offence discussed in Chapter Four. It may be recalled that this offence may be difficult to reconcile with the notion that only the blameworthy should be punished. A distinction was drawn between those acting in such a fashion and those who engage in harmful behaviour intentionally or recklessly (in the subjective sense). The objection raised was that although the individual may have been factually to blame for the victim's death it is debatable whether he was morally to blame if incompetence – even if extreme – led to the death. Corporate manslaughter also requires a gross breach of a duty of care, but here it is suggested that this is less objectionable. Corporate liability is distinctive from individual criminal liability in terms of the impact of a conviction. Both a company and an individual may face stigma (and anyone associated with the company may do so vicariously) but the punishment is far more significant for an individual who will likely face a lengthy custodial term rather than a financial penalty.

Despite this, is criminalisation warranted? If the hope was that corporations would take greater steps to maintain safety the deterrent effect of the offence is impossible to measure. There have only been a limited number of successful prosecutions which suggests that the impact will be marginal. That said, there is an argument that could be made that organisations may behave in a more rational way than individuals and so the threat of prosecution may lead to operational change. Victims may feel that justice would be better served if individuals were prosecuted, and, if convicted, punished, rather than corporations fined. Criminalisation in itself may not satiate demands for justice. It may intensify calls for greater punitiveness.

Criminalising behaviours that cause society harm is attractive politically due to its symbolic effect. In both the cases above the government were effectively seen to side with the law-abiding and powerless against the anti-social and dangerous corporations. There is also little political mileage in challenging such legislation as that could be seen as showing sympathy to the perpetrators. By pitting the responsible against the irresponsible in this way the government glossed over the fact that such a binary distinction is too simplistic. People view certain types of behaviour differently, so classifying some people as anti-social is arbitrary. So too is a determination that there was a gross breach of a duty of care by senior management. Yet the drive to criminalise was symptomatic of Labour's desire to control what it saw as deviant behaviour. The creation of a myriad of diverse new offences, measured in the thousands, has to be viewed alongside more invasive methods of responding to crime, particularly with regards to juvenile justice.

The approach was also crude. Whereas there should have been meaningful debate about whether it was appropriate to create an offence in any particular context it appears that criminalisation was practically the default position. The first explanation for this is political. Labour, particularly during its initial term, enjoyed a substantial parliamentary majority which limited the constraints on the executive. Opposition from the Conservatives was also muted as the party did not want to be seen as being on the wrong side of the debate. It was crucial to the Conservative's attempt to rebuild support that they did not cede ground on Law and Order which meant that the government could legislate in the knowledge that the Opposition would be unlikely to challenge the need for new offences. The effect of the unedifying appeal to popular punitiveness was that both parties became embroiled in a futile race that neither would win as it is always possible to devise a solution more draconian than your opponent's. Given their sizeable parliamentary advantage, Labour did not need to get drawn into this battle, but clearly they did not want to squander their majority by failing in their pledge to be tough on crime. There was also conviction behind Labour's position. According to Blair's memoirs:

> [Fighting] crime was a personal cause, it completely fitted a new politics beyond old right and left, and since no Labour person had ever made anything of it…the field was mine to play on. For once I was very confident of what I could do. And I was correct…I took a traditional Labour position, modernised it, made it popular and upended the Tories with it. (2010, 55)

Modesty aside, Blair's quote is telling as is displays a naive belief about the potency of the criminal law. It should not be forgotten that Labour also promised to be 'tough on the causes of crime', and valuable work was done to this end, but it would appear that the party's policy was a mixture of the opportunist and the simplistic. Of course, there is no reason why a democratically elected government should require an evidence base to determine social policy but the lack of debate and reflection on the expansion of the criminal law has significant implications.

The first is that any expansion of the criminal law increases the demands made on the criminal justice system unless there is a simultaneous process of decriminalising existing offences. Although some activities have been decriminalised in the past 20 years, these represent a fraction of the offences which have been created. Enforcement will suffer unless considerably more resources are made available to the relevant agencies; in fact budgets have been cut due to the coalition government's deficit reduction policy. This means that a criminal justice system which is already highly selective in the cases that are investigated and prosecuted will become more so. The threat that selectivity will lead to discrimination against marginalised groups therefore increases.

Second, previously law abiding citizens could experience the criminal justice system as offenders. There are obvious normative questions which we have addressed throughout this book about whether those who engage in particular activities are sufficiently blameworthy to deserve punishment. This is assumed too readily but needs to be considered on a case-by-case basis. There are, however, other implications for those convicted of a criminal offence. In some situations disclosure of a conviction may result in loss of employment or employment opportunities. More generally, however, it could be argued that the stigma associated with having been found guilty of an offence labels an individual in a way which may increase rather than decrease the likelihood of future criminality. This argument rests on the idea that the process of labelling reaffirms the individual's status as a deviant which makes it more difficult to reintegrate him or her back into society. Support for this thesis can be found in statistics which show routinely that the majority of those convicted of an offence re-offend within a short space of time. The effects of labelling may also explain why deterrence is hard to achieve.

A linked point is that if individuals suddenly find themselves being viewed with a different status by law enforcement agencies their overall perceptions of the criminal justice system may become more antagonistic. Speeding, unlike most forms of criminal activity, has the potential to kill, but, because of motorists complaining that 'they were being treated like a criminal', policing strategies have changed. The point here is that the resentment is unlikely to be channelled towards politicians but to those charged with enforcing the law. One could hardly blame the police for treading carefully if they know that the public will perceive their actions as heavy-handed but this could have the unfortunate effect of targeting police resources to crimes that are committed disproportionately by the disadvantaged in society.

Third, it is difficult to see how the rapid expansion of the criminal law facilitates progressive responses to criminal behaviour because it fosters a punitive environment. Conduct is criminalised so that it can be punished, despite the likely consequences outlined above. There are those, however, who argue that, although it is sensible to criminalise some behaviours, punishment is a brutal, degrading and inefficient response. Restorative justice in various guises has been offered as one possible alternative by penal theorists but, as this seeks to reintegrate the offender back into society in a way which respects his or her identity, it would be impossible to implement when a programme of rapid criminalisation was justified on the basis of a perceived need for punishment. It would appear illogical to increase the number of offences while at the same time raising concerns about the limitations of punishment. This might explain why the Green Party is the only

British political party which openly advances a policy of restorative justice and decarceration (Green Party, 2010, 24).

Finally, those who would have traditionally pursued a civil action may have been better served in that forum. It is an easy claim to make that victims want someone to be punished for their actions but what is sought is likely to be highly individualistic. Victims can easily be appropriated by those advocating criminalisation whether that is a lobby group or a political party. There is an associated danger that the state takes ownership of the dispute, leading victims to feel marginalised by the process. Although reparation is possible in the context of the criminal justice process, prosecution is brought in the name of the Crown and punishment is seen as a mechanism for repaying a debt to society. It is a matter of luck whether victims feel that the punishment imposed adequately reflects the harm that they suffered. Testifying at a criminal trial can also be a bruising experience for victims as the veracity of their testimony is subjected to searching cross-examination. A civil case may still entail confrontation but settlement out of court is common and, if the case does go to court, success is more likely because the standard of proof is lower in civil than in criminal cases.

From human rights to the International Criminal Court

In May 1915, following reports that Ottoman forces were engaged in the massacre of the Armenian population, the governments of Britain, France and Russia communicated the following message to the Grand Vizier in Istanbul:

> In view of these new crimes of Turkey against humanity and civilization, the allied Governments announce publicly to the Sublime Porte that they will hold personally responsible [for] these crimes all members of the Ottoman Government and those of their agents who are implicated in such massacres. (Cited in Schabas, 2012, 6)

The allied announcement represents the first attempt in the modern era to impose criminal responsibility for crimes against international law. At the end of the First World War the Treaty of Sevres was signed by the allies and Turkey. Under article 230 Turkey agreed to hand over to the allied powers those responsible for the massacres committed during the war. Furthermore, Turkey undertook to recognise an international tribunal established by the League of Nations (should it prove possible to do so) established for the purpose of trying such offences. No such tribunal was established and the government of the new Republic of Turkey never ratified the Treaty of Sevres. The vast majority of those responsible for the Armenian massacres went unpunished.

The Paris Peace Conference at the end of the First World War had been particularly concerned about how to deal with alleged breaches of the law and customs of war. In January 1919 a Commission on the Responsibility of the Authors of the War and on the Enforcement of Penalties was established. One of the matters it was required to investigate was the establishment of an appropriate tribunal to hear allegations of war crimes. The Commission recognised the fact that states individually could legitimately try individuals for war crimes but that an international tribunal was essential for the trial of certain offences: for example, atrocities in prison camps containing prisoners of war of more than one nationality; charges against persons of authority whose orders affected more than one nationality or operations against the armies of more than one of the Allies, and charges against the major enemy authorities and against any other persons whom it might not be desirable to try in any national court.

Article 227 of the Treaty of Versailles, concluded between the allied powers and Germany, proposed the establishment of a special tribunal for the trial of the former German Emperor. Again, no tribunal was established and Kaiser Wilhelm was able to gain asylum in the Netherlands.

The lack of successful prosecution of those accused of atrocities during the First World War led to a number of calls for the establishment of an international criminal tribunal. There was some concern that ad hoc tribunals established after the event were susceptible to claims that they were merely carrying out 'victor's justice'. A permanently established court would have greater legitimacy by appearing to be more genuinely independent. An international criminal court would also complement the newly established Permanent Court of International Justice (forerunner of the International Court of Justice) which had jurisdiction over disputes arising between states. During the 1920s and 1930s a number of organisations, including the Advisory Committee of Jurists established by the League of Nations and the International Law Association, called for the establishment of an international criminal court. Efforts to make such a court a reality were increased as the international situation became more unstable during the 1930s.

In October 1934 King Alexander I of Yugoslavia was assassinated in France. The suspects fled to Italy and attempts at extradition were unsuccessful. Three months earlier the Austrian Chancellor had been assassinated and an attempt had been made on the life of the Romanian prime minister. In response to growing concerns the League of Nations established an expert Committee for the International Repression of Terrorism (CIRT). The resolution which established the Committee noted that 'the rules of international law concerning the repression of terrorist activity are not at present sufficiently precise to guarantee efficiently international co-operation' (League of Nations, 1934, 1760). The Committee was charged with producing an international treaty to repress 'conspiracies or crimes committed with a political and terrorist purpose' (League of Nations, 1934, 1760), although the League provided no definition of terrorism. An International Conference on the Repression of Terrorism was held in Geneva in November 1937. Two treaties were signed at the end of the conference: the Convention for the Prevention and Punishment of Terrorism 1937 and the Convention for the Creation of an International Criminal Court 1937. Terrorism was defined as 'acts directed against a State and intended or calculated to create a state of terror in the minds of particular persons, or groups of persons or the general public'. In the event neither proposed treaty gained sufficiently widespread support. Twenty states signed the Terrorism Convention and out of those, 10 signed the Convention for the Creation of an International Criminal Court. Neither convention received sufficient ratifications to enter into force.

Within 10 years an international tribunal was established. The establishment of the International Military Tribunal at Nuremberg represented the first genuine attempt to hold the perpetrators of crimes against international law individually responsible. In 1950 the International Law Commission adopted the Principles of International Law Recognised in the Charter of the Nuremberg Tribunal and in the Judgment of the Tribunal. Principle I provides that:

> Any person who commits an act which constitutes a crime under international law is responsible therefor and liable to punishment.

Principle VI identifies the crimes as crimes against peace, war crimes and crimes against humanity. In January 1951 the Convention on the Prevention and Punishment of the Crime of Genocide 1948 (Genocide Convention) entered into force. The Genocide Convention confirms genocide as a crime under international law and requires states party to the treaty to undertake to punish the offence within their national jurisdictions. In 1948 the United Nations General Assembly voted in favour of the Universal Declaration of Human Rights which represented:

> [A] common standard of achievement for all peoples and all nations, to the end that every individual and every organ of society, keeping this Declaration constantly in mind, shall strive by teaching and education to promote respect for these rights and freedoms and by progressive measures, national and international, to secure their universal and effective recognition and observance, both among the peoples of Member States themselves and among the peoples of territories under their jurisdiction. (Preamble)

Following the adoption of the UDHRm work started to convert the Declaration into legally binding treaty law. The result of the work was the two International Covenants: the International Covenant on Civil and Political Rights 1976 and the International Covenant on Economic, Social and Cultural Rights 1976.

The period between 1945 and 1990 saw considerable development of international human rights law but little if any enforcement of international criminal law. The collapse of the Soviet Union and events in the former Yugoslavia and Rwanda at the beginning of the 1990s saw a renewed focus on international criminal law and individual responsibility. In Yugoslavia a series of political and economic crises led to the formal dissolution of the Socialist Federal Republic of Yugoslavia in 1992. Hostilities in Slovenia were followed by outbreaks of far more serious violence in Croatia and Bosnia-Herzegovina. Increasing reports of massacres, rapes and torture led the United Nations to appoint a Commission of Experts to investigate the situation. The Commission's Report detailed grave breaches of international humanitarian law and led the United Nations Security Council on 25 May 1993 to pass resolution 827 which formally established the International Criminal Tribunal for the former Yugoslavia (ICTY). Since that time 161 individuals have been indicted for serious breaches of international humanitarian law. Out of 141 cases concluded, 74 resulted in conviction and sentence.

In response to reports of atrocities occurring in Rwanda, the UN Security Council established the International Criminal Tribunal for Rwanda (ICTR) by resolution 955 of 8 November 1994. The ICTR was established for the prosecution of persons responsible for genocide and other serious violations of international humanitarian law committed in the territory of Rwanda between 1 January 1994 and 31

December 1994. It also has jurisdiction to deal with the prosecution of Rwandan citizens responsible for genocide and other such violations of international law committed in the territory of neighbouring States during the same period. The ICTR has dealt with 75 cases, 63 of which resulted in conviction although 16 of those are still pending appeal.

The establishment of the ad hoc tribunals for Yugoslavia and Rwanda appeared to give renewed impetus to attempts to create a permanent international criminal court. In 1998 the Statute of the International Criminal Court (ICC) was signed in Rome and the ICC came into effect in 2002 after the Statute had received the necessary number of ratifications. The ICC has jurisdiction to hear cases involving genocide, crimes against humanity, war crimes and the crime of aggression. Under the terms of the Rome Statute the ICC prosecutor can initiate an investigation on the basis of a referral from any state party to the Statute or from the United Nations Security Council. The ICC is currently investigating situations in Uganda, the Democratic Republic of the Congo, the Central African Republic and Mali (all parties to the Statute) and Darfur, and Libya — both non-States Parties. After a thorough analysis of available information, the Prosecutor has opened and is conducting investigations in all of the above-mentioned situations.

Although it is rarely specifically mentioned, we would suggest that an understanding of blame is key to the relationship between international human rights law and international criminal law. Arguably both are underpinned by a desire to make the world a better, more secure place. The preamble to the United Nations Charter provides:

We the peoples of the United Nations determined
- to save succeeding generations from the scourge of war, which twice in our lifetime has brought untold sorrow to mankind, and
- to reaffirm faith in fundamental human rights, in the dignity and worth of the human person, in the equal rights of men and women and of nations large and small, and
- to establish conditions under which justice and respect for the obligations arising from treaties and other sources of international law can be maintained, and
- to promote social progress and better standards of life in larger freedom.

Protecting human rights and the dignity and worth of the human person is an underlying purpose of criminal law as much as it is the focus of human rights law. Yet the focus of the two systems of law is different. Criminal law tends to be directed towards individuals by imposing individual criminal responsibility. That is reflected in the often quoted statement from the Nuremberg Tribunal:

> Crimes against international law are committed by men, not by abstract entities, and only by punishing individuals who commit such crimes can the provisions of international law be enforced. (International Military Tribunal, 1947, 223)

International criminal law is about allocating criminal responsibility, blame, to individuals. Human rights law focuses on the wider society and the state. As we have seen elsewhere in the book, allocating blame can be comforting, as by blaming the few we can exonerate the many (including ourselves). As we saw in Chapter Five, atrocities occur in a particular context. Putting those directly responsible for them on trial may satisfy an immediate desire for 'justice', yet it does little to prevent similar events happening elsewhere in future. The focus on blame leads, we argue, to an increasing criminalisation at the international, as much as the national, level. The danger is that the emphasis on criminalisation might be at the expense of positive work promoting human rights.

EIGHT

Blamestorming and blamemongers

Using blame as a means for evaluating the criminal justice system has proved fruitful, even if the picture that emerges defies easy summary. Blamestorming reminds us that the allocation of blame is a process, as is the criminal justice system. In both processes it would be hoped that the attribution of liability is subject to careful reflection in the knowledge that a finding of culpability is profound in terms of stigma and often in other material respects. The reality, though, can be very different. Blamestorming can be haphazard, instinctive and can lead to scapegoating. At the same time, the supposed due process safeguards embedded in the criminal justice system which are designed deliberately to protect the innocent have often been marginalised by crime control priorities. The crime control model does not set out to convict the innocent, but it should be obvious that, by relaxing the impediments to convicting the guilty, one heightens the risk of convicting the innocent. Viewing the criminal justice process as an exercise in blamestorming removes much of the legal mystique and exposes what is in essence a system designed to attribute responsibility. There may be rules which specify how the exercise is to take place (and these depend in part on time, place and culture) but discretion and subjective assessments are rife.

Blamestorming operates throughout the process. Law makers responding to perceived harms may consider culpability, perhaps drawing on media and popular assessments. If an offence is created, law enforcement officers become engaged in a blamestorming exercise every time they are faced with an incident. Many policing decisions such as who to stop, who to search, who to arrest and who to charge, are influenced by this type of calculation. Prosecutorial agencies facing decisions about bringing charges will also review the evidence to see whether the individual could be held blameworthy. It is at trial that blamestorming becomes most overt as the prosecution and defence present alternative accounts which test the defendant's culpability. Finally, sentencing involves a further exercise in quantifying the seriousness of the offence which requires a consideration of the offender's culpability. In sum, determinations of blame dictate all key stages of the criminal process.

There is, though, a surreptitious danger with blamestorming: the process starts from an assumption that someone is to blame for an incident and then seeks to find out who that person is, but often no one is directly responsible and so the search for an individual to hold to account is no more than an exercise in scapegoating. There is a difference between blamestorming in the knowledge that no one is personally culpable and blamestorming in the knowledge that identifying the culprit will be difficult. The former represents a cynical abuse of power and is a clear case of scapegoating while the latter carries the possibility, however remote, of finding a blameworthy person. Many police investigations carry little chance of success but that does not mean that they should be abandoned. In the criminal justice sphere, with the threat of punishment, proceeding with the knowledge that no one is to blame is morally repugnant even though the authorities can face horrendous pressure to act when a major incident occurs. Acting when identification will be difficult is perfectly justifiable provided adequate safeguards exist to stop wrongful convictions. As society seems ever more willing to criminalise behaviour and demonstrates a greater readiness to assign blame, it is concerning that the government continues to reduce the protection afforded to those who have been arrested or who face trial.

In this final chapter, we expand on some of the most important themes that emerged from the work, drawing together some central themes about how blame can inform a criminological analysis of the criminal justice system. It is our belief that our focus on blame has exposed some novel issues worthy of further criminological consideration and has provided some original insights on more enduring concerns. Blamestorming is a process but it is not, nor can it be, a value-neutral process. The chapter concludes with some thoughts about how blame may not only inform an understanding of contemporary criminal justice but can be used as a basis for creating a more progressive and humane response to harmful behaviour.

Defining blame

Mary Douglas (1992), suggested a society without blame is not possible. She associates blame with a human need to seek explanations for situations. If someone dies, we need to know why they died. In earlier societies it was sufficient to explain the death in terms of the supernatural: 'she died because she has offended the ancestors, she had broken a taboo, she had sinned' (p 4). The belief that we have ever increasing control over our own lives and destinies has led to a rejection of such explanations and a focus on causes and explanations closer to home. This search for explanations has led to the emergence of blamestorming. Increasingly, society wants to know why harm occurred; why more was not done to prevent the harm occurring; what assurances can be provided that the harm will not occur in the future. Ultimately, death cannot be prevented yet the increasing desire to apportion blame could sometimes be seen as a denial of this fundamental fact.

In this book we have taken a broad view of blame. We have suggested that there is no practical difference between blame and culpability and have demonstrated the close links both have with responsibility and accountability. Blame is an evaluative response but it is not simply an objective evaluation, it is connected to desire, emotion, expectation and disposition. We accept the view that the blamer is doing more than simply making an objective entry on some form of moral ledger. Blame is linked to resentment but it is a distinctive emotional response. We would support Sher's view that '[Blame] is a stance or attitude that a person takes toward himself or another on the basis of a judgment that that person has in some way failed to conform to some moral standard' (Sher, 2006, 7) and further 'To blame someone…is to have certain affective and behavioural dispositions, each of which can be traced to the combination of a belief that that person has acted badly or has a bad character and a desire that this not be the case' (p 115). It is clear that to blame someone is to think less of them.

Typically, blame is seen as backward looking and responsive: blame relates to events that have already occurred. Yet there is also a future dimension to blame. Kathleen McGraw's study (McGraw, 1991) of the blame management strategies of elected public officials focuses on how officials seek to maximise praise and minimise blame through the use of accounts or explanations. McGraw argues that officials manage public perceptions through the use of accounts or explanations. McGraw found that while accounts which conveyed positive character information about events could minimise blame, poor accounts could actually increase the amount of blame. For McGraw, 'It is clear that blame entails much more than attribution of responsibility for a past event but also future liability for censure or punishment' (p 1149). This future dimension to blame suggests that far from being a single objective evaluation, blaming is an ongoing process. We have seen in the reactions to incidents of child abuse that allocating blame to those directly responsible is often insufficient to halt the blaming process and, through inquiries and reviews, others become sucked into the blamestorm. Our appetite for blame demands not only the conviction of the abusers, but the resignation of the Director of Social Services and the dismissal of social workers.

Legal determinations about blame

Although this book offers a criminological critique, this cannot be divorced from earlier decisions about what amounts to criminal behaviour. It is not simply a question, as some criminologists appear to think, about what conduct is defined as criminal but also a matter of how offences are then structured. Deciding, for example, whether an offence can be committed recklessly is important, but determining what constitutes reckless behaviour is also vital. This determination serves as a useful example. Unjustified risk-taking can lead to significant harm, so there is a moral basis for criminalising such conduct. Is it fair, however, to conclude that someone who did not see an obvious risk was acting in a reckless manner?

Where the risk appears obvious and the harm is significant, factual blame may be easy to find. In the leading English case of *R v G* [2003] UKHL 50 (see Chapter Four) burning paper led to damage valued at £1 million. Despite that, it is the case that some vulnerable people cannot foresee a risk for various reasons. The case in question involved two young boys and it was accepted that they failed to see the possibility that the fire would spread. The issue that faced the House of Lords was whether recklessness encompassed conduct which would pose an obvious risk to the reasonable man even though the defendant had not personally foreseen this. Although the House of Lords had due regard to earlier authorities, they were effectively engaged in a blamestorming exercise: would it be proper to hold the boys to account for causing this damage? Recognising the importance of individual culpability, the court held that the test for recklessness should be subjective: someone who did not perceive a risk should not be viewed as blameworthy and should not be seen to be acting recklessly as a result. What this demonstrates is that blamestorming can be considered and careful.

Notions of blameworthiness may help explain some decisions which appear to be at odds with standard notions of criminal liability. Motive should be irrelevant when considering whether a defendant intended a particular result. (The prosecution and defence may, however, consider motive at trial as evidence to support or disprove a claim that the conduct was intentional.) Yet, when highly atypical cases present themselves, motive is not discounted but is used to justify a conclusion that there was no intention. Here blamestorming may function in a benign fashion – it would have been outrageous if the defendants in the cases discussed further in Chapter Four were held criminally liable – but we should not be blind to the fact that a broader perception of justice is taking precedence over the standard rules for establishing liability in these, admittedly rare, cases.

There are, however, many instances when questions of blame should be irrelevant to the criminal law; with strict liability offences the individual is liable if he or she engages in the prohibited conduct or fails to fulfil a duty regardless of the reason. Many strict liability offences are minor and of a regulatory nature so the consequences of conviction may not be significant. Yet the courts are prepared on occasion to require that an element of mens rea is read into the offence. Again this interpretation serves as a mechanism to protect those who are perceived to be blameless in situations where the law is unclear and where the effect of a conviction would be more than minimal. A somewhat artificial distinction is drawn between 'real' offences and regulatory offences. According to the courts, attention is given to whether stigma would follow conviction as well as the likely penalty. These factors recognise that society should be slow to convict blameless individuals of offences where the outcome, both reputational and punitive, is potentially profound. In this context, the courts are again interpreting the law in a way that protects the blameless in more serious offences when there is ambiguity about how an offence should be interpreted.

The debate surrounding strict liability offences centres on the extent to which it is just to punish those who lack culpability and whether other aims, such as the need to regulate some forms of behaviour for the common good, should override this concern. An allied matter is whether it is right to criminalise incompetence. Many offences are satisfied when negligent conduct occurs, however these offences are often comparatively trivial so can potentially be justified on similar grounds to most strict liability offences. Whereas the courts have generally interpreted statute in a restrictive fashion so as to guard against convicting the blameless (at least of more serious offences), it is the House of Lords in England and Wales which provided for manslaughter by gross negligence. It goes without saying that this is a serious offence; the maximum penalty is life imprisonment. It is also important to stress that there is a distinction between negligence and gross negligence, though the fact that this is left to be determined by the jury on a case by case basis hardly inspires confidence. The extent to which someone's conduct departed from what was reasonable to expect is in one sense irrelevant: an individual may be blameless even if his conduct was outrageous when measured objectively.

When an individual dies as a consequence of someone breaching a duty of care, it is often easy to apportion factual blame and it may be appropriate for that person to be held liable in the civil courts. Is factual blame sufficient to warrant criminal liability even in extreme cases, however? Factual blame and moral blame would appear to be in danger of becoming conflated. It is also difficult to see an alternative basis for the offence as competence is unlikely to be achieved through deterrence and the public can be protected from those unable to perform at an acceptable standard in other ways. When responding to strict liability offences, the courts deserve credit for recognising the impact of a conviction and using that to ensure that the blameless are not held liable for serious criminal offences unless that is the stated intention of parliament. The blamestorming exercise here is far cruder and prioritises the harm caused at the expense of moral blame. The gravity of the harm is used to justify manslaughter by gross negligence whereas the severity of the stigma and punishment acts as a restraint in strict liability cases.

There are two interconnected processes at work: the way in which the criminal law allocates blame; and the way in which the criminal justice system allocates blame. For too long this has not been fully recognised in part because legal academics concentrated on the first and criminologists on the second. Academic criminal lawyers often fail to recognise that, even where the elements of an offence are made out, the arbitrary nature of the criminal justice process has a significant impact on who is subsequently convicted. Criminologists, on the other hand, frequently downplay the complexity of the criminal law thereby missing subtle but important processes which also determine who enters the criminal justice process. Neither process is value-neutral but this is not necessarily a problem, provided that the aims can be justified. Nor does the system have to espouse the same values at every stage; as well as being impractical there may be reasons why, for example, greater due process is required at points where individuals are especially vulnerable.

Describing the processes as interconnected was deliberate as it is too simplistic to view them as linear. Many procedural stages (arrest, prosecution and so on) are determined with regard to the law. Blamestorming in the context of the criminal law is a process which decides what conduct is criminal and, equally, what conduct escapes censure. Individual culpability influences the criminal law in diverse ways even leading to apparent conflicts with standard principles on occasion. These decisions have implications for the criminal justice system and it is to this that this chapter now turns.

Blame and procedural decision-making

One of the perceptions that was challenged in Chapter Two is that the standard response to criminal activity involves a prosecution and trial and, if a conviction follows, the imposition of punishment. In reality the trial process is reserved for only a small proportion of individuals and many law-breakers are diverted from prosecution at an early stage. If a meaningful assessment of the importance of blame in society's response to harmful behaviour is to be conducted, diversionary processes need to be considered alongside the trial process. It remains a moot point whether it is best to view diversionary measures as distinct processes in their own right or as part of a broader process for responding to crime.

An obvious starting point is whether the grounds for diverting some forms of activity while prosecuting others are sound. From a normative perspective, it would surely be offensive if more serious forms of delinquency were diverted and more trivial offences prosecuted yet there are instances where this seems to be the case. Objectively, tax evasion and the breach of health and safety regulations cause significant harm and, at least in the case of tax evasion, often entail deliberate, sophisticated planning. Prosecution, however, is reserved for a minority of serious cases. A more general policy of diverting minor crimes on grounds of proportionality and expediency is more defensible. Limited resources forces selectivity which means that prioritisation becomes a necessity. Proportionality is an appropriate guiding principle. Decisions about who should be diverted, whether at a macro or a micro level, could be classified as an exercise in blamestorming. It can be difficult to discern what guides these decisions though guidelines often suggest that individual culpability is a relevant concern alongside the gravity of the harm.

Blame is also of critical importance when one considers the cases that are dealt with in the orthodox fashion. It first has an impact on the decision as to whether prosecution is in the public interest. If prosecution is not seen as appropriate, the individual may be diverted but there is also the possibility that no further action will be taken. Deciding which court should hear the case depends broadly on offence-severity, but this is not only a question of quantifying the harm that was caused. Individual culpability is also a relevant variable.

Determining sentence shows that blamestorming can arise post-conviction. The statutory framework and the guidelines that sentencers should follow in England and Wales delineate a system where the seriousness of the offence is of primary concern. Parliament recognised that offence-severity could not be measured if the offender's culpability was ignored (Criminal Justice Act 2003, s143(1)). The sentencing statistics provide evidence that there remains a high degree of subjectivity in quantifying the seriousness of any given offence and then determining what would constitute a proportionate sentence. Various factors may explain disparity such as court culture or the frequency with which sentencers are faced with a particular offence. The difficulty of measuring severity has, however, to be admitted.

Blame, luck and diminished responsibility

We began this book with a discussion of the case of Mrs Inglis. The case raises important questions about the nature of blame and has a particular relevance to the issues discussed in Chapter Three. Blame is often presented as unproblematic and objectively identifiable. The increasing centrality of retribution to sentencing policy has led to the increasing importance of blame to criminal justice. Yet, as we have pointed out, it remains a topic which has been subject to limited analysis. In Chapter Three we saw that cognitive ability, self-control and resistance to peer pressure are key factors in the decision to commit wrongful acts. Since the commission of wrongful acts may lead to blame, levels of cognitive ability, self-control and resistance to peer pressure should logically be taken into account when assessing blame. We may not blame a three-year-old for taking a toy that belongs to another because we do not believe that a three-year-old necessarily has the ability to understand concepts of property rights and ownership. We expect adults to demonstrate higher levels of self-control than children and we are less surprised when a group of teenagers succumb to peer pressure than when a group of adults behave similarly.

What is surprising perhaps is the fact that research that has been undertaken into developmental and cognitive psychology appears not to have informed decisions about blame and its place in the criminal justice system. While the setting of a minimum age of criminal responsibility may be influenced by perceptions of childhood and adolescence and the conflict between the child-as-victim and the child-as-threat, attitudes to mental illness might be expected to be more scientifically informed. Yet here, too, we saw how desire for retribution and the attribution of blame may outweigh objective assessments of criminal responsibility. The partial defences of diminished responsibility, loss of control and the offence of infanticide may have their origins in a desire to provide courts with the possibility of mitigating sentence where the normal imposition of a mandatory sentence was required. Yet a serious investigation of the extent to which 'abnormal mental function' should reduce blame, and therefore affect sentence, is surely long overdue. Given the fact that the prison population as a whole has considerably lower levels of educational attainment and higher levels of mental illness than the population as a whole, one might question the extent to which current sentencing policy truly reflects levels of culpability.

The extent to which factors such as age and mental function may influence assessments of blame can sometimes appear something of a lottery. The concept of moral luck indicates that attribution of blame may be much more extensively a matter of chance. Often the consequences of any particular act or omission may be a matter of luck. The consequences of criminal activity are usually dependent on a combination of linked occurrences. We saw in the case of Mrs Inglis how a tragic combination of factors contributed to the death of Thomas Inglis. Had Edward Drummond been treated by different medical practitioners it is possible that he would have survived being shot by Daniel M'Naghten and students of criminal law would have no M'Naghten Rules to consider. The Kantian solution would be to blame only the intention and take no account of the act, yet ascertaining intention is no easy task. We often surmise intention from the act. The driver who intentionally breaks the speed limit may intend to arrive more quickly at the destination. The level of blame attaching to a speeding driver who hits and kills a child will be considerably more than that attaching to the speeding driver who hits and kills a rabbit. Both drivers will be blamed more than the speeding driver who arrives safely without incident at the destination. Even if we consider self-blame here it seems likely that the speeding driver who kills the child will feel the greatest self-blame.

Precursory conduct and the attribution of blame

Chapter Six presented a number of scenarios (involvement in paramilitary activity or gang membership, purchasing illegal drugs and the use of intoxicants) as a continuum based on the likelihood that crime would ensue. While joining a criminal enterprise may or may not be intrinsically unlawful, it demonstrates clear intention to offend. At the other extreme, despite considerable evidence showing a correlation between intoxication and crime, few drinkers set out to offend and the causal link between intoxication and offending is weak and elusive. Another observation was made, however: those scenarios where the causal link appears weakest arise most frequently.

This means that ignoring the earlier behaviour would have a greater aggregate effect.

Blame can easily be imputed in an uncritical manner. The best example in this context is the way in which the concept of **involvement in a criminal enterprise** has been expanded from situations where someone is a willing participant in the enterprise to include those indebted to a drug dealer. Drug deals are illegal activities, but is it accurate and fair to categorise the purchaser as someone involved in a criminal enterprise? It is not difficult to provide an alternative account of a desperate individual fearing violent retaliation who commits an offence in which he would otherwise have played no part. In any event, surely there is a normative difference between an eager recruit to a criminal gang and someone who only offends under duress?

This example also shows how blame is often ascribed broadly. There are virtues in having a uniform approach to particular situations: a lack of uniformity exacerbates diverse outcomes which can lead to significant individual injustice. Certainty also allows for a considered debate about the approach adopted, although it becomes obvious that devising a uniform position can involve crude categorisation which often masks considerable variety. Returning to the drug user coerced into offending by a dealer, would justice be better served if courts recognised that factual situations may differ to the extent that sympathy is warranted in some cases but not in all? If the availability of a defence depends on the individual's blame, over-broad categorisation would threaten a meaningful assessment of this key determinant in individual cases. Categorisation may then be crude and over-inclusive. It may also unravel when subjected to detailed analysis as is the case with the arbitrary distinction drawn between **strict** and **basic liability** offences in English law. But what of the central question? What blame should attach to behaviour, sometimes lawful, sometimes unlawful, which heightens one's risk of committing an offence?

If there is a sufficient causal link between the precursory conduct and the crime – and this should be established rather than assumed – and if there is subjective awareness of the link, it would appear reasonable to attribute blame. This may legitimate an offence of, for example, joining a paramilitary organisation. Mere association does not cause harm in such a case, the mischief is the harm that would subsequently be caused. Other offences may perhaps reflect both the present condition and the increased potential for harm; the offence of being drunk and disorderly provides an example. More controversially, there is the German offence of 'total intoxication'. This offence identifies the culpable behaviour (that is, the act of getting intoxicated) and, arguably, responds to that in a proportionate manner. In so doing, it recognises the difficulty of establishing a causal link between intoxication and offending, although, as the offence definition requires a criminal harm to occur, an element of moral luck survives. Harm which can factually but not legally be attributed to the individual determines liability. Equating factual blame with moral blame in this manner is problematic.

Perceptions of justice remain important. The *Daviault* case in Canada demonstrates that genuine incredulity can follow the acquittal of a 'blameworthy' individual. It is far from an isolated example. The law should not be driven solely by public perceptions which are often ill-informed and partial. One cannot sensibly gauge opinion on many issues and there is a danger that the most vocal are seen to be speaking on behalf of the majority. It is also a truism that bad cases do not make good law, and it is bad cases that generally excite the public. Nonetheless, popular sentiment can provide a useful barometer of whether the law is seen to operate in a just manner. Where the offender had engaged in conduct prior to the offence which appeared to have led to the offence, it would come as no surprise if the public viewed this behaviour as aggravating and demanded a more severe response. This is speculation. No studies that we are aware of have tested this hypothesis. One dated study into Australian sentencers' perceptions (Potas, 1994) found a marked divergence of opinion about whether intoxication should aggravate or mitigate a sentence. If this finding is of more general applicability, government, the judiciary and commentators need to exercise caution before justifying policy on the basis of a perceived popular perception of blame.

Quantifying blame

> Blame is an elusive concept, and its ubiquity in common language makes its measurement quite difficult. (McGraw, 1991, 1149)

The Criminal Justice Act 2003 indicates that when deciding on sentence the sentencer much begin by considering the seriousness of the offence. S143(1) of the Act provides:

> In considering the seriousness of any offence, the court must consider the offender's culpability in committing the offence and any harm which the offence caused, was intended to cause or might foreseeably have caused.

According to the Sentencing Guidelines Council (2004) four levels of culpability can be identified:

Where the offender:

i) has the intention to cause harm, with the highest culpability when an offence is planned. The worse the harm intended, the greater the seriousness.

ii) is reckless as to whether harm is caused, that is, where the offender appreciates at least some harm would be caused but proceeds giving no thought to the consequences even though the extent of the risk would be obvious to most people.

iii) has knowledge of the specific risks entailed by his actions even though he does not intend to cause the harm that results.

iv) is guilty of negligence.

Even in cases of strict liability and where no culpability needs to be proved it will still be relevant in determining the seriousness of the offence. Few would argue with the view that greater blame attaches to those who act intentionally than to those who are merely negligent. The Sentencing Council has provided more detail as to how culpability might be assessed although it accepts that assessing the seriousness of an offence (harm + culpability) is 'a difficult task' particularly where there is an imbalance between culpability and harm. As we saw in Chapter Three, moral luck may result in more or less harm being caused than was intended. In Chapter Five we discussed the factors that may increase or decrease seriousness. The impression here is that sentencing can be the scientific application of objective tests in which the sentencer quantifies the seriousness of the offence and determines the sentence. It may be 'a difficult task' but it is not an impossible one. Having accomplished the task the determined sentence will be proportionate and will reflect the level of blame the offender deserves.

Yet as we have argued throughout this book, blame is far more complex than the impression given in the Sentencing Council's guidelines. It is:

as common as water and as transparent to the gaze. We all know what it is but we cannot explain what we know by describing the experience. Often there is no experience to describe. We also cannot explain what we know by

> specifying blame's purpose, since genuine blame is always impotent because always after the effect. Given its ubiquity, its elusiveness, and its evident moral importance, we might expect philosophers to have scrutinised blame carefully. But strikingly, they have not. (Sher, 2006, vii)

Social psychologists may argue that it is almost impossible to separate harm from culpability. Studies investigating the attribution of blame consistently find it linked to perceived harm caused (Ohbuchi et al, 1989; Frederickson, 2010). There is evidence, too, that blame may be linked to perceived characteristics of the offender and the victim and the relationship between the two. Much of the research has been done in relation to attitudes to rapists (see, for example, Pollard, 1992; Whatley and Riggio, 1993). Less blame seems to attach to offenders when the victim is perceived as less respectable or is known to the offender. The maximum amount of blame is reserved for those who rape 'respectable' strangers. Yet as Birkbeck and Gabaldon (2001) point out: 'Much interesting research remains to be done on the situational referents affecting the attribution of blame to offenders' (p 100).

A far greater understanding of blame attribution and blame quantification is required if sentencing is to become a truly scientific and objective process. A greater understanding would also contribute to an understanding of offending behaviour since offenders also carry a conception of blame. Birkbeck and Gabaldon (2001) considered the research on offender morality to investigate whether offenders constructed blame differently from non-offenders. They identified a number of different types, but found that offenders often do engage in moral calculation before engaging in offending behaviour. It seems clear that the truly spontaneous, thoughtless act is rare (although more common among adolescents – see Chapter Three). The classic plea of the arrested criminal is 'Why are you wasting your time with me? You should be out catching the real criminals.' Many reduce self-blame by applying excuses and justifications to their actions or by comparing their actions to similar actions of others: 'I may be bad but I am not as bad as them.'

This ability to recalibrate one's moral compass and thus affect blame attribution is seen most starkly in relation to those who commit genocide or crimes against humanity. Chapter Five discussed how many of those engaged in the most horrendous activities during the Second World War led perfectly respectable, mostly law-abiding lives before and after the commission of war crimes and crimes against humanity. Most of those who worked in the concentration camps were not deranged sociopaths. For the most part they were ordinary citizens. They were able to commit the most atrocious acts because they did not believe that what they were doing was immoral or blameworthy: many felt they were acting for a greater good, others viewed their victims as less than human. The purpose of much propaganda during times of armed conflict is to demonise and dehumanise the enemy: if the Hutus/Jews/Gays/and so on are less than human then little or no blame can be attributed if we do them harm. The Sentencing Guidelines Council (2004) recognises that the qualities of the victim affect culpability. We would argue that without a clear understanding of blame and how to quantify it, this presents a potential danger. If it is more blameworthy to target certain victims it must surely be less blameworthy to target other victims. This clearly has important implications for society as a whole.

Swiss cheese

In Chapter One we referred to an apparent growth in blame culture which in turn has led to an increasing focus on litigation and, in some areas, criminalisation. 'Where there's blame, there's a claim' captured the public imagination precisely because it appeared to chime with the growth in blame. Increasingly when bad things happen we seek out bad people to blame. Yet identifying the bad people does not seem to stop the bad things happening. Some suggest that this focus on the individual might be part of the problem. Often it can be easier, and more comforting, to allocate blame than to investigate the true causes of a bad event. The act of blaming allows us to separate the good from the bad, leaving us on the side of the good. Studies of human error identify two main approaches: the person approach, which generally involves blaming, and the system approach. The tradition within the medical domain has been to adopt the person approach. This was the approach adopted in respect of Beverly Allitt referred to in Chapter One. It has also tended to be the approach adopted in respect of many of the inquiries into child abuse. The person approach 'views... unsafe acts as arising primarily from aberrant mental processes such as forgetfulness, inattention, poor motivation, carelessness, negligence, and recklessness' (Reason, 2000, 768):

> If something goes wrong, it seems obvious that an individual (or group of individuals) must have been responsible. Seeking as far as possible to uncouple a person's unsafe acts from any institutional responsibility is clearly in the

interests of managers. It is also legally more convenient, at least in Britain. (p 768)

The system approach, by contrast, sees human error as normal, expected behaviour and focuses instead on changing the conditions under which humans operate. It is credited with having led to major improvements in aviation safety. This approach focuses on a layered series of defensive barriers and safeguards:

> In an ideal world each defensive layer would be intact. In reality, however, they are more like slices of Swiss cheese, having many holes – though unlike in the cheese, these holes are continually opening, shutting, and shifting their location. The presence of holes in any one 'slice' does not normally cause a bad outcome. Usually, this can happen only when the holes in many layers momentarily line up to permit a trajectory of accident opportunity – bringing hazards into damaging contact with victims. The holes in the defences arise for two reasons: active failures and latent conditions. Nearly all adverse events involve a combination of these two sets of factors. (Reason, 2000, 769)

Active failures do usually arise from conduct of individuals with direct contact with the system and this may involve rule violation. Latent conditions are:

> [The] inevitable 'resident pathogens' within the system. They arise from decisions made by designers, builders, procedure writers, and top level management. Such decisions may be mistaken, but they need not be. All such strategic decisions have the potential for introducing pathogens into the system. Latent conditions have two kinds of adverse effect: they can translate into error provoking conditions within the local workplace (for example, time pressure, understaffing, inadequate equipment, fatigue, and inexperience) and they can create longlasting holes or weaknesses in the defences (untrustworthy alarms and indicators, unworkable procedures, design and construction deficiencies, etc). Latent conditions – as the term suggests – may lie dormant within the system for many years before they combine with active failures and local triggers to create an accident opportunity. Unlike active failures, whose

specific forms are often hard to foresee, latent conditions can be identified and remedied before an adverse event occurs. Understanding this leads to proactive rather than reactive risk management. (Reason, 2000, 769)

The Swiss cheese model does not deny that active failures may arise from malice on the part of individuals but that an overemphasis on blame can lead to a failure to consider latent conditions and system flaws. Being 'tough on crime and the causes of crime' does have the potential of considering both active failures and latent conditions. Yet, as we argued in Chapter Seven, the emphasis has been crime rather than its causes. It is more comforting to prosecute and blame individuals for genocide than to look for the underlying causes.

The blamemongers: from process to value

This book set out to provide a criminological account of the role blame plays in the operation of criminal justice at a national and supra-national level. Our justification for taking this approach was broadly two-fold. First, while aspects of criminal justice had been explored in this way, there was a strong case for a more sustained analysis that included some hitherto unexplored and under-explored areas of criminal justice. Second, criminology draws on a number of disciplines, some of which have much to contribute to a study of blame. A criminological approach not only enabled us to draw on this literature, but compelled us to do so, even when this challenged our disciplinary comfort zones. Inevitably we drew more heavily from some areas than from others – in many cases not those that were originally anticipated. Issues emerged which demanded incorporation or expansion and, inevitably, this came at the cost of other arguments which we deemed less valuable.

Philosophy and criminal law theory provided especially rich literatures and it is therefore apt that the book ends not with comment about the process of attributing blame but rather with a plea: given that the process of blamestorming appears inevitable, and that the process often has a disproportionate impact on the already disadvantaged, continual vigilance is required if the process of criminalisation can be morally justified.

Attributing blame is not a value-neutral process. Decisions have to be made which can have far-reaching consequences, not only to the person whose conduct is or is not adjudged to be culpable. Other stakeholders are affected, perhaps most notably those directly harmed by the incident: the attribution of blame may change the sense in which they are seen to be victims. More broadly, society is affected by our readiness to apportion blame and by the consequences which follow such a finding. A central claim made in this work is that there is an increasing demand for an individual (or other legal actor) to be held to account for a harmful event and that this trend has been amplified by a similar demand that the blameworthy are then punished. As a consequence, the reach of the criminal law has extended which should be a matter of concern to all those who respect individual liberty.

This is not to say that criminalisation is never warranted. Conduct which results in significant harm has sometimes been neglected shamefully. Recent attempts to address human trafficking provides an example. Other offences may be necessary as a response to emerging threats such as cyber crime. If examples can be found of new offences which can be justified the book documents numerous insidious developments. Intervention is often based on perceived harm. Some forms of harm which have been recognised, for example, violence in a domestic setting, do indeed justify either criminalisation or more rigorous enforcement. Not all harms should result in criminalisation, however. In some cases a de minimis rule should apply: criminal justice involvement is unnecessary on grounds of proportionality. In other cases, the harm lacks the specificity that should determine criminal liability. Anti-social behaviour, to take the most infamous example, can have an extremely adverse effect on quality of life, but deeming ostensibly lawful conduct anti-social represents a significant curtailment of liberty. Most significantly, over-reliance on harm as a determinant of criminal liability masks the potentially uncomfortable truth that people are not always to blame for harmful events. Blame is a concept of significant rhetorical value and one with profound consequences for those whose conduct satisfies the blamemongers. A concept of such subjectivity lends itself to distortion and over-simplification. Sometimes this manipulation would appear cynical and deliberate, but it would be wrong to deny that this is always the case. Blame is complex and contestable.

At a time when recourse to the criminal law continues apace, blame can fulfil another function. It can act as a restraint. The Criminal Justice Act 2003, the most important statute on sentencing in England and Wales, states correctly that the seriousness of an offence should be measured with reference both to harm and to individual culpability. This recognises that someone who causes serious harm may nonetheless have limited culpability. Neither harm nor blameworthiness can determine the seriousness of an offence in isolation. This insight is also relevant when decisions are made about criminalisation. Both harm and blameworthiness should be considered before a new offence is created. Other factors are relevant; most notably, would another strategy yield greater benefits? These should not be absolute requirements – social regulation may justify the existence of strict liability offences in some instances, for example. Ultimately, however, there should be a significant onus on policy makers to explain why conduct which causes no harm or which can be committed by the blameless should be criminalised.

A critique of the process by which blame is assigned is vital in understanding how criminal justice operates. Claims, some of which are fair but others baseless, that individuals are blameworthy, are central to the enterprise. Used thoughtfully, though, blame provides more than an analytical tool. It has the potential to provide a normative basis for challenging the boundaries of the criminal law and the operation of the criminal justice system. These are vital tasks.

Glossary

ACTUS REUS Every criminal offence specifies the conduct that is prohibited. All aspects of the definition must be satisfied in order to secure a conviction. A distinction is drawn between actus reus and mens rea requirements. The actus reus relates to the prohibited conduct. Taking the example of theft in English law, s1 Theft Act 1968 states that theft is the dishonest appropriation of property belonging to another with the intention to permanently deprive the other of it. The actus reus requires the appropriation of property belonging to another.

BASIC INTENT Criminal offences in England and Wales are classified as offences of basic or specific intent. In cases involving basic intent offences, evidence of voluntary intoxication is irrelevant and must be ignored when determining whether the defendant satisfied the mens rea of the offence. There is debate about how offences should be classified but generally offences that can be committed recklessly are basic intent offences.

BENEFITS AND BURDENS THEORY An account of retributive justice associated with Herbert Morris and Jeffrie Murphy. It relies on the assumption that law-breakers can an unfair advantage through their offending whilst we can all benefit from the law abiding behaviour of others. The task of the criminal justice system is therefore to provide a balance between the benefits and burdens of conformity with the law so we all benefit.

BLAME REQUIREMENT Not all offences require the defendant to be blameworthy (see Strict Liability). However, courts have felt uneasy convicting the blameless of more serious offences, particularly where it is felt that conviction carries stigma and / or the likely punishment is significant. In such cases the courts have introduced a blame requirement unless it is clear that parliament intended otherwise.

BLAMELESS CRIME Most criminal liability (and blame) is dependent upon some element of intention on the part of the offender. Blameless crime refers to those situations where the action alone can give rise to liability irrespective of intention. The most common example is provided by strict liability offences. Arguably too, imposing liability for reckless behaviour also involves an element of blameless crime.

BLAMEMONGERS The issue of who is allocating blame, and their right to do so, can often be significant. Blamemongers refers to those who apportion and allocate blame.

BLAMESTORMING Identified by the Oxford English Dictionary for the first time in 2003, Blamestorming refers to the increased tendency today to seek to apportion and allocate blame following any perceived failure.

BUSINESS CONDITION We use the term Blamemonger to refer to those who engage in allocating blame. The Business Condition is one of four conditions identified by Bell as a necessary requirement for the legitimate claim to blamemonger status. According to Bell, we can only legitimately blame another when it is our business to do so: we need to have some interest in the action/inaction attracting blame. Privacy also dictates that we have no 'business' in certain private acts of others.

CAUSAL LUCK One of four types of moral luck identified by Thomas Nagel. Causal luck has similarities with Circumstantial Luck and Constitutive Luck. The question arises as to the extent one can be blamed for actions that are the result of causes outside one's control.

CIRCUMSTANTIAL LUCK One of the four types of moral luck identified by Thomas Nagel. Circumstantial luck refers to the fact that the circumstances one finds oneself in can be a matter of chance and outside one's control. Individuals are blamed for actions they take or fail to take and little account is taken of what might have happened had circumstances been different.

COMMON SENSE Like Blame, Common Sense is a concept which superficially appears to be intuitive and unproblematic. Common sense is often used as a substitute for real, cogent evidence. This, for example, in debates about the minimum age of criminal responsibility the idea that children cannot distinguish between right and wrong is dismissed as 'flying in the face of common sense'. The appeal to common sense is used to justify the lack of more scientific inquiry.

CONSTITUTIVE LUCK One of four types of moral luck identified by Thomas Nagel (and others). Constitutive luck refers to qualities we possess over which we have no control. To a large extent our personality is dependent on luck. Given that our personality has an influence on how we behave and how we act, to some extent our actions are therefore dependent on Constitutive Luck.

CONTEMPORARY CONDITION A necessary condition identified by Bell to be satisfied by those seeking to allocate blame. The legitimacy of one's blame diminishes the further one is in terms of time and space from the target of that blame.

CRIME CONTROL In a seminal article about the criminal justice process, Howard Packer distinguished between crime control and due process values. The crime control model prized systemic efficiency and was designed to facilitate the conviction of the guilty. Packer's models originate in the late 1960s and have attracted criticism in the intervening period but it is agreed that they represent a valuable means of exploring the tensions inherent in the criminal justice process.

CRIMINAL CULPABILITY In order to establish criminal culpability all of the requirements of an offence have to be proved. Moreover, criminal culpability is avoided if a valid defence exists. In England and Wales, for example, a nine-year-old cannot be criminally culpable even if he satisfied all of the requirements of a given offence. Criminal culpability therefore depends wholly on legal determinations about the scope of offences and defences; if the nine-year-old satisfied all of the requirements of an offence in Scotland he would be criminally liable.

CRIMINAL ENTERPRISE For the purposes of this book, a criminal enterprise is taken to mean a group or organisation set up to engage in criminal activity. This term is deliberately broad and would include both a gang of shoplifters and Mafia organisations.

CRIMINAL OFFENCES Conduct defined by the law as illegal, the breach of which can result in conviction and punishment. A vast range of conduct is criminalised; no-one knows how many offences exist but there are many thousand. Although many offences have a long pedigree, the criminal law evolves. New offences are created whilst other conduct is decriminalised. Countries also criminalise different types of behaviour. There is legitimate debate about what forms of behaviour should be criminal. Not all offences require blameworthy conduct on the part of the offender and this is a key theme in this book. Another contention made is that the growth in the number of offences can be explained by a greater readiness to attribute individual blame to harmful events.

CRIMINOGENIC This term denotes factors which heighten the risk of offending.

DISHONESTY Many property offences (e.g. fraud and theft) require the defendant to have acted dishonestly. It is a mens rea requirement of these offences. There has been debate about whether dishonesty should be assessed objectively or subjectively. Both of these approaches are problematic and, in England and Wales, a hybrid position has been adopted whereby an initial determination is made about whether the conduct was dishonest by the standards of reasonable and honest people. If it was, dishonesty is found if the defendant would have realised that reasonable and honest people would have regarded it thus.

DUE PROCESS The second of Howard Packer's models of the criminal justice process. Due process was taken to mean that procedural safeguards were put in place at crucial junctures to ensure that the innocent were not convicted. These protections could impede crime control values as the factually guilty could also benefit. Although recent criminal justice legislation often appears driven by crime control concerns, due process rights are often embedded in human rights conventions.

EXTRAORDINARY CRIMES Mass killings, crimes against humanity, genocide and grave breaches of human rights have frequently been referred to as Extraordinary Crimes; the level and scale of violence seemingly taking such activities beyond the sphere of the normal or ordinary. The instances of such violence perhaps suggests that such crimes are sadly less extraordinary than is claimed. In any event, such crimes are committed by 'ordinary' people. It does appear, however, that extraordinary crimes attract a higher level of blame.

GUIDELINE JUDGMENTS Prior to a more formal system of sentencing guidelines, the Court of Appeal issued a series of guidelines on sentencing particular offences or on generic sentencing issues such as determining whether an offence is sufficiently serious to warrant a custodial sentence. The coverage of offences was patchy and concentrated on the most serious offences which would ordinarily attract lengthy terms of imprisonment. Guideline judgments were particularly ineffective when giving advice on more generic issues such as determining the seriousness of an offence for sentencing purposes.

INTENTION Some offences specify that the defendant must have intended a particular result. In England and Wales, for example, murder requires an intention to kill or to cause grievous bodily harm. Intention is conceptually problematic and this has generated considerable case law on the topic. Intention covers situations where it is someone's purpose or aim to achieve a particular end. The problematic cases have centred on situations where the result was virtually inevitable. Can intention be inferred? The current law in England and Wales allows the jury to infer intention if they conclude that the defendant realised that the outcome was a virtual certainty of his actions.

JUST DESERTS The level of blame may be reflected in the amount of punishment imposed. Retributivist accounts of punishment require that any sanction is proportionate to the seriousness of the offence so that the offender receives what he or she justly deserves.

MENS REA Most, though not all, offences specify a state of mind which must have been present at the time of the offence. Intention, recklessness and dishonesty are common examples. The exception are strict liability offences which specify no mens rea requirements. How mens rea terms are defined in statute or by the courts is of central importance to this study as the tests employed may or may not encompass blameless behaviour.

MORAL LUCK A concept particularly associated with Thomas Nagel and Bernard Williams, moral luck refers to the situation where blame may be allocated or withheld for reasons outside the control of the moral actor.

NON-COMPLICITY CONDITION Bell argues that this needs to be met before one can legitimately allocate blame. If one has been complicit in the wrongdoing complained of, one loses the right to allocate blame.

NON-HYPOCRISY CONDITION Identified by Bell, this refers to the argument that one has no standing to blame another for conduct one is guilty of oneself.

OBJECTIVITY A central dilemma for the criminal law is whether certain mens rea requirements, particularly dishonesty and recklessness, should be determined using an objective or a subjective test. An objective test relies upon the perceptions of a hypothetical reasonable person as distinct from the particular defendant. Potential injustice occurs when the defendant's competency departs from that of the reasonable person. Adopting an objective test raises questions about the acceptability of convicting those who are, for whatever reason, unable to reach the objective standard required.

PROFESSIONAL OFFENDING The Sentencing Council identifies professional offending as a category of offending that attracts higher levels of blame. The increased levels of premeditation and planning are associated with higher levels of culpability.

PUTTING ONESELF IN HARM'S WAY In this book the authors use the term to denote a variety of circumstances whereby individuals embark on conduct which heightens the risk that they will subsequently offend. Examples include becoming intoxicated and joining a criminal gang. Other commentators have considered these behaviours in isolation but our contention is that issues of blame link them and that a wider assessment is warranted.

QUASI-CRIMINAL This is a term of art used to describe conduct prohibited by the criminal law which is not perceived as properly criminal in character. The distinction between quasi-criminal and criminal behaviour would appear to depend more on questions of blame than on the harm or potential harm associated with the offence as many regulatory offences which would be classed as quasi-criminal nonetheless carry the risk of serious harm occurring.

REASONABLE PERSON The reasonable person is an important legal construct, particularly in the civil law. However, the reasonable person is also relevant to the criminal law most notably when an objective test is employed to determine liability. Generally the reasonable person has no specific characteristics but in certain situations gender and age may be taken into account. The specific defendant may then share few characteristics with the reasonable person, sometimes through no fault of his own.

RECKLESSNESS Risk-taking can be both blameworthy and dangerous depending on the context. Some forms of risky conduct may be highly dangerous but cannot be regarded as morally blameworthy; emergency surgery may serve as an example. Many offences can be committed recklessly which recognises the blame that attaches to such behaviour. An enduring concern is whether recklessness demands subjective appreciation of risk or whether an objective recognition should suffice. English law has vacillated between the two approaches but, after a series of cases where blameless individuals were convicted, it is now incumbent on the prosecution to prove that the defendant foresaw the risk.

RESULTANT LUCK One of four types of moral luck identified by Thomas Nagel. Resultant luck refers to a situation where two people may act in the same way with identical intent yet their action has very different results. Resultant luck raises important questions as far as the allocation of blame is concerned since whether or not harm is done becomes a matter of chance.

SCAPEGOATS Historically, scapegoats were those who took the blame for the wrongdoing of others. Increasingly its meaning has been widened to include those who may carry some element of blame. Sometimes the search for scapegoats following criminal activity will go beyond the direct perpetrators.

SENTENCING COUNCIL The Sentencing Council is a body charged with providing guidance on sentencing particular offences or on more general sentencing issues. Most members of the Council are judges though there are members representing criminal justice agencies, victim organisations and academia. Sentencers are bound to follow guidelines unless it is contrary to the interests of justice to do so. It is difficult to assess whether this occurs from the sentencing statistics.

SPECIFIC INTENT In English criminal law offences are classified as either basic intent or specific intent offences. The distinction becomes relevant in cases involving voluntary intoxication as the relevance of evidence of intoxication differs depending upon classification. With regards to specific intent offences, evidence of voluntary intoxication can be considered when determining whether the defendant satisfied the mens rea of the offence. Diverse, and potentially incompatible, means of classification exist but specific intent offences generally require proof that the defendant intended a particular result.

STRICT LIABILITY Certain offences, often comparatively minor in nature, require no fault on the part of the defendant. These offences are classified as strict liability offences. The courts recognise that blameless individuals can (indeed should) be convicted of these offence if the other requirements are met. In certain situations, however, the courts have imposed a blame requirement due to the impact of a conviction in terms of reputation and punishment.

SUBJECTIVITY Whilst an objective test relies upon the hypothetical reasonable person, a subjective test assesses whether the individual defendant foresaw risk or realised that his actions were dishonest. This removes the objection that an objective test can impose unrealistic standards and lead to the conviction of the blameless. In the leading cases on dishonesty and recklessness the courts considered in depth the importance of blameworthiness in the criminal law.

TOTAL INCAPACITATION The German Criminal Code contains an offence of Total Incapacitation which is an alternative verdict when the requirements of another offence are not satisfied as the defendant's intoxication at the time compromised his ability to form an intention to cause a particular harm or foresee the harm as a possible consequence of his actions. The offence carries a maximum penalty of five years' imprisonment.

UNIT FINES Unless financial penalties take account of an offender's financial means the punishment will impact disproportionately on those on modest incomes. The Criminal Justice Act 1991 introduced a system of unit fines to accommodate disparity. Sentencers would determine the gravity of an offence and allocate it a unit value. The amount of the fine would be calculated with regard to the number of units and the offender's disposable income. After sustained (and sometimes misleading) media criticism, unit fines were abolished in the Criminal Justice Act 1993. The general principle that fines should reflect an offender's means remains.

References

Aldridge, J, Measham, F, Williams, L, 2011, Illegal leisure revisited: Changing patterns of alcohol and drug use in adolescents and young adults, London: Routledge

American Psychological Association, 2004, www.apa.org/about/offices/ogc/amicus/roper.pdf

Arnett, J, 1992, Reckless behavior in adolescence: A developmental perspective, *Developmental Review* 12, 4, 339–73

Arnett, J, 2000, Emerging adulthood: A theory of development from the late teens through the twenties, *American Psychologist* 55, 5, 469–80

Ashworth, A, 2005, *Sentencing and criminal justice*, Cambridge: Cambridge University Press

Ashworth, A, 2009, *Principles of criminal law*, 6th edn, Oxford: Oxford University Press

Ball, C, 2004, Youth justice? Half a century of responses to youth offending, *Criminal Law Review*, 167–80

Barker, DJ, 2009, The moral limits of consent as a defense in the criminal law, New Criminal Law Review 12, 1, 93–121

BBC, 2013, 'Paedophilia not criminal condition' says Durban cardinal, www.bbc.co.uk/news/world-africa-21810980

Becker, HS, 1963, *Outsiders: Studies in the sociology of deviance*, New York: The Free Press

Beckman, M, 2004, Crime, culpability, and the adolescent brain, *Science* (30 July), 305, 5684, 596–99

Bell, M, 2013, The standing to blame: A critique, in DJ Coates and NA Tognazzini (eds) *Blame: Its nature and norms*, pp 263–81, Oxford: Oxford University Press

Bennett, T, Holloway, K, Farrington, D, 2008, The statistical association between drug misuse and crime: A meta analysis, *Aggression and Violent Behavior*, 13, 2, 107–18

Birkbeck, C, and Gabaldon, LG, 2001, Offender Morality and the Criminal Event, in R Meier, LW Kennedy and VF Sacco (eds) *The process and structure of crime: Criminal events and crime analysis*, Piscataway, NJ: Transaction Publishers

Birmingham Safeguarding Children Board, 2013, *Serious Case Review in respect of the death of Keanu Williams*, www.lscbbirmingham.org.uk/images/stories/downloads/executive-summaries/Case_25__Final_Overview_Report_02.10.13.pdf

Blair, T, 2010, *A journey*, London: Hutchinson

Boden, JM, Fergusson, DM, Horwood, LJ, 2012, Alcohol misuse and violent behavior: Findings from a 30-year longitudinal study, *Drug and Alcohol Dependence* 122, 1, 135–41

Boden, JM, Fergusson, DM, Horwood, LJ, 2013, Alcohol misuse and criminal offending: Findings from a 30-year longitudinal study, *Drug and Alcohol Dependence* 128, 1, 30–6

Bradfield, M, Aquino, K, 1999, The effects of blame attributions and offender likableness on forgiveness and revenge in the workplace, *Journal of Management* 25, 5, 607–31

Braithwaite, J, 2002, *Restorative justice and responsive regulation*, Oxford: Oxford University Press

Braithwaite, J, Pettit, P, 1990, *Not just deserts: A republican theory of criminal justice*, Oxford: Clarendon Press

Branwyn, G, 1997, Jargon watch, *Wired Magazine*, February, 5.02, http://archive.wired.com/wired/archive/5.02/scans.html?pg=5

Brooks, L, 2011, An ugly totem for the abject failure of our criminal justice system, *Guardian*, 18 March, www.theguardian.com/commentisfree/2011/mar/18/justice-10-age-criminal-responsibility

Browning, CR, 2001, *Ordinary men: Reserve Police Battalion 101 and the final solution in Poland*, London: Penguin

Brownstein, HH, Crimmins, SM, Spunt, BJ, 2000, A conceptual framework for operationalizing the relationship between violence and drug market stability, *Contemporary Drug Problems* 27, 4, 867–90

Bucher, R, 1957, Blame and hostility in disaster, *American Journal of Sociology* 6, 467–75

Butler Committee, 1975, *Report of the Committee on Mentally Abnormal Offenders* Cmnd 6244, London: HMSO

Cammiss, S, 2009, *Determining mode of trial: Exploring decision making in magistrates' courts*, Saarbrucken: VDM Verlag

Cammiss, S, 2013, Courts and the trial process, in A Hucklesby, A Wahidin (eds) *Criminal justice*, 2nd edn, Oxford: Oxford University Press

Card, R, 2012, *Card, Cross and Jones Criminal Law*, 20th ed, Oxford: Oxford University Press

Cavender, SJ, 1989, The Lords against Majewski and the Law, *Bracton Law Journal* 21, 9–16

Centre for Social Justice, 2012, *Rules of Engagement: Changing the heart of youth justice*, www.centreforsocialjustice.org.uk/UserStorage/pdf/Pdf%20reports/CSJ_Youth_Justice_Full_Report.pdf

Cipriani, D, 2009, *Children's rights and the minimum age of criminal responsibility: A global perspective*, Farnham: Ashgate

Coates, DJ, Tognazzini, NA, 2013, *Blame: Its nature and norms*, Oxford: Oxford University Press

Cohen, S, 2002, *Folk devils and moral panics*, 3rd edn, Abingdon: Routledge

Coventry Safeguarding Children Board, 2013, *Serious Case Review: re Daniel Pelka*, http://www.coventrylscb.org.uk/files/SCR/FINAL%20Overview%20Report%20%20DP%20130913%20Publication%20version.pdf

CRC (UN Committee on the Rights of the Child), 2007, Children's rights in juvenile justice, *CRC General Comment No 10*, 25 April, CRC/C/GC/10, Geneva: United Nations Human Rights

Cree, V, Clapton, G, Smith, M, 2014, Moral panics, Jimmy Savile and social work: A 21st century morality tale, *Discover Society* 4, http://www.discoversociety.org/wp-content/uploads/2014/01/DS4_Cree1.pdf

Crofts, T, 2009, Catching up with Europe: Taking the age of criminal responsibility seriously in England, *European Journal of Crime, Criminal Law and Criminal Justice* 17, 4, 267–91

CPS (Crown Prosecution Service), 2013a, *The Director's guidance on charging*, 5th edn, May 2013 (revised arrangements), London: CPS

CPS (Crown Prosecution Service), 2013b, *CPS Conditional Cautioning Data, Quarter 1 2013/2014*, April–June 2013, London: CPS

Curtis, R, Wendel, T, 2007, You're always training the dog: Strategic interventions to reconfigure drug markets, *Journal of Drug Issues* 37, 4, 867–91

Daily Telegraph, 2008, 'Blamestorming' and new office buzzwords, 28 July, www.telegraph.co.uk/news/uknews/1576877/Blamestorming-and-new-office-buzzwords.html

DfE (Department for Education), 2011, *The Munro review of child protection: Final report. A child-centred system*, https://www.gov.uk/government/uploads/system/uploads/attachment_data/file/175391/Munro-Review.pdf

DH (Department of Health), 2013, *A promise to learn – a commitment to act: Improving the safety of patients in England*, London: DH, www.gov.uk/government/uploads/system/uploads/attachment_data/file/226703/Berwick_Report.pdf

Dingwall, G, 2006, *Alcohol and crime*, Cullompton: Willan Publishing

Dingwall, G, 2006/2007, From principle to practice: Reconstructing the nature of sentencing guidance, *Contemporary Issues in Law* 8, 4, 293–318

Dingwall, G, 2008, Deserting desert? Locating the present role of retributivism in the sentencing of adult offenders, *Howard Journal of Criminal Justice* 47, 4, 400–10

Dingwall, G, Harding, C, 1998, *Diversion in the criminal process*, London: Sweet and Maxwell

Dingwall, G, Koffman, L, 2008, Determining the impact of intoxication in a desert-based sentencing framework, *Criminology and Criminal Justice* 8, 3, 335–48

Donoghue, J, 2011, Truancy and the prosecution of parents: An unfair burden on mothers?, *Modern Law Review* 74, 2, 216–44

Douglas, M, 1992, *Risk and blame: Essays in cultural theory*, London: Routledge

Douglas, T, 1995, *Scapegoats: Transferring blame*, London: Routledge

DrugScope, 2013, How much crime is drug related?, www.drugscope. org.uk/resources/faqs/faqpages/how-much-crime-is-drug-related

Ericson, RV, 2007, *Crime in an insecure world*, Cambridge: Polity Press

Erikson, KT, 1976, *Everything in its path: Destruction of community in the Buffalo Creek flood*, New York: Simon and Schuster

Farrier, D, 1976, Intoxication: Legal logic or common sense?, *Modern Law Review* 39, 5, 578–81

Feinberg, J, 1970, *Doing and deserving: Essays in the theory of responsibility*, Princeton: Princeton University Press

Feld, LP, Frey, BS, 2007, Tax compliance as the result of a psychological tax contract: The role of incentives and responsive regulations, *Law and Policy* 29, 1, 102–20

Ford, JA, 2005, Substance use, the social bond, and delinquency, *Sociological Inquiry* 75, 1, 109–28

Fox, D, Dhami, MP, Mantle, G, 2006, Restorative final warnings: Policy and practice, *Howard Journal of Criminal Justice* 45, 2, 129–40

Franzoni, LA, 2004, Discretion in tax enforcement, *Economica* 71, 283, 369–89

Frederickson, JD, 2010, 'I'm sorry, please don't hurt me': Effectiveness of apologies on aggression control, *Journal of Social Psychology* 150, 6, 579–81

Gardner, MR, 1993, The mens rea enigma: Observations on the role of motive in the criminal law past and present, *Utah Law Review* 635–750

Gardner, S, 1995, Manslaughter by gross negligence, *Law Quarterly Review* 111, 1, 22–7

Garland, D, 2001, *Culture of control: Crime and social order in contemporary society*, Oxford: Oxford University Press

Genocide Watch, 2012, *Countries at Risk Report – 2012*, Washington, DC: Genocide Watch, www.genocidewatch.org/images/Countries_at_Risk_Report_2012.pdf

Gilchrist, E, 2006, Deciding to prosecute, in MR Kebbell, GM Davies (eds) *Practical psychology for forensic investigations and prosecutions*, Oxford: Wiley

Glover, J, 1970, *Responsibility*, London: Routledge and Kegan Paul

Golash, D, 2005, *The case against punishment*, London: New York University Press

Goldson, B, 1997, Children in trouble: State responses to juvenile crime, in P Scraton (ed) *Childhood in 'crisis'?*, London: UCL Press

Goldson, B, 2013, 'Unsafe, unjust and harmful to wider society': Grounds for raising the minimum age of criminal responsibility in England and Wales, *Youth Justice* 13, 2, 111–30

Goldson, B, Peters, E, 2000, *Tough justice: Responding to children in trouble*, London: The Children's Society

Goldstein, PJ, 1985, The drugs/violence nexus: A tripartite conceptual framework, *Journal of Drug Issues* 15, 4, 493–506

Green Party, 2010, *Fair is worth fighting for: Green Party general election manifesto 2010*, London: The Green Party

Greenawalt, K, 1986, Distinguishing justifications from excuses, *Law and Contemporary Problems* 49, 3, 89–108

Haidt, J, 2001, The emotional dog and its rational tail: A social intuitionist approach to moral judgment, *Psychological Review* 108, 4, 814–34

Haji, I, 1998, *Moral appraisability: Puzzles, proposals, and perplexities*, Oxford: Oxford University Press

Hart, HLA, 1968, *Punishment and responsibility*, Oxford: Clarendon Press

Hendrick, H, 1994, *Child welfare: England 1872-1989*, London: Routledge

Hillyard, P with Pantazis, C, Tombs, S, Gordon, D, 2004, *Beyond criminology: Taking harm seriously*, London: Pluto Press

Hirschi, T, Gottfredson, M, 1983, Age and the explanation of crime, *American Journal of Sociology* 89, 3, 552–84

Hirst, M, 2008, Causing death by driving and other offences: A question of balance, *Criminal Law Review*, 339–52

HM Revenue and Customs, 2013, *Landfill Tax Guidance*, www.hmrc.gov.uk/manuals/lftmanual/lft19020.htm

HMSO, 1967, *Report of the Tribunal appointed to inquire into the disaster at Aberfan on October 21st 1966*, HL 316, HC 553, London: HMSO

HMSO, 1974, *Report of the Committee of Inquiry into the care and supervision provided in relation to Maria Colwell*, London: HMSO

Home Office, 2011, *Crime in England and Wales 2010/2011*, London: Home Office

Hudson, BA, 1995, Beyond proportionate punishment: Difficult cases and the 1991 Criminal Justice Act, *Crime, Law and Social Change* 22, 1, 59–78

Husak, D, 1989, Motive and criminal liability, *Criminal Justice Ethics* 8, 1, 3–14

Husak, D, 2005, Strict liability, justice, and proportionality, in AP Simester (ed) *Appraising strict liability*, Oxford: Oxford University Press

Husak, D, 2010, *The philosophy of criminal law: Selected essays*, Oxford: Oxford University Press

ILC (International Law Commission), 2001, *Draft articles on responsibility of States for internationally wrongful acts, with commentaries*, New York: United Nations, http://legal.un.org/ilc/texts/instruments/english/commentaries/9_6_2001.pdf

International Military Tribunal, 1947, *Trial of the major war criminals before the International Military Tribunal*, 1, 223, Nuremberg: International Military Tribunal

Jones, O, 2011, *Chavs: The demonization of the working class*, London: Verso

Kahneman, D, 2003, A perspective on judgment and choice: Mapping bounded rationality, *American Psychologist* 58, 9, 697–710

Kant, I, 1959, *Foundations of the metaphsyics of morals*, Indianapolis, IN: Bobbs-Merrill

Kaufman, WRP, 2003, Motive, intention, and morality in the criminal law, *Criminal Justice Review* 28, 2, 317–35

Kessler, K, 1994, The role of luck in the criminal law, *University of Pennsylvania Law Review* 142, 2183–237

Kirchengast, T, 2010, *The criminal trial and discourse*, Basingstoke: Palgrave Macmillan

Klepper, S, Nagin, D, 1989, Tax compliance and perceptions of the risks of detection and criminal prosecution, *Law and Society Review* 23, 2, 209–40

Koffman, L, 2006a, The rise and fall of proportionality: The failure of the Criminal Justice Act 1991, *Criminal Law Review*, 281–99

Koffman, L, 2006b, The use of anti-social behaviour orders: An empirical study of a new deal for communities area, *Criminal Law Review*, 593–613

Koffman, L, Dingwall, G, 2007, The diversion of young offenders: A proportionate response?, *Web Journal of Current Legal Issues*, 2, www.bailii.org/uk/other/journals/WebJCLE/2007/issue2/koffman2.html

League of Nations, 1934, *Official Journal* 15

Leviner, S, 2008, An overview: A new era of tax enforcement – from 'big stick' to responsive regulation, *Regulation and Governance* 2, 3, 360–80

Luoma, JB, Twohig, MP, Waltz, T, Hayes, SC, Roget, N, Padilla, M, Fisher, G, 2007, An investigation of stigma in individuals receiving treatment for substance abuse, *Addictive Behaviors* 32, 7, 1331–46

Macdonald, S, 2008, Constructing a framework for criminal justice research: Learning from Packer's mistakes, *New Criminal Law Review* 11, 2, 257–311

Mathiesen, T, 2006, *Prison on trial*, 3rd edn, Winchester: Waterside Press

Matza, D, 1964, *Delinquency and drift*, Oxford: Wiley

McConville, M, Hodgson, J, Bridges, L, Pavlovic, A, 1994, *Standing accused: The organisation and practices of criminal defence lawyers in Britain*, Oxford: Clarendon

McCord, D, 1990, The English and American history of voluntary intoxication to negate mens rea, *Journal of Legal History* 11, 3, 372–95

McGraw, KM, 1991, Managing blame: An experimental test of the effects of political accounts, *American Political Science Review* 85, 4, 1133–57

McMurran, M, Hollin, CR, 1989, Drinking and delinquency: Another look at young offenders and alcohol, *British Journal of Criminology* 29, 4, 386–94

Menard, S, Mihalic, S, Huizinga, D, 2001, Drugs and crime revisited, *Justice Quarterly* 18, 2, 269–99

Meredith, B, 2009, The art (or not) of blamestorming, 2 March, www.batimes.com/articles/the-art-or-not-of-blamestorming.html

Merthyr Express, 1966, *The last day before half-term*, www.nuffield.ox.ac.uk/politics/aberfan/chap1.htm

Milgram, S, 1974, *Obedience to authority*, New York: Harper

Milgram, S, 1977, Some conditions of obedience and disobedience, reprinted in S Milgram, *The individual in a social world reading*, Boston, MA: Addison Wesley

Ministry of Justice, 2013, *Statistical notice: Further breakdown of cautions*, London: Ministry of Justice

Moore, MS, 1997, *Placing blame: A theory of the criminal law*, Oxford: Oxford University Press

Moore, MS, 2009, *Causation and responsibility: An essay in law, morals and metaphysics*, Oxford: Oxford University Press

Moore, P, 1981, Scroungermania again at the DHSS, *New Society*, 22 January, 55, 949, 138–39

Morris, H, 1968, Persons and punishment, *Monist* 52, 475–501

Muncie, J, 1999, *Youth and crime*, London: SAGE

Murphy, JG, 1973, Marxism and retribution, *Philosophy and Public Affairs* 2, 3, 217–43

Nagel, T, 1979, *Mortal questions*, Cambridge: Cambridge University Press

New South Wales Sentencing Council, 2009, *Sentencing for alcohol-related violence*, Sydney: New South Wales Sentencing Council

Newbury, A, 2011, I would have been able to hear what they think: Tensions in achieving restorative outcomes in the English youth justice system, *Youth Justice* 11, 3, 250–65

Newbury, A, Dingwall, G, 2013, It lets out all my demons: Female young offenders' perceptions about the impact of alcohol on their offending behaviour, *International Journal of Law, Crime and Justice* 41, 4, 277–91

Norrie, A, 1992, Subjectivism, objectivism and the limits of criminal recklessness, *Oxford Journal of Legal Studies* 12, 1, 45–58

NSPCC, 2013, *Giving victims a voice, A joint MPS and NSPCC report into allegations of sexual abuse made against Jimmy Savile under Operation Yewtree*, www.nspcc.org.uk/news-and-views/our-news/child-protection-news/13-01-11-yewtree-report/yewtree-report-pdf_wdf93652.pdf

Ohbuchi, K, Kameda, M, Agarie, N, 1989, Apology as aggression control: Its role in mediating appraisal of and response to harm, *Journal of Personality and Social Psychology* 56, 2, 219–27

Old Bailey, 1843, Trial of Daniel M'Naughten, www.oldbaileyonline.org/browse.jsp?id=def1-874-18430227&div=t18430227-874&terms=daniel#highlight

ONS (Office for National Statistics), 2007, *Mortality statistics: Deaths registered in 2007*, London: ONS

Ormerod, D, 2011, *Smith and Hogan's Criminal Law*, 13th edn, Oxford: Oxford University Press

Ormerod, D, Williams, DH, 2007, *Smith's Law of Theft*, 9th edn, Oxford: Oxford University Press

Orviska, M, Hudson, J, 2003, Tax evasion, civic duty and the law abiding citizen, *European Journal of Political Economy* 19, 1, 83–102

Packer, H, 1968, *The limits of the criminal sanction*, Stanford, CA: Stanford University Press

Padfield, N, 2011, Intoxication as a sentencing factor, in JV Roberts (ed) *Mitigation and aggravation at sentencing*, Cambridge: Cambridge University Press

Paris Principles, 2007, *The principles and guidelines on children associated with armed forces or armed groups*, www.icrc.org/eng/assets/files/other/parisprinciples_en[1].pdf

Parker, H, 1996, Young adult offenders, alcohol and criminological cul-de-sacs, *British Journal of Criminology*, 36, 2, 282–98

Peuch, K, Evans, R, 2001, Reprimands and warnings: Popular punitiveness or restorative justice?, *Criminal Law Review*, 794–805

Pollard, P, 1992, Judgments about victims and attackers in depicted rape: A review, *British Journal of Social Psychology* 31, 4, 307–26

Potas, I, 1994, Alcohol and sentencing of violent offenders, in *National Symposium on Alcohol Misuse and Violence: Report 6A*, Canberra: Australian Government Publishing Service

Quinn, JF, Sneed, Z, 2008, Drugs and crime: An empirically based, interdisciplinary model, *Journal of Teaching in the Addictions* 7, 1, 16–30

Reason, J, 2000, Human error: Models and management, *British Medical Journal* 320, 7237, 768–70

Robinson, PH, Darley, JM, 2007, Intuitions of justice: Implications for criminal law and justice policy, 81 *South California Law Review* 81, 1, 1–68

Rome Statute, 2002, 1998 document A/CONF.183/9 of 17 July 1998, www.icc-cpi.int/nr/rdonlyres/ea9aeff7-5752-4f84-be94-0a655eb30e16/0/rome_statute_english.pdf

Room, R, 2005, Stigma, social inequality and alcohol and drug use, *Drug and Alcohol Review*, 24, 2, 143–55

Sanders, A, Young, R, Burton, M, 2010, *Criminal justice*, 4th edn, Oxford: Oxford University Press

Scanlon, TM, 2008, *Moral dimensions: Permissibility, meaning, blame*, Cambridge, MA: Harvard University Press

Schabas, W, 2012, *Unimaginable atrocities: Justice, politics and rights at the War Crimes Tribunals*, Oxford: Oxford University Press

Selby-Brigge, LA (ed), 1960, *Hume: A treatise of human nature*, Oxford: Oxford University Press

Sentencing Council, 2009, *Definitive guidelines on attempted murder*, London: Sentencing Council

Sentencing Council, 2012a, *Allocation: Definitive guideline*, London: Sentencing Council

Sentencing Council, 2012b, *Attitudes to sentencing sexual offences*, London: Sentencing Council

Sentencing Guidelines Council, 2004, *Overarching principles: Seriousness*, London: Sentencing Guidelines Council

Sentencing Guidelines Council, 2008, *Magistrates' court sentencing guidelines: Definitive guideline*, London: Sentencing Guidelines Council

Sher, G, 2006, *In praise of blame*, Oxford: Oxford University Press

Simester, AP, 2005a, *Appraising strict liability*, Oxford: Oxford University Press

Simester, AP, 2005b, Is strict liability always wrong?, in AP Simester (ed) *Appraising strict liability*, Oxford: Oxford University Press

Simester, AP, Spencer, JR, Sullivan, GR, Virgo, GJ, 2010, *Simester and Sullivan's criminal law: Theory and doctrine*, 4th edn, Oxford: Hart

Simon, J, 2007, *Governing through crime: How the war on terror transformed American democracy and created a culture of fear*, Oxford: Oxford University Press

Simons, KW, 1997, When is strict criminal liability just?, *Journal of Criminal Law and Criminology* 87, 4, 1075–137

Smart, JJC, 1973, An outline of a system of utilitarian ethics, in JJC Smart, B Williams (eds) *Utilitarianism for and against*, pp 3–77, Cambridge: Cambridge University Press

Smith, AM, 2007, On being responsible and holding responsible, *Journal of Ethics* 2, 4, 465–84

Smith, AM, 2013, Moral blame and moral protest, in DJ Coates, NA Tognazzini (eds) *Blame: Its nature and norms*, Oxford: Oxford University Press

Smith, JC, 1976, Comment on Majewski, *Criminal Law Review*, 375–78

Strawson, PF, 2008, *Freedom and resentment and other essays*, Abingdon: Routledge

Sykes, GN, Matza, D, 1957, Techniques of neutralization: A theory of delinquency, *American Sociological Review*, 22, 664–70

Tajfel, H, Turner, JC, 1986, The social identity theory of intergroup behaviour, in S Worchel, WG Austin (eds) *Psychology of intergroup relations*, Chicago, IL: Nelson-Hall

UN (United Nations), 1985, *Standard minimum rules for the administration of juvenile justice adopted by the General Assembly resolution 40/33 of 29/11/85*, Geneva: UN

UN (United Nations), 1999, *Report of the Independent Inquiry into the actions of the United Nations during the 1994 genocide in Rwanda*, Geneva: UN, www.securitycouncilreport.org/atf/cf/%7B65BFCF9B-6D27-4E9C-8CD3-CF6E4FF96FF9%7D/POC%20S19991257.pdf

Veltfort, HR, Lee, GE, 1943, The cocoanut grove fire: A study in scapegoating, *Journal of Abnormal and Social Psychology* 38, 2S, 138

Virgo, G, 1993, The Law Commission consultation paper on intoxication and criminal liability. Part 1: Reconciling principle and policy, *Criminal Law Review*, 415–25

Von Hirsch, A, 1992, Proportionality in the philosophy of punishment, *Crime and Justice* 16, 55–98

Von Hirsch, A, 2000, *Censure and sanctions*, Oxford: Oxford University Press

Von Hirsch, A, Bottoms, A, Burney, E, Wikstrom, PO, 1999, *Criminal deterrence and sentencing severity*, Oxford: Hart

Von Hirsch, A, Ashworth, A, Roberts, J, 2009, *Principles of sentencing: Readings in theory and practice*, 3rd edn, Oxford: Hart

Walklate, S, 2009, Gender and the criminal justice system, in A Hucklesby, A Wahidin (eds) *Criminal Justice*, Oxford: Oxford University Press

Waller, J, 2007, *Becoming evil: How ordinary people commit genocide and mass killing*, Oxford: Oxford University Press

Whatley, MA, Riggio, RE, 1993, Gender differences in attributions of blame for male rape victims, *Journal of Interpersonal Violence* 8, 4, 502–11

White, HH, Gorman, DM, 2000, Dynamics of the drug–crime relationship, *Criminal Justice*, 1, 15, 1–218

Wilkinson, C, Evans, R, 1990, Police cautioning of juveniles: The impact of Home Office Circular 14/1985, *Criminal Law Review*, 165–76

Williams, B, 1981, *Moral luck*, Cambridge: Cambridge University Press

Williams, B, Hall, M, 2009, Victims in the criminal justice process, in A Hucklesby, A Wahidin (eds) *Criminal justice*, Oxford: Oxford University Press

Williams, G, 1981, Recklessness redefined, *Cambridge Law Journal* 40, 2, 252–283

Williams, G, 1983, *Textbook of criminal law*, 2nd edn, London: Stevens and Sons

Williams, G, 1988, The unresolved problem of recklessness, *Legal Studies* 8, 1, 74–91

Wilson, W, 2011, *Criminal law*, 4th edn, Harlow: Longman

Zimbardo, P, 1972, Pathology of imprisonment, *Society* 9, 6, 4–8

Zimbardo, P, 2007, *The Lucifer effect: How good people turn evil*, London: Routledge

Zimmerman, M, 1988, *An essay on moral responsibility*, Totowa NJ: Rowman and Littlefield

Zimring, FE, 1998, Toward a jurisprudence of youth violence, in M Tonry, M Moore (eds) *Youth violence: Crime and justice. A review of research*, Volume 24, pp 447–501, Chicago, IL: University of Chicago Press

Case list

Andrews v DPP [1973] AC 566

Attorney-General's Reference (No 3 of 2003) [2004] EWCA Crim 868

Attorney-General's Reference (No 2 of 1999) [2000] 3 All ER 182

Attorney-General's Reference (No 6 of 1980) [1981] QB 715

B (A Minor) v Director of Public Prosecutions [2000] 2 WLR 452

Coleman v The Queen (1990) 47 A Crim R 306

Cundy v Le Cocq (1884) 13 QBD 207

Director of Public Prosecutions v Majewski [1977] AC 443

Elliott v C [1983] 1 WLR 939

Erdemović (IT-96-22-A)

Gammon (Hong Kong) Ltd v Attorney General of Hong Kong [1985] 1 AC 1

Gillick v West Norfolk and Wisbech Area Health Authority and Department of Health and Social Security [1986] 1 AC 112

HM Advocate v Savage [1923] JC 49

M'Naghten Rules (1843) 10 CI & Fin 200

Montana v Egelhoff 518 US 37 (1996)

R v Abrahams (1980) 2 Cr App Rep (S) 10

R v Adomako [1994] 3 WLR 288

R v Ali [2008] EWCA Crim 716

R v B, C and Jason Owen [2009] (unreported, Central Criminal Court, 22 May 2009)

R v Bradley (1980) 2 Cr App Rep (S) 12

R v Brown [1994] 1 AC 212

R v Burgess [1991] 2 QB 92

R v Caldwell [1982] AC 341

R v Chaulk (1990) 2 CR (4th) 1

R v Peter William Coonan (formerly Sutcliffe) [2011] EWCA Crim 5

R v Cox (1993) 14 Cr App Rep (S) 749

R v Cunningham [1957] 2 QB 396

R v Daviault (1994) 93 CCC (3d) 21

R v Dias [2002] Crim LR 490

R v Doughty [1986] EWCA Crim 1

R v G [2003] UKHL 50

R v Hasan [2005] UKHL 22

R v Heath [2000] Crim LR 109

R v Howe [1987] 1 All ER 771

R v Inglis [2010] EWCA Crim 2637

R v Kai-Whitewind [2005] EWCA Crim 1092

R v Latif [1996] 1 All ER 353

R v Martin (Anthony Edward) [2003] QB 1

R v Parkhouse [1999] 2 Cr App Rep (S) 208

R v Sharpe [1987] 1 QB 853

R v Spence (1982) 4 Cr App Rep (S) 175

R v Steane [1947] KB 997

R v Sullivan [1984] AC 156

R v Watson [1989] 1 WLR 684

R v Windle [1952] 2 QB 826

Roper v Simmons 543 US 551 (2005)

Stapleton v R (1952) 86 CLR 358

Sweet v Parsley [1970] AC 132

Walters v The Queen [2007] NSWCCA 219

Yip Chin-Cheung v R [1994] 3 WLR 514

Index

Index

Index

Howard, Michael 57
Howe 117–18
human error, approaches to 166–8
human rights 149–51
Hume, David 18–19
Hutchinson, William 62
hypocrisy 12

I

ICC 59, 150
incapacitative sentencing 44
inchoate offences 71–4
incompatibilists 17–18
incompetence 86–92, 98, 157
Independent 23
indictable offences 37
infanticide 65
Infanticide Act 1938 65
Inglis, Frances 1–3, 70–1
Inglis, Thomas 1–3, 70–1
insanity, defence of 62–5
intention 175
  ascertaining 161, 175
  basic intent 171
  and criminal liability 72–4, 77–8
  and intoxication 125–6, 127–8,
    129–30
  and manslaughter 88–9, 142–3
  and mens rea 77–8
  and moral assessment 53, 72–3
  and motive 78, 79–83, 156
  and resultant luck 74, 177
  and sentencing 164
  specific intent 177
International Conference on the
    Repression of Terrorism 148
International Covenant on Civil and
    Political Rights 149
International Covenant on Economic,
    Social and Cultural Rights 149
International Criminal Court (ICC)
    59, 150
international criminal courts 59, 147,
    150
international criminal law 146–51
and age of criminal responsibility
    59–60
International Criminal Tribunals
    149–50
international human rights law 149–51
International Law Commission 148
Draft Articles on State Responsibility
    68, 69
International Military Tribunals 113,
    148
intoxication
  and blame 124–33, 162–3
  and sentencing 130–3, 163

total intoxication 128, 162–3, 178
intuition 108–9
involuntary manslaughter 88

J

Jones, O. 35
Jones, Ray 136
Jozefow, massacre at 111
just deserts 40, 102, 175
justifications 67–70
juveniles
  and alcohol 124–5
  and cautions 28
  and criminal responsibility 53–61
  doli incapax 58
  and international criminal law 59–60
  and pre-trial diversion 28–9, 49
  and recklessness 85–6, 156
  and reprimands 28, 29
  and warnings 28–9
  see also children

K

Kahneman, D. 109
Kant, I. 72, 102
Kaufman, W.R.P. 80
Kessler, K. 72–3
Koffman, L. 29, 132–3, 140–1

L

Labour Party 139–40, 141, 143–4
Langford, Mark 23
League of Nations 148
Legal Aid, Sentencing and Punishment
    of Offenders Act 2012 30–1
Leviticus 13
liability *see* criminal liability
Local Safeguarding Children Boards
    135–6
luck 70–6, 161–2, 172, 175, 177
Luoma, J.B. 123

M

Macdonald, S. 48
Mackay, Lord 90
magistrates' court 37–9, 51
Magistrates' Court Sentencing
    Guidelines 39
Magistrates' Courts Act 1980 38
Mail on Sunday 7
Main, John 24
Majewski 127
Major, John 7
Mandela, Nelson 25
manslaughter 88–91
  corporate manslaughter 141–3
Martin, Tony 70
massacres 110–11, 146–7